HIGHER

RMPS

MORALITY & BELIEF

Joe Walker

The publishers would like to thank the following individuals, institutions and companies for permission to reproduce copyright material:

Photo credits: p.2 © almagami – 123RF; **p.3** © alphaspirit - iStock via Thinkstock/Getty Images; **p.11** © Stockdisc/Corbis/Legal SD176; **p.14** © wernerimages – iStock via Thinkstock/Getty Images; **p.19** (left & right) © The Forgiveness Project/photo by Brian Moody; **p.20** © The Forgiveness Project/photo by Brian Moody; **p.27** © stevanovicigor – iStock via Thinkstock/Getty Images; **p.30** (left) © ChiccoDodiFC – iStock via Thinkstock/Getty Images; (right) courtesy of Shelka04 via Wikipedia (http://creativecommons.org/licenses/by/3.0/); **p.31** © Chuck Nacke/Alamy Stock Photo; **p.42** © jax10289 – iStock via Thinkstock/Getty Images; **p.43** © jessekarjalainen – iStock/Getty Images; **p.50** © Christopher Furlong/Getty Images; **p.55** © Design Pics Inc/Alamy Stock Photo; **p.62** © habari1 – iStock via Thinkstock/Getty Images; **p.66** © Manuel Faba Ortega – iStock via Thinkstock/Getty Images; **p.67** © Bernadette Delaney/Alamy Stock Photo; **p.71** © Nabil BIYAHMADINE – Fotolia; **p.72** © MrKornFlakes – iStock via Thinkstock/Getty Images; **p.78** © namyen026 – iStock via Thinkstock/Getty Images; **p.85** (top) © wareham.nl (sport)/Alamy Stock Photo; (left) © Lordn – iStock via Thinkstock/Getty Images; (right) © Trevor Snyder – Fotolia; **p.91** © xavigm – iStock via Thinkstock/Getty Images; **p.92** (left) © KeremYucel – iStock via Thinkstock/Getty Images; (right) © akova – iStock via Thinkstock/Getty Images; **p.94** © filipefrazao – Fotolia; **p.100** © NASA/JPL; **p.106** © Ryan Rodrick Beiler/Alamy Stock Photo; **p.114** © overcrew – Fotolia; **p.116** © Jim West/Alamy Stock Photo; **p.124** © Justin Kase z12z/Alamy Stock Photo; **p.130** © KatarzynaBialasiewicz – iStock via Thinkstock/Getty Images; **p.133** © Stockbyte – Getty Images; **p.134** © London News Pictures/REX Shutterstock; **p.139** © photka – Fotolia; **p.141** © André Quillien/Alamy Stock Photo; **p.144** © Scott Heavey/REX Shutterstock; **p.149** © CandyBox Images – Fotolia; **p.151** © Matthew Chattle/REX Shutterstock; **p.152** © Pete Riches/Demotix/Corbis; **p.156** © Frantab – iStock via Thinkstock/Getty Images; **p.157** © Custom Medical Stock Photo/Alamy Stock Photo; **p.159** © Spiegl/ullstein bild via Getty Images; **p.167** © Jeff J Mitchell/Getty Images; **p.170** © My Life, My Death, My Choice (www.lifedeathchoice.org.uk); **p.174** © Alchemy/Alamy Stock Photo; **p.178** © sudok1 – iStock via Thinkstock/Getty Images; **p.183** © Sebastian Kaulitzki – 123RF; **p.185** © Zoya Fedorova – 123RF; **p.190** © science photo – Fotolia; **p.199** © Oleg_Zabielin – Fotolia; **p.201** © Alistair Linford/REX Shutterstock; **p.205** © michaelfitz – Fotolia; **p.207** © luchschen – iStock via Thinkstock/Getty Images; **p.209** © MacX – Fotolia; **p.211** © Petrovich9 – iStock via Thinkstock/Getty Images; **p.216** © MAHMOUD TAHA/AFP/Getty Images; **p.217** © Hulton-Deutsch/Hulton-Deutsch Collection/Corbis; **p.218** © Artur Widak/NurPhoto/REX Shutterstock; **p.224** © Rachel Megawhat/Alamy Stock Photo; **p.226** © STRINGER/epa/Corbis; **p.227** © Rachel Megawhat/Demotix/Corbis

Image on pages 1, 232, 237, 242 © 9245953 – Fotolia; pages.9, 10, 19, 30, 39, 49 © Meinzahn – iStock via Thinkstock/Getty Images; pages 61, 62, 70, 77, 84, 91 © narith_2527 – iStock via Thinkstock/Getty Images; pages 99, 100, 110, 120, 129, 138 © pixbox77 – iStock via Thinkstock/Getty Images; pages 147, 148, 156, 166, 173, 183 © bestdesigns – iStock via Thinkstock/Getty Images; pages 195, 196, 204, 215, 223 © zabelin – iStock via Thinkstock/Getty Images

Acknowledgements:

Course assessment and marking guidance content in pp 232–236 has been adapted from SQA course specification and support notes and marking instructions © Scottish Qualifications Authority. The exam-type questions are not derived from any SQA specimen or past papers.

Orders: please contact Bookpoint Ltd, 130 Park Drive, Milton Park, Abingdon, Oxon OX14 4SB. Telephone: +44 (0)1235 827720. Fax: +44(01235) 400454. Lines are open 9.00a.m.–5.00p.m., Monday to Saturday, with a 24-hour message answering service. Visit our website at www.hoddereducation.co.uk. Hodder Gibson can be contacted direct on: Tel: 0141 848 1609; Fax: 0141 889 6315; email: hoddergibson@hodder.co.uk.

First published in 2016 by
Hodder Gibson, an imprint of Hodder Education
An Hachette UK Company
2a Christie Street
Paisley PA1 1NB

Impression number 5 4 3 2 1
Year 2020 2019 2018 2017 2016

Cover photo © ktsdesign – 123RF
Illustrations by Sarah Arnold Illustrations
Typeset in Cronos Pro Light 11/13.2 pt by Aptara inc.
Printed in Slovenia

A catalogue record for this title is available from the British Library
ISBN: 978 1 4718 6372 1

Contents

Acknowledgements

Thanks first and foremost to Lorna and David. David was not long born when I started my first book and is now a 24-year-old highly qualified sports scientist and fellow swimming coach – from whom I learn loads. Lorna has managed to build up a dazzling variety of academic qualifications over the years while still doing the things I'm pretty rubbish at (tiling, decorating, laminate flooring and the like – but I do the cooking …). Thanks to both for your patience, love and understanding over the years.

I would also like to thank a range of people who have commented on drafts of the book – although any errors remain mine: Dr Naomi Appleton for looking through the materials related to Buddhism; Barbara Coupar for commenting on the Roman Catholic perspective; Rev Ken Coulter, for commenting upon the Church of Scotland perspective and Gary McLelland, for keeping a watchful eye on the Humanist perspective.

Finally, I would like to thank John Mitchell, in his final year at Hodder Gibson. Hundreds of thousands of learners across Scotland have, for many years, benefited from John's commitment to supporting the Scottish curriculum and his contribution to learning in Scotland cannot be over-stated. I have welcomed his support and guidance for the past twenty-five years or so and he will be sorely missed by all the Hodder Gibson authors as he, probably quite literally, sails into the sunset and finally hangs up his laptop – an end of an era not only in publishing lunch terms but in so many other ways.

Note to teachers

This book has been written to support the Scottish Qualifications Authority course in Religious, Moral and Philosophical Studies (RMPS) at Higher – and should be of use therefore for National 4 and 5 levels too – 'Morality and Belief'.

I often receive comments about books along the lines of: 'You should have said more about …' and 'There should be more detail on …'. It is important to remember that each of these topics (and each part of each topic) could easily be a book in itself – or a single book of around 50,000 pages.

It's best therefore to consider this book as a 'starter for ten'. The aim here is to open up the topic areas – give a basic outline of the background to each one and start learners on the journey of reflection, consideration and analysis and so learning about and from religion and other belief systems. I continually strive to avoid expressing my own opinion on any of these matters – rather presenting facts, views, opinions and beliefs neutrally and allowing learners to reach their own conclusions. What I think, or any other teacher thinks, about each topic is not relevant – our job is to assist learners to make sense of some very difficult issues and reach their own conclusions (bearing in mind that this is a lifelong process). So inevitably there is a great deal of selection going on in this book, which is unavoidable. Also, in terms of illustrative religious and philosophical perspectives I have been deliberately selective to keep it all manageable. I have focused on Christianity (and the Church of Scotland and the Roman Catholic Church in particular) and Buddhism (though here I have not separated out Theravada/Mahayana traditions or any other branch of Buddhism). For 'non-religious' perspectives, I have used Utilitarianism and Humanism. However, although I have chosen to illustrate each issue with these religious and non-religious perspectives, you are perfectly free to use any others you think the SQA will accept.

Our job is to help learners develop the skills, attributes and knowledge-base to make sense of an increasingly complex world. Arguably, we are living in an age which is more information-rich than at any time in the past. For my first book – started in 1991 – I made many a visit to university and other libraries – now the information of the world is at my fingertips on the iPad sitting next to my computer and I have drawn upon it, of course. I have, at all times, tried very hard to make sure that the information and views outlined in this book are drawn from authoritative sources and will be happy to put right anything which has gone astray in that respect.

Please also remember to keep up to date with any changes to the course which the SQA puts into place. During the writing of this book, 'Moral Relativism' was removed from the course specification – so keep your eyes well and truly peeled for any updates from the SQA.

NB: The questions and activities in this book are designed to support learning and teaching – so, other than section 26, they may not always reflect SQA question stems and prompts. Use your professional judgement in this matter and ensure that your learners are aware of the kinds of questions SQA can and cannot ask in formal assessment contexts.

Note to learners

Welcome to RMPS – good choice. This book covers one-third of your course (though you'll only study one section in it!). I have tried to keep it light and to help you learn while enjoying yourself. The book is designed to set you off in your thinking – not to provide 'an answer' for everything (or anything for that matter) and you will want to research further to fill in the detail wherever possible – though think carefully about what's out there online and so on – some of it is very helpful and some isn't. If you can, engage with followers/adherents of the religious and philosophical perspectives you explore (good luck finding some Utilitarians), but remember to be careful to separate out fact from opinion and evidence from viewpoint and to reflect critically on what you learn. This book, and this course, is designed to support your learning – so that you can achieve whatever it is in life you want to achieve and so make the world a better place. Enjoy the challenge and enjoy the course.

1 Morality and belief

It is 3016, and three young people have reached the magical age of 16 years old. In 3016, it is recognised that the world is a better place when everyone does what is right, although it is also recognised that forcing anyone to do what is right is wrong. So, invented by the genius John Burbleblott, a chemical potion has been created which tastes a bit like lentil soup. However, this potion is a one-off drink for life. At 16 you are offered a choice – you can drink a mug of this potion … or not. No one will force you to drink it and no one will judge you for choosing not to drink it. Once you have drunk this potion, its chemicals will go to work on your brain immediately … and irreversibly. The potion will affect an area of your brain identified by John Burbleblott and named by him as the 'Burbleblott spot'. This bit of the brain is where all your decisions about right and wrong are made. The potion will work on this area of your brain and after drinking it … you will never be able to think or do anything wrong again – for the rest of your life.

The three young people who must now make the choice about drinking the potion or not are typical young people in 3016 … they love their holographic interface, their atmospheric sensory suits and, of course, their neurological media implants – well what young person wouldn't? Interestingly, like all young people in 3016, beliefs are central to their life and of the three, one is a Christian, one a Buddhist and one a Humanist. Although much has changed in the world (and in the other planetary systems people now regularly holiday in), Christianity, Buddhism and Humanism remain much as they have done in the past, and so each young person makes decisions about life based on their understanding of Christianity, Buddhism or Humanism. Each has just received a priority neurological communication confirming the date when they must choose to drink the potion … or not.

Talk Point

What should they do?

What is morality?

At its simplest, morality is about right and wrong. Being a 'moral person' would mean living a good life and being an 'immoral person' would be the opposite. The difficulty is in deciding what is and is not 'moral', and then deciding how to live – and even if it is important to live – a moral life. In different times, places and in different cultures still today, some might think of something as perfectly moral and others might think the opposite about the same thing! Some people think that there are things which are 'morally neutral' while others might think that these very things are very 'morally charged'. Some think your morality is determined by the situation and others think it is determined by laws, rules or guidance from divine beings and so on. Some think we are born with a 'program' in our brains about what is right and wrong and others think we are born like blank canvases and we have to learn what we think is right and wrong by trial and error and by being guided by others in a variety of ways. Morals are sometimes summed up in laws and rules which we follow – and these vary according to where and when we live. Morals may also be summed up in codes and sets of guidance which are based on the communities we are a part of and any belief system we follow.

What is belief?

Our beliefs are the things we think about life, the universe and everything. Again, some think we are born with beliefs and others think these are things we 'pick up' and develop throughout our lives. Our beliefs are often very closely linked to our upbringing, the culture we live in, the time we live in and so on. Some people probably constantly think about and challenge and reassess their beliefs – while others maybe just 'go with the flow' a little more. Some beliefs are very strongly held by some – and for others beliefs are just there in the background. How much belief affects action is a matter of debate – and there are varying views about this. Beliefs may come through experience, through being taught or through membership of communities and groups such as religious and other belief groups.

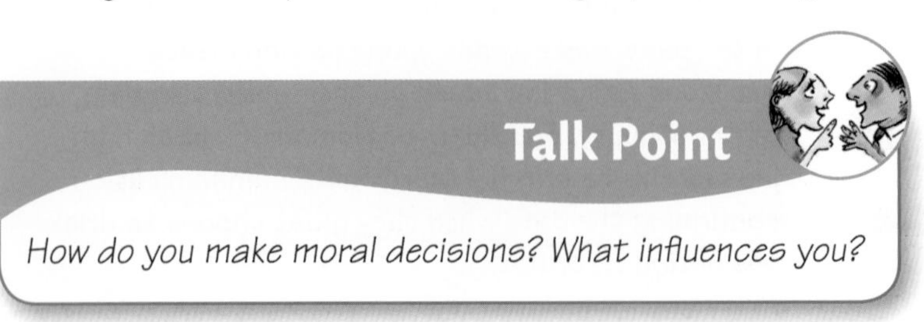

Talk Point

How do you make moral decisions? What influences you?

The link between morality and belief

In some ways these two words can be interchangeable – what you think is right is also what you believe to be right and so morality can = belief. However, the relationship between these isn't always simple because sometimes belief comes before morality: I believe X so this makes me choose Y. Sometimes belief comes after morality: I do X therefore I believe (or must believe) Y. This course is based on the idea that morality and belief are closely linked: the topics you will study in this course are going to make you think very carefully about your morality and your beliefs – and about how the two are related. All of the topics in this course can produce very fierce debate and strong emotions. Each topic can also lead to a very different range of views which depend upon a very wide range of issues, facts, opinions ... and so on. There won't be anything you're likely to study that will be all that simple and it will almost certainly come with a dazzling variety of beliefs and moral viewpoints based on ... well, that is for the rest of this book.

Making decisions about moral issues

We each probably make decisions about right and wrong many times every day. For example, you're reading this when you could be doing something else (daydreaming perhaps) – so you have made a choice about studying in RMPS or letting your mind wander away to other things. Many of our moral decisions are pretty straightforward ones and others are very complex. Some of the moral issues in this book are issues which you might never face – and others are. What you will be learning throughout the course
are the very important life skills of being able to make reasonable, thoughtful decisions.
This is a skill which is important throughout your life. You will have to learn about the evidence, weigh up arguments, consider different viewpoints and then put that all together to make sense of your own response to the topic or issue. This will help you to develop very important skills for learning, life and work. In this course you might cover science, technology, economics, social issues and so on – and you will draw upon a range of beliefs and viewpoints to help you make sense of these very complex issues and topics – this won't be easy, but it will be rewarding.

Moral responses

For each of the topics you will examine in this course, you are expected to be able to consider them in relation to the following:

- Responses from religious authority
- Responses from non-religious viewpoints.

You will be required to understand, explain and evaluate a range of religious and non-religious viewpoints about the topic you choose to explore. Now, this doesn't mean that you can consider the topics in relation to 'my granny who follows voodoo' or 'my auntie Margaret who doesn't believe in any religion'. We will be considering *authoritative* responses from both these positions. These authoritative responses might be from a religion's sacred scriptures or a non-religious belief group's agreed position about something. Authoritative responses might also include the teachings of key religious figures past and present and statements made by the 'ruling bodies' of such religions. For non-religious belief groups, authoritative responses might include the viewpoints of key figures past and present and statements from groups and organisations which are nationally or internationally representative of this belief group. Now there are many varieties of religious belief around the world and there are many different non-religious philosophies and 'stances for living', so to keep it as manageable as possible, we will be drawing upon teachings, beliefs and views from the following:

Religious authority: Christianity

Christian moral responses are reached by individual Christians and Christian groups in a variety of ways:

- **Reading sacred scriptures** In this case, the Bible. Christians will be likely to read this and then try to work out what it teaches about right and wrong.
- **Key religious figures** In Christianity, the teachings of Jesus are central – and his teachings contain a great deal about moral behaviour and choices. There are other key figures in Christianity whose teachings and views Christians might draw upon when considering moral issues. The first disciples, the apostles, saints, theologians past and present and so on. While scriptures and key figures are important, linking this to modern moral topics is not always straightforward – because many of the moral issues facing us today were not written about in the Bible, or dealt with specifically by any key religious figure.
- **Prayer** Individual Christians may also seek direct guidance from God on moral choices. They will pray and wait for answers and guidance. How they recognise and interpret this will be their choice.

However, for most Christians, learning from other Christians in denominations and churches is another way to make sense of difficult moral decisions – and in this course we will use two specific Christian denominations when exploring moral issues (although in your course you are free to use any religious viewpoint to respond to moral issues).

Religious authority: The Church of Scotland

A member of the Church of Scotland might draw upon the views of the Church when making moral choices. A member of the Church of Scotland may take part in Bible study, listen to sermons and other teachings in his/her own church and learn from other members of the church. As an organisation, the Church has a number of 'councils, committees and departments' which regularly prepare very detailed documents exploring particular moral issues. These documents are prepared along with experts in the field they relate to – as well as theologians. These documents basically link Christian teaching to moral issues and may make recommendations to the Church's highest body, the General Assembly. The General Assembly meets once a year and is made up of commissioners – members of the Church who hold positions in local churches – such as elders, deacons and ministers. The Assembly debates and discusses the papers presented and may vote to accept them or not. Once 'passed' by the Assembly the paper would be considered to be 'The Church's view on ...'. However, individual members of the Church of Scotland can still choose to accept this view or not and the Church leaves a great deal of room for 'individual conscience'. This book tries very hard to represent Church of Scotland teachings and views, but it is not in any way 'officially approved' by the Church of Scotland and the issues it deals with change all the time. So, if you are a member of the Church of Scotland, check out the Church's position with your minister or by contacting 121 George Street, Edinburgh, the Church's headquarters.

Religious authority: The Roman Catholic Church

A member of the Roman Catholic Church may take part in Bible study, listen to the views of individual priests and teachers and pray and reflect, just like a member of the Church of Scotland. However, in Catholicism there are a number of other ways in which individuals will arrive at moral decisions. The Catholic Church has, throughout its history, drawn upon a range of theologians – sometimes referred to as 'Doctors of the Church' – who have interpreted biblical and Church teaching on various matters. It has also had 'Councils' involving the highest levels of the Catholic priesthood (cardinals, archbishops, bishops and so on), for example, the Councils of Trent and the first and second Vatican Council:

at these Councils, many doctrinal issues have been agreed and therefore have become 'Church teaching'. One major source of Catholic teaching we will refer to in this course is the Catechism of the Catholic Church (CCC). This is a comprehensive document finally published in 1992, which contains key Catholic teachings on a wide range of issues.

Unlike the Church of Scotland, where the 'leader' is the moderator, chosen only for a year, the head of the Catholic Church is the Pope – from the moment of selection this is a lifelong role (although recently, and unusually, Pope Benedict retired from the role). The Pope is also the Bishop of Rome and head of the Vatican State. The Pope is viewed as a final authority in matters of Catholic belief and he issues teachings in a variety of ways – for example, Papal Bulls and Encyclicals, which are documents issued by the Vatican and which outline Church teaching on specific matters. Of course, things that the Pope says are often reported in the media – but his views are only Church teaching if they are issued in official Papal declarations (*ex cathedra*) and therefore represent the *magisterium* of the Church. Of course, Catholics are invited to accept and follow the teachings of the Church, but like other Christians, the role of individual conscience is still important. Catholics believe that the teachings of the Church are not to be thought of just as a set of dry rules or instructions but as something more. A good way to think of it is that Catholics believe that the Church is a mother and a teacher. A mother cares for you, looks out for you and wants to protect you from harm; in that way she also becomes your teacher. So it's not some list of 'dos and don'ts' but loving guidance about how best to live your life. It is important to point out that this book does not have any official 'seal of approval' from the Catholic Church – so if you are a Catholic it would make sense to make sure your RMPS teacher and/or your parish priest supports your understanding of Catholic teaching on these complex issues.

Religious authority: Buddhism

Buddhists too will meditate, reflect and study sacred scriptures in order to make moral choices. They will consider the teachings of Buddha and of key figures within Buddhism past and present. There are Buddhist scriptures too and writings from Buddhism past and present which Buddhists may draw upon when considering their responses to moral issues. Like the other religions, though, many of the moral issues covered in this course were not around when these scriptures were written – so Buddhists will have to try to link the general principles in their scriptures with modern moral issues – which will be easier at some times than others. Like other religions, Buddhism also has a number of denominations and other groups within the religion – Theravada and Mahayana for example, but also Zen and Pure Land and others. In this book, Buddhism will be covered as a single religion rather than going into detail about different versions of Buddhism. This, again, is just to keep things manageable in a book that you won't need to transport into school in a wheelbarrow. You are more than welcome to explore all the different varieties of Buddhist thought and teaching on each issue and build your own understanding further – and if you are a Buddhist you will probably want to do this anyway.

Talk Point

Within your class, what role is played by religion when your classmates are making moral decisions? How well or badly does this reflect the place of religion in society as a whole?

Non-religious viewpoints: Humanism

Humanist Society Scotland has referred to itself as a belief group. Humanists make moral choices in a variety of ways. There are no agreed central sources of teaching for Humanists – certainly no 'scriptures' of any sort – and there is not any particular agreement on who any 'key figures' in Humanism might be. Humanist organisations like Humanist Society Scotland and the British Humanist Association do publish materials expressing 'Humanist views on ...', but individual Humanists are free to accept or reject these views as they see fit. For Humanists, the principle way to make moral choices is to gather as much evidence as possible and then approach this evidence using reason to reach a conclusion. According to Humanist Society Scotland, Humanists *'are people who trust science and rational inquiry to help explain the universe around us, and who do not resort to supernatural explanations'*[1]. Humanism is therefore a philosophy, an approach and a way of life – but each Humanist can reach their own conclusions about moral issues. Humanists may make use of the views of 'key figures in Humanism' such as Bertrand Russell, Carl Sagan, Richard Dawkins and others – but these key figures do not have the same place in Humanism as key figures generally do in religion.

Non-religious viewpoints: Utilitarianism

Utilitarianism is a philosophical perspective. Generally speaking it is based on the principle that any moral choice should result in 'the greatest good/happiness for the greatest number'. This can also be expressed as 'the best consequences for the greatest number'. This means that Utilitarians always have to weigh up the benefits and costs linked to each moral choice in relation to who they affect and how they affect them. Utilitarian thinking appears in the writings of two of its founding fathers, Jeremy Bentham (1748–1832) and John Stuart Mill (1806–73). Utilitarianism can also be broken down into two types of Utilitarianism: *act* Utilitarianism, which uses the consequences (real or predicted) of actions to decide what is right or wrong; and *rule* Utilitarianism, which is a set of rules (or a rule) that are applied to decide what to do in certain situations to maximise happiness for the greatest number.

Moral complexity

Moral issues are often very complex and require a good understanding of the background as well as everything else linked to it. As an example, let's consider the environment. To make a moral decision about the environment you would probably need to consider:

- a range of scientific claims about the environment and the effect of human activities on the environment
- a range of views about the impact of human psychology, behaviour, social structures, politics, economics (to name but a few) on the environment
- how far all of these views/opinions/facts and figures agree/disagree about the causes and consequences of human activity for the environment
- the key teachings/viewpoints of your religion or belief group and perhaps the key teachings/viewpoints of key figures and representatives of this religion/belief group and how far your religion/belief group is 'agreed' on its approach to human interaction with the environment
- your own understanding of all of this! (Then you can decide whether to recycle your jotters from last year or chuck them in the bin ...)

Perhaps the next time anyone suggests that RMPS is easy you might like to mention these five bullet points ...

Nevertheless, although moral choices are not easy to make, it is vital that we make them – and that we make them as carefully as possible. All of the issues in this course are complex, sometimes very sensitive and usually very difficult. The consequences of our actions (or inaction) might also be very serious, so it is everyone's responsibility perhaps to make carefully judged moral decisions. This course is not just about passing Higher RMPS (though that's important) – it's about helping you to take your place as a member of society who is informed about the big issues and who can have a positive impact on the world. It's important to understand the world in which we live – but it's also important to work towards making it a better place for all: your part in that is just as vital, just as important, as anyone else's.

Personal Reflection

- *How do you make moral choices?*
- *What role does religion/belief play in your life?*
- *Would you take John Burbleblott's potion?*

Active learning

Check your understanding

1. What might be the characteristics of a 'moral person'?
2. Why doesn't everyone agree about what is and isn't moral?
3. Describe two sources or methods a Christian might use to help make moral decisions.
4. For one of these sources/methods, explain one benefit and one drawback of using this to help make moral decisions.
5. What differences are there between how a member of the Church of Scotland and a Roman Catholic might make moral decisions?
6. Why might the scriptures of religions not be easily applied to moral issues in the twenty-first century?
7. In what different ways might people who are not religious make moral decisions?
8. What is the difference between act and rule Utilitarianism?
9. Why might making moral choices be a difficult process?
10. Explain how you decide what is right and wrong.

Investigate

1. Carry out a survey in your class/school to find out how people make decisions about right and wrong. Make sure the answers are treated as confidential. You could ask people about how far their choices in life are guided by religious or other kinds of belief. You could collate and display your findings.
2. By this stage in your learning you will have learned a lot about Christianity. You may have learned about Buddhism and Humanism. Carry out your own research into Buddhism and/or Humanism and create a report on one/both of these. You should find out about their history, their key beliefs/views and how Buddhists and Humanists make decisions about right and wrong.
3. Although you will have learned about Christianity throughout RME, you may be less familiar with the Church of Scotland and/or the Roman Catholic Church. Carry out your own research into one of these and create a PowerPoint or other visual presentation about the denomination you have chosen.
4. To help you develop your understanding of the religious and belief 'landscape' of Scotland, you should carry out research to produce a poster about religion and beliefs in Scotland. What is the spread of religion and beliefs like in the twenty-first century? How has it changed in recent times? How central is belief in the life of modern Scots?

Analyse and Evaluate

1 What are the key similarities and differences between how the religious and philosophical perspectives in this section reach moral decisions?
2 Followers of religions draw upon a range of sources when deciding what is right and wrong – often including direct 'revelation' from their divine figure. What should a religious person do if they thought their divine figure was telling them to do something which all the teachings of the religion pointed to as being wrong?
3 Discuss each of the following statements in pairs and then in your class consider the responses people give:
   - The sacred scriptures of religion come from so long ago that they aren't really very helpful to people trying to make moral choices in the twenty-first century.
   - Most moral issues are far too complex for anyone to understand and make decisions about – we should leave it to the experts.
   - No one has the right to suggest what anyone else should believe.
   - Everyone is responsible for their own moral choices – we can't blame anyone else.
   - Even if a 'key figure' or famous person says we should do something, we still need to work it out for ourselves.
   - Following a religion or a belief system is just an easy way to avoid making decisions for yourself.

Apply

Having now considered the religious and other perspectives you will explore in this course, in groups, come up with a range of simple moral dilemmas (don't use anything you might cover in this book), for example, 'You have accidentally dropped your wee brother's favourite toy and it has smashed into a thousand pieces'. For each of these moral dilemmas explain what a Christian, Buddhist, Humanist and Utilitarian might advise and what sources they might draw upon in giving their advice. You can go into as much detail as you like.

RELIGION
AND
JUSTICE

2 The causes of crime

Imagine the following fictitious situation: James Carron has been found guilty of murder for which he can now face life imprisonment. Before sentencing, the judges hear final statements from the defence and prosecution …

Defence: My Lords, there is no doubt that the crime committed by James was a truly horrific one. James has acknowledged that and is deeply sorry for his actions. James understands and accepts that he must be punished for his actions. However, the defence argues that a life sentence is not in order here. It would be easy to think of James as simply a thoughtless monster who carried out a terrible action, but of course the truth is far more complex than that. From birth, James did not receive the opportunities in life that many in this courtroom would have enjoyed. His abusive father was in and out of prison many times, before abandoning his wife and children. James's mother herself had a difficult life, battling addiction brought on by her abusive relationship. The young James had to grow up quickly and his difficult life fostered in him a deep anger towards the world, an anger which would erupt uncontrollably for the slightest of reasons. This inevitably led to James missing a great deal of his education and therefore losing out on making himself desirable to any employer. This in turn led him to cope through drug addiction and a series of petty crimes – crimes designed to enable him to support his younger brothers in avoiding his course in life. As a society, we all share the blame for James's circumstances – his downward spiral was there for all to see, but he was no one's concern. Unsurprisingly, anger and resentment built up in James, and this anger, clouded by his drug dependency, ultimately led to the actions for which he is being sentenced today. It would be easy to think that James could have exerted some control over his circumstances to avoid his crime – easy for us to say, but not for James, a victim of a series of dreadful circumstances which might have pushed any one of us to our limits. For this reason the defence calls for leniency in sentence – an expression of society's responsibility for the circumstances of life against which we did not do enough to protect James.

Prosecution: My Lords, the prosecution does not, for a moment, minimise the difficulties of Mr Carron's life. We recognise the failings on the part of many others which led to his difficulties throughout life. We recognise that there were times when his judgement was less than it could be as a result of his drug dependency. We recognise that Mr Carron's circumstances were far from ideal. While all this is undeniable, however, it does not excuse Mr Carron from the enormity of his heinous actions. Many people experience great hardship in life, many are neglected by parents, fail in their educational aspirations, are excluded from working life and as a result fall victim to seeking escape through drug dependency. We do not wish to minimise this negative set of life experiences which Mr Carron has experienced. However, while many share the unfortunate nature of his life experiences, this does not automatically lead them to become killers. It is not inevitable that dreadful circumstances in life make one a murderer. No, we argue that Mr Carron, despite his tragic circumstances, ultimately had a choice. In choosing to carry out his vile crime he chose the wrong path. For this, he must be punished to the full extent of the law. All face difficulties in life – some certainly have more than their share of hardship – but to accept that this can be turned to as a way of excusing the taking of life is not acceptable. Mr Carron made many poor choices, and it is for these choices that we call for a sentence of life imprisonment. Any other sentence would express contempt for Mr Carron's victims, and open the door for all to claim that equally atrocious events were somehow not their responsibility …

What is crime?

James Carron has committed murder – the taking of innocent life without justification – which is regarded as a crime everywhere. But what makes it a crime? To make things simple, let's think of crime as anything which breaks the law. Laws are different around the world of course, so what counts as a crime in one country might not in another. So to keep things simple, we'll stick with Scots law – so crime is anything which breaks the law in Scotland. Unsurprisingly, it's still not that simple because crime can be committed on purpose (or intentionally), such as *murder*, or it can be unintentional, such as dangerous driving causing death, in which case it is more likely to be *culpable homicide* than murder. It is also a crime to attempt to do certain things (such as *attempted murder*) – and it is a crime to *aid and abet* the committing of crime. There are many crimes, and some are considered by the courts to be more serious than others, such as murder and assault, compared with parking on a double yellow line or making a fraudulent insurance claim. While most are likely to agree that some crimes are far more serious than others, there can still be different views about how criminal 'lesser' crimes are, such as taking certain classes of 'recreational drugs' for example. Throughout this section, we will assume that anything which breaks the current laws in Scotland is a crime.

Talk Point

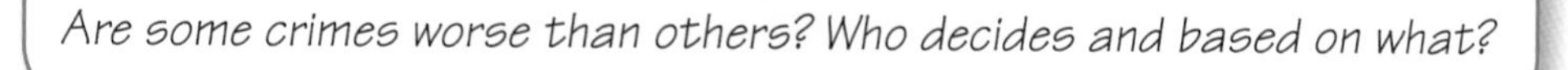

Are some crimes worse than others? Who decides and based on what?

The causes of crime: simple or complex?

Imagine you were one of the judges. What sentence would you give James Carron? For some, the causes of crime are relatively straightforward and quite simple, for others they are far more complex and difficult to disentangle. When courts in Scotland make decisions about sentencing they do take into account a range of factors through 'background reports'. This can be anything from the guilty person's mental state to other circumstances of their life. The aim of the courts is to find out if there are any mitigating circumstances. Defence solicitors may also give a plea in mitigation, which basically amounts to trying to get as light a sentence as possible because you put before the judges a range of factors which affected your client's actions. During court cases solicitors and advocates are likely to be very skilled in introducing doubt into judges' and juries' minds about the guilt of the accused. One way this can be done is by highlighting life circumstances which may have contributed to the actions of the accused. Judges and juries should be making their decisions about whether or not the accused is guilty based on the facts alone, but of course all involved are human, and introducing the idea that somehow the accused 'couldn't help themselves' may well appeal to human nature. Your guilt should be linked only to *whether or not* you committed the crime, but in reality perhaps it's a bit more complicated because it might be hard for judges and juries to ignore *why* you might have committed the crime. Throughout this section it is important to be aware that the causes of one kind of criminal activity may be very different to the causes of another – or they could be exactly the same.

Possible individual causes of crime

It is not always easy to separate individual causes from wider social circumstances because there will be interaction between both. However, some possible individual causes of crime might be:

Personality factors

Is there such a thing as a 'criminal personality' – are some people 'born criminals'? Is there a gene for being a criminal? Psychologists and neuroscientists are likely to disagree about this – partly because what makes your personality is itself very complex. But let's say that something about your personality makes you more likely to commit crime. Let's say that in your DNA, there is a code for being a criminal – does that then mean you are not responsible for your actions? Should we screen for this DNA before birth – and if we find it, what should we do? Would everyone who had this DNA automatically (and unavoidably) commit crime? Could there be DNA for theft, for murder – for parking on double yellow lines? It would be very difficult to isolate any such DNA and point to it contributing to one crime more than another, but perhaps in the future – who knows?

As well as possible direct DNA causes for 'a criminal personality', could DNA contribute to something else which then leads to criminal action? For example, aggression levels in individuals may be linked to hormonal balance (which in turn might be caused by genetic factors). It is suggested, for example, that there is a link between high testosterone levels and aggression. Dabbs *et al.* (1995) found that male offenders with high testosterone levels were more likely to be in prison for violent crime (in 1997, Dabbs and Hargrove found the same applied to female persons in custody). In both studies, however, it is difficult to say if the high testosterone levels caused violent crime or if violent crime caused high testosterone levels. So, might high levels of this hormone make you more likely to commit violent crime? If so, could you 'blame' your testosterone levels, over which you have no control?

As well as hormonal factors, there could be a range of other individual factors which lead to criminal behaviour. For example, those labelled 'psychopaths' or 'sociopaths' may be more likely to commit serious, often violent, crime but the causes of psychopathological and sociopathological behaviours are not at all clear, so how far we can think of them as causes of crime – over which the criminal has little or no control – is not clear.

Of course, personality style may be a complex mixture of nature and nurture, and may be the result of the interaction between biological/psychological factors and social factors. Picking all this apart to decide what has caused criminal activity is not going to be easy.

One other factor is important here: some crimes are planned carefully and the criminal has a clear understanding of what they are doing and why. They also have a clear knowledge of all the possible outcomes of their activity. Other crimes are very much in the 'heat of the moment' – they are unplanned, unforeseen and, perhaps, less in the control of the person doing them – and maybe even 'unintentional'. How much of a difference does this make? Are the causes of planned crimes the same as those which are done in the heat of the moment? Should courts take this into account? How important is the *intention* of your actions in relation to the *outcome* of your actions?

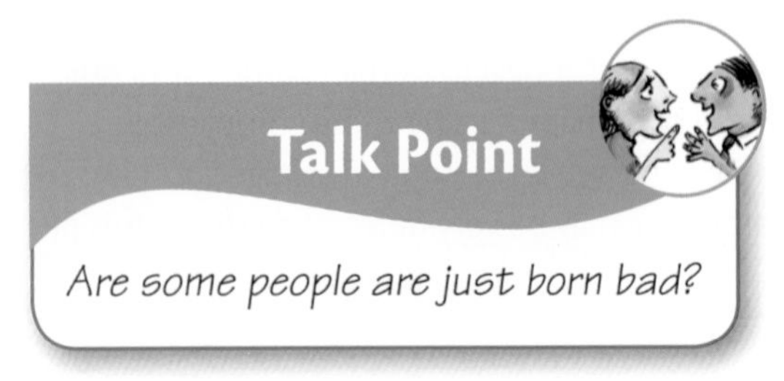

Individual circumstances

Every individual is a unique combination of a range of experiences, events and choices in life. Whatever our life experiences, our individual responses to these are many and varied and could lead to some responding by engaging in criminal activity and others not doing so. What goes into this complex mix itself will be varied across individuals and how each individual responds to this complex mix might determine how likely they are to be a criminal. For example, some psychologists argue that early childhood experiences have a large effect on adult behaviour. Certain experiences may be more likely to lead to criminal activity than others; for example, childhood abuse has been suggested as a strong possible cause of later antisocial and criminal behaviour. However, the link is not simple or clear: some people who experience childhood abuse engage in criminal behaviour while many do not – equally, many who have never experienced any kind of childhood abuse engage in criminal behaviour.

Some psychologists argue that the role of *mediating factors* is an important one. Mediating factors are things which might reduce (or of course increase) the effect of something. So, for example, imagine a child neglected by his parents at an early age – a mediating factor would be whether or not he was taken into care as a result of this and the quality of his care. Perhaps having loving and caring foster parents would 'undo' any damage done to the child through his natural parents' neglect. So the effect of early childhood experiences on later life may be able to be 'put right' by a range of other factors and so reduce the harmful effect of early experiences. However, again, this raises the important question of how far anyone can 'blame' their early childhood – or any events in their life – for their actions.

Again too, such early childhood experiences (or indeed any experiences in life) might have a secondary effect in leading people to a range of 'coping mechanisms'. These coping mechanisms might be the result of a range of experiences in life and are a way of helping you to cope with what has happened. This could involve a range of addictions and other forms of unhealthy lifestyle. Perhaps, it is argued, in order to 'feed' such addictions, individuals are more likely to engage in crime. For example, feeding a drug addiction is costly – paying for regular fixes might require more than the average pay packet can stretch to. Also, as a drug addict you are probably less likely to be able to secure any normal form of employment, so getting the money you need might lead you to turn to crime as a quick and effective way to get hold of a lot of money fast. When you add to this the fact that the thinking processes of drug addicts are often negatively affected by their addiction, then this can lead to the possibility that crimes will be a lot less 'controlled' than they otherwise could be – which could lead to crimes becoming violent.

Possible social causes of crime

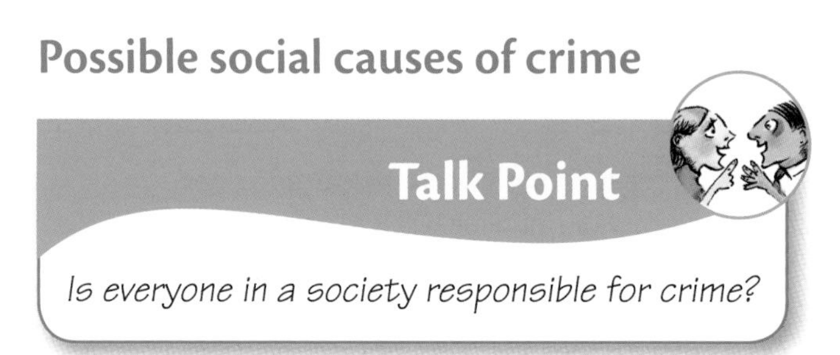

The individual possible causes you've thought about do not exist in a vacuum. All of our individual actions are linked to our interactions with others, with situations, and so on. Various *social processes* can be mediating factors which make crime more or less likely, and how individuals experience and respond to a range of social circumstances is going to have an effect on whether or not they commit crimes. The contribution of social factors to causing crime is also very complex and hard to pick apart. Crimes are generally carried out by individuals, but they may be the end result of a long and complex set of interacting factors which led to the crime and over which they had little control.

Social learning theories

Some argue that crime breeds crime (and so, in fact, prisons are simply schools for learning to be a better criminal!). Social learning theories say that we learn our behaviours through observing and copying others where we see them rewarded for their actions. So if we see 'people getting away with it' we are more likely to try it for ourselves. So the causes of crime include imitation of others – a simple process where we do what seems to work for others. Of course, the punishment of crime has a role in putting us off such imitation of criminal behaviour (its deterrence value) and if we see criminals punished then this should make us less likely to commit crime. This does seem to work, of course, but not for everyone – more of that in the next section.

Economic issues

Some turn to crime because they want a better life – they want to be rich. Others turn to crime because they see it as the only way to make ends meet. For example, if your family were starving and you thought the only way to feed them was to steal something, what would you do? For some, this is a major cause of crime in some situations and means that the responsibility for crime belongs with everyone who ignores the needs of the poor. Perhaps if societies were organised in such a way that no one was in need, then certain crimes might never happen. It is generally agreed that crime rates go up in times of economic recession, so perhaps this cause of crime could be dealt with by reducing economic inequality (and all the other forms of inequality which might lead to economic inequality). This might require laws, or it might just require people to care more about the needs of others. On the other hand, of course, it is far from true that anyone who is poor is going to engage in criminal activity, and it is also true that many people you would think of as being wealthy engage in criminal activity. Being underprivileged does not automatically mean that you will become a criminal because of the influence of many other factors – however, some argue, it remains a possible contributory factor in crime, so one way to reduce crime is to promote greater economic fairness in society.

Power imbalances and other factors

Some argue that one of the major causes of crime is the imbalance of power in society. The argument is that because some have power and others don't, then this leads to resentment, anger, envy and a feeling of wanting to take what you don't have. Power imbalances come around in a number of ways – for example, some might argue that certain sectors of society 'look after their own' and that you are more likely to get on in life if you come from a particular class, race, social group, gender, city, country and so on. Such differences within and between societies and social groups have the potential – it is argued – to lead to instability in society, which in turn is more likely to lead to crime. The solution therefore is to make sure that everyone in society has an equal opportunity to have a good life so that society becomes more stable and crime less likely. Again, individual responses to this suggested cause of crime will play a great part in whether or not criminal activity follows and a whole range of mediating factors will be important here.

The role of freedom of choice

In all of the discussion about the possible causes of crime so far, one theme is common: how far can and does each individual have freedom over their choice to engage in criminal activity or not? Free will is a very complicated philosophical and psychological idea, but it is an important one in this case. Are we free to make choices about everything and what does such freedom mean? It is very hard to say how much freedom anyone has about any choices they make in life, because all of our choices have a wide range of possible causes and contributing factors. Are all of our choices linked to our DNA, our personality, our social circumstances, our experiences, the chemicals running through our bodies, the structure and function of our brain? Can we think of any criminal act as something which someone has freely chosen to do? Are we ever 'in our right mind' when we carry out a crime? For some, this is the central issue, and it takes us right back to James Carron: how free were his choices and how much were they 'imposed' on him by factors which were not in his control? Perhaps, of course, the causes of crime are not important – perhaps we should consider only the outcomes. Does it really matter why James Carron committed murder – should his punishment simply fit the crime and ignore the possible causes of the crime?

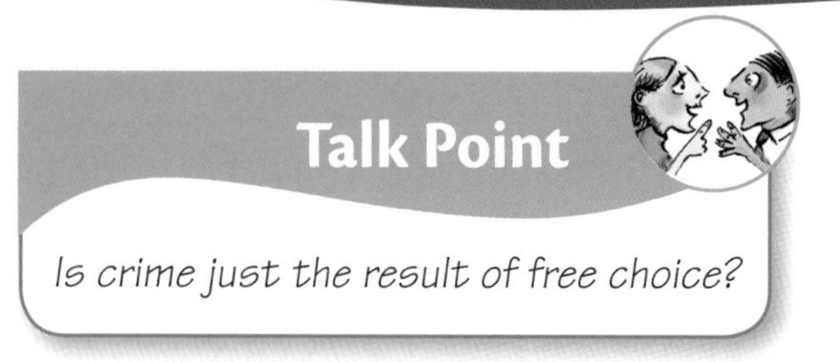

Some religious and philosophical reflections on the causes of crime

Christianity

Within Christianity a range of viewpoints are likely about the causes of crime. Some will argue that all crimes are a result of the fallen nature of humanity – humans are sinners and crime of any kind is a sin. It is therefore important for Christians themselves to resist any urge to engage in criminal activity and support others to do the same. However, while Christians would agree that criminal acts are a result of our sinful human nature, many Christians might argue that the causes of crime are far more complex than just the result of sin. They would point to injustice in society, poverty and inequality as contributory factors in crime – though they would be unlikely to allow people to use them as excuses for crime.

The Roman Catholic Church

The Catechism of the Catholic Church draws upon the Ten Commandments to state what counts as a crime. The Church would consider the cause of crime as the sin which lies behind the action. (CCC 865–69). It states that *'the fifth commandment forbids direct and intentional killing as gravely sinful.'* (2268) It supports the seventh commandment, which states quite clearly that *'You shall not steal.'* (Exodus 20:15) The Catechism states: *'The seventh commandment forbids unjustly taking or keeping the goods of one's neighbour and wronging him in any way with respect to his goods.'* (2401) So Church teaching on murder seems very clear, however it does go on to say that: *'the deliberate murder of an innocent person is gravely contrary to the dignity of the human being, to the golden rule and to the holiness of the Creator.'* (2261) This means that while the murder of an innocent person is considered criminal, it might allow that the killing of someone who is 'not innocent' may be possible in some circumstances (though whether this counts as murder or not is a matter for debate). The Church also qualifies its views on theft with the use of the word *'unjustly'*, because some could take this to mean that there might be times when taking something which is not yours is justified. However, in Scotland, the Roman Catholic Church would support the law of Scotland in relation to crime. As to the possible causes of crime, the Roman Catholic Church is very aware of the pressures on those who are in poverty, but it would be unlikely to condone them engaging in criminal acts because they are poor. It suggests that crime is part of our sinful nature and it is every individual's responsibility to reject sin, although it is equally everyone's responsibility to understand and show compassion towards the sinner.

The Church of Scotland

The Church of Scotland would have a broadly similar view to that of the Roman Catholic Church. It would be against any actions which broke any of the Ten Commandments and would support the law of Scotland in its handling of crime. The Church of Scotland would also accept, as does the Roman Catholic Church, that the causes of crime are many and complicated and might include individual and/or social contributory factors. They would also accept that the Christian's role is to oppose crime, support justice for all, and to understand and help rehabilitate those who have committed crimes. The Church of Scotland would not accept someone using their circumstances in life as an excuse for committing crime, but is also aware of the fact that there is often a close relationship between social and economic factors and criminal activity. The Church would argue that a fair, just and equal society would be likely to lead to reductions in crime, but that the fallen nature of humanity probably means that crime will be with us until we all put right our relationship with God.

Buddhism

Buddhists also accept the laws of the land in which they live, so would be likely to oppose anything which broke the law. Buddhists would also accept that there are complex causes of crime, which have both a social dimension and an individual one. Imbalanced, uncaring and unkind societies where people are lacking in equality, opportunity and perhaps hope are likely to be breeding grounds for crime. However, in Buddhism, individual causes of crime are also central. The key to the causes of crime are probably linked to the second of the four noble truths: *all suffering is caused by desire.* Perhaps, therefore, one common cause of crime is our desire – or greed – which is fuelled by our attachment to things. This could be physical attachment – so that we are always wanting things and if we cannot satisfy those wants through the normal channels in life (such as working to be able to pay for things), then some will resort to crime to get what they want. It could also be psychological attachment – perhaps, for example, to wanting to be better than others – which might result in criminal activity to 'prove it'. In Buddhism, the three root poisons *hatred, greed and delusion* are key causes of crime because they lead to unskilful actions and it is probably true to say that most crimes involve some mixture of the three root poisons.

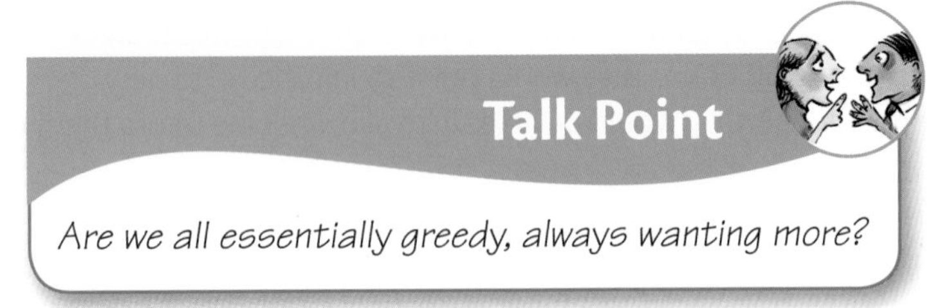

Humanism

The British Humanist Association states that: *'Actions can be morally wrong without being illegal, and illegal without being morally wrong, but many actions are clearly both.'*[2] Although Humanists argue that people should work to challenge unjust laws, until they are changed they should follow them. Humanist values are summed up for many in the Amsterdam Declaration (2002)[3] which sets out the values of Humanism worldwide. This contains seven fundamental values, one of which includes *'Humanists insist that personal liberty must be combined with social responsibility.'* So Humanists oppose crime, however they also understand that its causes can be very complex. They would argue that the causes of crime need to be researched carefully so that we are making judgements about the causes of crime based on the evidence. Although the causes of crime are complex, they are not unalterable as the Amsterdam Declaration states: *'By utilising free enquiry, the power of science and creative imagination for the furtherance of peace and in the service of compassion, we have confidence that we have the means to solve the problems that confront us all.'* Humanists would be likely to argue that the causes of crime are probably a complicated mixture of the interaction between individual and social factors. They do not believe that there is anything naturally 'good' or 'bad' about human nature, but that human survival depends on biological and social factors.

Utilitarianism

Utilitarianism is based on the principle of maximising happiness for the greatest number, though this does not automatically mean ignoring the happiness of the minority – because, certainly in relation to crime, it is very possible that both are closely linked. The consequences of crime are definitely not causes of happiness for victims and, while they might cause some kind of happiness for 'successful' criminals, for those convicted of crime it's unlikely that they will be happy about it. Utilitarians generally argue that a society which balances the needs of the majority with the rights of the minority is most likely to be the happiest form of society. Certainly if a contributing factor in crime is individual or social circumstances for the minority (as criminals are) and this has damaging implications for others then this needs to be put right. Most Utilitarians would accept that the causes of crime can be complex and that an unhappy society is probably likely to contain more crime. In this case, the task is to create as happy and contented a society as possible, which should therefore result in reduced crime as people feel less need to break the law to achieve their desired outcomes. Of course, Utilitarians would be aware that some crime might simply be related to individual characteristics and would occur no matter how happy the society (successful and wealthy people commit crimes too). Their hope would be that if you followed a utilitarian philosophy then you would carefully judge the likely consequences of your actions – and this would probably lead to less crime.

Personal Reflection

* *What do you think are the most likely causes of crime and do you think these causes might be different for different crimes?*
* *Some say that given the right conditions anyone would commit a crime. What do you think?*
* *Is it ever possible for judges to take into account all the possible causes of crime when deciding on sentencing for crime?*

Active learning

Check your understanding

1. What are the possible individual causes of crime?
2. How might circumstances lead to criminal behaviour?
3. In what ways might social factors be linked to crime?
4. How far do you think committing crime is a matter of free choice?
5. Why might someone argue that religions and belief groups allow people to make excuses for criminal behaviour?
6. In what ways might human greed and ignorance be linked to crime?
7. In what ways might 'an unhappy society' lead to more crime?
8. What do you think are the major causes of crime?
9. Should religious people be less likely to commit crime than non-religious people?
10. Do you think crime will ever disappear from human society?

Investigate

1. Before sentencing in Scotland's courts, judges may call for background reports on the guilty person. What kinds of things do these reports cover? Are there things these reports do not cover which you think they should?
2. What evidence is there for and against the view that there is a 'criminal personality type'?
3. Carry out your own research in your school either using interviews or questionnaires (your findings should be anonymous). In this research you should aim to find out people's views about the causes of crime. Are there any differences of views between groups (e.g. adults and school pupils; males and females, etc.)? You should produce a short report of your findings.
4. Using newspapers, the internet and TV news reports, analyse how the media reports crime. Some questions you could explore are:
   - Which crimes are most/least often reported?
   - How often is the crime 'sensationalised' and how is this achieved?

- How often is the accused/guilty person portrayed as a 'monster' or as someone at the mercy of his/her circumstances?
- What is the balance of reporting about male and female criminals and in what ways are these categories reported differently?
- Which groups in society are most often reported as being involved in crime and how far is this reporting possibly biased?
- How far do the sentences for the crimes match how serious the crimes were (in your opinion)?

5 Using the internet find out in what ways (and if) the religions/denominations/philosophies you have studied in this section help either the victims of crime or the rehabilitation of criminals.

Analyse and Evaluate

1 Using the religious and non-religious perspectives you have studied in this section, how do you think each would respond to the following statements:
   - The responsibility for crime lies with society.
   - Crimes are often caused by people who are just 'born bad'.
   - Once a criminal, always a criminal.
   - It is never acceptable to excuse crime because of someone's life history.
   - The causes of crime are so complex that we could never hope to work them out.
   - No matter how good society is, there will always be crime.

2 Imagine a drug was produced which stopped anyone ever committing a crime. Should taking this drug be compulsory for everyone? What do you think?

3 How far do religious and non-religious perspectives agree that the causes of crime are mostly not under an individual's control?

Apply

Imagine that the Scottish Government wanted to produce some guidance for judges to help them work out what to take into account when sentencing someone found guilty of a crime. The Scottish Government wants this guidance to reflect psychological and social factors which may be linked to the causes of crime, but also wants to include views from religious and non-religious groups about the possible causes of crime. In a group, produce this guidance document. It should be straightforward and clear and assist judges in knowing what they might take into account when sentencing.

3 Perspectives on punishment

Just before Christmas in 2008, Scottish nurse Magdeline Makola was violently abducted from her home by Justice Ngema. Justice was a friend of someone she knew and he had called at her house. He threatened to kill her, tied her up and threw her in the boot of her car. He took all the money from her bank account using an ATM and demanded more. She was sure he planned to kill her. However, he left her in the boot of her car and she soon realised that he wasn't coming back. She was drifting in and out of consciousness and could hear people's voices as they passed the car, but no one responded to the weak sounds she made to try to attract attention through the tape over her mouth. As the temperatures plummeted she prepared herself for death. She didn't feel angry though, she just wanted to calmly die. At one point, however, she heard voices and made one final attempt to chew through the tape over her mouth and made a weak call for help. This time she was heard and rescued, though she was suffering from severe frostbite. She says: 'Because of the joy of being found alive, I have never again felt any hatred towards Justice Ngema, but I have felt a deep sadness. We were both South Africans in a foreign country, and we should have helped one another, like brother and sister'. She added: 'It's hard to understand why he did what he did. He wasn't on drugs, he wasn't drunk, and he didn't have mental problems. He was just a human being motivated by greed and desperation. My hope now is that in prison he comes into contact with people who can help him so that he can understand the harm that he did and change his life. You have to be positive to open up ways for someone to become a better person'.

Shad Ali, a British Pakistani, was brutally assaulted after coming to the aid of two Pakistani women who were being racially abused. During the assault the attacker repeatedly stamped on and kicked his face. Had the attacker not been pulled off by passers-by it is likely Shad would have been killed. The right side of his face remains filled with metal plates, and after the attack he had long complex surgery and experienced significant psychological trauma. His friends wanted retribution, but he told them that this was not the answer. In fact, he wanted to forgive his attacker. He says: 'I received a huge amount of criticism and confusion from friends and family who didn't understand why I wanted to forgive – especially from my wife who initially felt nothing but hatred for this man … After years of requesting to visit him, I was finally allowed to exchange letters with him and I found out that he was full of remorse and wanted to meet me too. I tried not to have any expectations of what the day would bring. Once we shook hands, we spontaneously hugged, which was totally unexpected, and I became

very emotional and started crying ... we shared our individual experiences of the day of the attack and also a bit of our life stories. By the end of the meeting it felt like we had become friends.

Edinburgh man Eric Lomax was brutally tortured for three and a half years while he was a Japanese prisoner of war. In 1982, Eric found out that the man who tortured him, Nagase Takashi, was working for a charity and had built a Buddhist temple. Eric thought if he ever met Nagase Takashi he would probably kill him. Five years later, Eric's wife wrote a letter to Mr Nagase and Mr Nagase responded. Eric felt that Mr Nagase's letter was so full of compassion that he began to wonder if the two of them meeting might be the right thing to do. In 1998 they did meet and Mr Nagase trembled, cried and bowed repeatedly, expressing his deep regret for what he had done. Over the course of a few days the two men chatted and laughed together. They remained friends until Eric died in 2012. Eric had said: 'Forgiveness is possible when someone is ready to accept forgiveness. Some time the hating has to stop.'

Based on stories at **www.theforgivenessproject.com**

Perspectives on punishment: forgiveness

Three remarkable stories which describe forgiveness, reconciliation and people who chose to leave hatred and anger behind. Could you have done this in their situation? In the cases of Shad Ali and Eric Lomax, the men who behaved so terribly towards them craved their forgiveness, and Shad and Eric chose to forgive them. Magdeline's attacker is said never to have shown any remorse for his actions and although Magdeline chose never to meet him again, she nevertheless forgave him for his actions. When someone has committed a terrible crime, it can often be very hard to imagine forgiving such a person for their actions – especially for the victims of crime – but in each of these cases this is exactly what happened.

Many religions stress the importance of forgiveness, no matter what the crime. Most require that the person guilty of the crime shows remorse for their actions, seeks forgiveness and, of course, makes clear that they will never behave in such a way again. Many non-religious perspectives also believe in the value of forgiveness, suggesting that forgiveness is better for the victim, the criminal and society generally, because it puts an end to a potentially destructive cycle of retribution and counter-retribution, and brings peace of mind to all involved. For some, forgiveness is the most positive and constructive response to crime, because it puts an end to the hatred which is more likely to feed further crime.

Forgiveness is a perspective on punishment although, of course, it is in some ways the opposite of punishment. What questions does forgiveness raise as a response to crime?

What makes one person able to forgive and another unable to do so?

As with many of the issues you study in this course, this question is not easy to answer. Perhaps individual personality types make people more likely to be forgiving than others. Perhaps this combined with social factors make people likely to forgive. For example, if you are brought up always to forgive no matter what, then obviously forgiveness is more likely to be your response to crime. Your beliefs will play an important part here because if you are brought up in a religion or philosophy which stresses the importance of forgiveness, then you are more likely to forgive. It might simply be that forgiving others is a rational and reasonable decision you reach when you carefully think through all the possible reactions to crime – reaching the conclusion that forgiveness is the best response. Alternatively, it might be a very emotional response, which just feels like the right thing to do – even if others, and maybe even you, don't understand why you are forgiving. Some argue that forgiveness brings benefits to all – the criminal is shown that hatred and anger are not necessary responses (which might help them avoid repeating their crimes) and the person forgiving does not need to 'hold on to' any hatred or anger – which might be better for their own state of mind.

Why does one person respond to crime with love and understanding and another with hatred and loathing?

Gandhi said: *'The weak can never forgive. Forgiveness is an attribute of the strong.'* Perhaps forgiveness is a more likely possibility where you can empathise with people and see things from their perspective. Perhaps those who see crime as caused by many different factors are less likely to respond to criminals with hatred and anger and seek retribution. Maybe people with a strong sense of our common humanity are more likely to be forgiving than others who think in very 'either/or' terms – or who see no link with other human beings. Perhaps those who forgive just think of it as a more positive and creative response to crime – one which could break a vicious cycle of hatred.

Is forgiveness the same as being 'let off' for crime?

Of course, some think that forgiveness is not only difficult, it is not helpful. Perhaps, they might argue, forgiveness is just seen by criminals as weakness and is more likely to make them commit further crimes because they might think that in some way, being forgiven is the same thing as being 'let off the hook'. A forgiving society might give criminals the wrong message about the seriousness of crime and so perhaps make crime more likely. In 2015, the Churches' Child Protection Advisory Service[4] suggested that convicted sex offenders were seeking new victims by targeting churches on their release – because of the views of church members about forgiveness. However, forgiveness does not need to be thought of as an alternative to punishment, but as something which works alongside certain types of punishment. Many people who choose to forgive also support the idea of justice being done and proper punishments being in place for crime. They would argue that you can forgive someone, but that they can still, at the same time, receive punishment for their actions. This approach would mean that people would not think of forgiveness as a 'soft touch' approach because it would go hand in hand with the normal handing out of justice through punishment as part of any society's laws and rules. Some argue that forgiveness and trust do not need to co-exist. You can forgive someone, but you don't need to trust them again and it certainly doesn't mean that you think their actions were in any way right – or that you would allow them to continue with their actions.

Talk Point

Does forgiving a criminal make them more or less likely to repeat their crime?

Is forgiveness the 'right' response to crime?

Some argue that forgiveness is always the right emotional response to crime, because of its benefits for both victim and criminal. They might say that it is an approach which is far more likely to lead to a positive and productive outcome, something which is less likely with retribution and hatred. They could of course argue that forgiveness can also involve proper punishment and so thinking of it as in any way a weak response to crime is wrong. Some may say that forgiveness is important for the victim, because it allows them to 'move on' from the trauma of crime. Perhaps, in such a view, the criminal does not matter, because the forgiveness is an act of self-compassion carried out by the victim, not an act of compassion towards the criminal. Clearly, forgiveness without any wrongs being put right by the criminal (either through some form of punishment or restorative actions) could be seen as a weak response to crime and unlikely to put an end to crime – but instead perhaps it should be seen as part of a wider response to crime and criminals involving both forgiveness and justice.

Perspectives on punishment: retribution

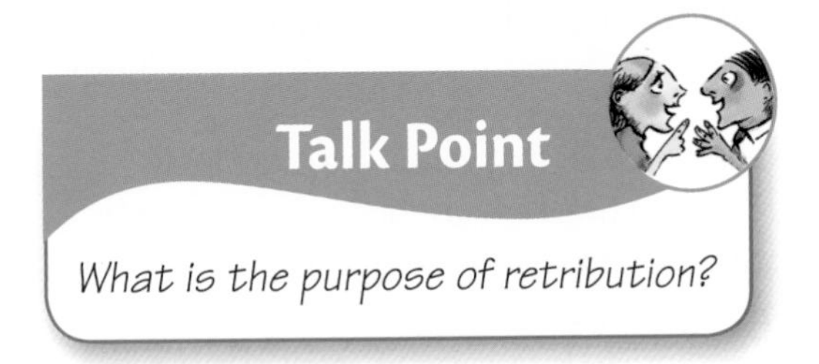

In many ways, retribution is the opposite emotion to forgiveness, because it wants to 'balance up the books' by making the criminal suffer in some way to make up for the suffering they have caused. Often retribution is thought of in an *'eye for eye, tooth for tooth'* way, as described in the Bible/Jewish scriptures. The point is to make the criminal suffer in exactly the same way as the victim – so for a murderer, this would mean that they would lose their life too. In some systems this might be a token retribution – for example, in some cultures, theft might result in the cutting off of your thieving hand. Even prison can be based on a society's requirement that retribution is taken for crime committed – because this is 'hitting back' by removing the criminal's freedom.

What makes some people want retribution?

Some people probably feel that retribution 'balances things up' because the criminal pays for what they have taken or done. In some cultures, blood feuds are very much part of the culture and this can lead to an endless cycle of violence – because each act of violence or crime means that the victim's family feels the need to respond in the same way. So-called 'honour killings' may also have an element of retribution – because they are about getting someone back for something they are thought to have done to bring 'dishonour' to an individual, family, culture or way of life. Of course, being angry about crime is a pretty reasonable response to crime – and perhaps the more serious the crime, the greater the anger is likely to be – but does this mean that this anger should spill over into yet more hatred, violence and perhaps further crime?

Why do some reject retribution as an approach to crime?

Although anger is a reasonable enough response to crime, is it a positive emotion for the victim, the criminal or society? Some argue that it is not a positive response, because it could make the victim behave in as bad a way as the criminal (even if they just support retribution rather than carry it out) and so become 'criminals' themselves. Some say that 'like for like' retribution is a funny way to show that the original crime was wrong – because it just repeats the original crime, which is made to look like a reasonable response. Some say too that retribution leads to an unending cycle, because every act of retribution leads to someone else needing to take retribution for that and so on – endlessly.

Is retribution the 'right' response to crime?

Some argue that it is. It shows that society will not tolerate crime and it means the criminal has to 'pay back' for what they have done. This balances things up, makes society safer and is the right response to crime. It also has a *deterrent value* – which means that it will put the criminal off repeating the crime and, importantly, it will put others off doing the crime (or similar crimes, or indeed any crime) because of the example which has been set by the act of retribution on the criminal by society (or individuals or families, etc.).

Some disagree – they argue that retribution just meets our emotional needs for balance, but isn't productive, helpful or kind. It sends out the wrong message to everyone about what it means to be human and does not take into account the individual circumstances of a crime – for example, the difference between a crime committed in the heat of the moment and a coldly planned and executed crime. Also, retribution does not necessarily make the victim feel better – if anything, it will make them feel worse – because they will know that they have been responsible for the same level of suffering as the person who committed the crime in the first place. There is also an important point to be made about getting it right if retribution is the method of punishment. Many guilty verdicts are overturned – sometimes after many years – as new evidence comes to light (or the limitations of original evidence become more obvious). What happens in these situations if retribution has been taken? Would the 'criminal' now become the 'victim' and would this new 'victim' be entitled to take retribution? It would all get very complicated and some say that for this reason, retribution as a response to crime doesn't make sense.

Perspectives on punishment: proportionality

In eighteenth-century England, the 'Bloody Code' was a set of laws which included 222 crimes for which you could be executed. Crimes included: impersonating a Chelsea pensioner; being a pickpocket, 'strong evidence of malice' in children 7–14 years old; writing a threatening letter; and stealing a sheep. If you think the death sentence for such crimes is a bit extreme, then you already understand what is meant by proportionality. Proportionality has two key meanings, each of which raises a number of questions:

The punishment should fit the crime

This means that the seriousness of the crime should be reflected in the seriousness of the punishment. For example, it could mean that the death penalty is only applied when a crime has resulted in a life being taken – not for writing a threatening letter. This shows that a society has a balanced approach to crime and sentencing, because the crime and the punishment 'match up' in some way. The problem here, however, is who decides 'how serious' a crime is? Different crimes are regarded as more serious by some, and in some countries are more serious than in others – and of course, nowadays some crimes are not thought of as serious as they were in the past. So the problem here is 'matching up' the crime and punishment because first you have to agree a 'value' for each crime and each punishment (which could be difficult to agree about). Proportionality in this sense is linked to the deterrence value of punishment because if you know that a certain crime will result in an equally severe punishment, then you might think twice about carrying out the crime and will be deterred from (put off) committing the crime in the first place.

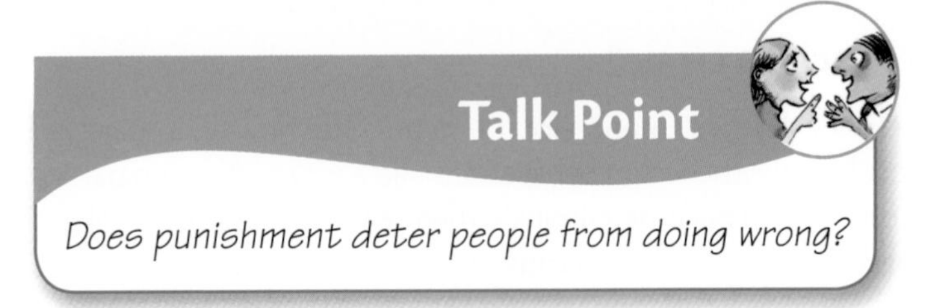

The punishment should only go as far as is necessary

This means that any punishment should do what it intends to do and no more. For example, the punishment should punish and be as severe as necessary, but not wildly out of proportion to the crime. The trouble with this again is who decides what 'out of proportion' might mean? Let's take murder as an example: some argue that the taking of the murderer's life is the correct (and proportionate) response to the crime. However, international laws state that capital punishment should be swift, dignified and as painless as possible. In the past there have been some truly gruesome methods of slow and painful execution – were these slow horrible deaths out of proportion even to the crime of murder? Some will argue again that the deterrence value of punishment is important here: they would say that the more terrible the punishment, the more likely it is that people will be put off committing the crime in the first place. In fact, this would mean that a disproportionate punishment would be considered a good idea by some. Others would argue that even criminals have rights and that disproportionate sentencing goes against those rights. Proportionality, they would argue, means that the crime is suitably punished but no more and that society does the right thing by the criminal in proportionate sentencing. Those who argue for proportionate sentencing might also point out the issue of leaving room for errors – for example, where guilty verdicts are subsequently overturned at a later date: if the punishment has been disproportionate then this might lead to added problems for society in responding to the now 'not guilty' decision, because a greater punishment than was required was carried out.

Most legal systems in the world would probably argue that their sentencing is proportionate – because their sentences match how serious they think the crime is and how important it is for them to punish the crime in a way they think is appropriate.

Some religious and philosophical views on punishment

Christianity

While the Old Testament quite clearly states 'eye for eye, tooth for tooth', and many Christians today would accept this straightforward link between crime and punishment, others would stress the importance of forgiveness, after the words of Jesus who, when asked about the 'eye for eye' passage, responded that you should 'turn the other cheek'. (Matthew 5:38–39) Many Christians argue that while individual Bible passages can be used to support retribution and disproportionate responses to crime, the underlying theme across Christian teaching is forgiveness.

The Church of Scotland

Forgiveness

The mother and close relatives of Grangemouth Church of Scotland Minister, Aftab Gohar, were killed in a suicide bombing attack on a church in Pakistan. The Rev Gohar said: *'It is wrong what these people did but I forgive them … Forgiving is what we learn from the Lord Jesus Christ. That is why I forgive.'*[5] Perhaps the most central prayer in Christianity is likely to be recited each week in the Church of Scotland. In this prayer, the Lord's Prayer, which came directly from

Jesus, there is a line which states *'forgive us our sins, as we forgive those who sin against us'.* This line reminds Christians that they should forgive others just as God forgives them. For Christians in the Church of Scotland – as for other Christians – the Bible is full of stories about the importance of forgiveness, including the parable of the lost son. However, for Christians, perhaps the most significant teaching came from Jesus while on the cross. Here, as he was dying he uttered the words: *'Father, forgive them, for they do not know what they are doing'.* (Luke 23:34) So, if Jesus can forgive even at this moment then it is also clear that Christians should forgive too.

Retribution

Given the importance of forgiveness within the Church of Scotland, it is unlikely that the Church of Scotland would ever support punishment as retribution. Retribution keeps hatred alive and it would be hard to see how further evil coming as a result of evil would ever be considered acceptable in the Church of Scotland. Christians do believe in the importance of justice and that those who commit crimes should make amends for their crimes – but such restorative justice is not retribution. Citing the story of Zacchaeus, The Church of Scotland states: *'No point is served in the life of human society, no truth is revealed about the justice of God, if release from past sin cannot be offered or restoration accomplished.'*[6] How far someone can be forgiven without asking for forgiveness is probably a matter for debate within the Church of Scotland.

Proportionality

The Church of Scotland therefore combines its beliefs about forgiveness with its beliefs about justice and urges a positive, creative and forgiving response to crime and so would probably support proportional responses to crime. However, there may be differences of opinion on this within the Church. In 2014, the Church produced a document called 'Our vision, imagining Scotland's future'. In this are a number of views expressed within the Church at focus group events, including views about crime and punishment: for example, some members of the Church of Scotland had *'mixed attitudes as to whether the correct balance between punishment and rehabilitation is currently being achieved, with some advocating a stronger emphasis on rehabilitation, whereas others focused on a need for a more robust attitude to crime.'*[7]

The Roman Catholic Church

Forgiveness

In January 2015, Pope Francis said: *'God always forgives us. He never tires of this. It's we who tire of seeking forgiveness ... there is no sin which God will not pardon. He forgives everything.'*[8] So if God forgives, then Christians should too according to Pope Francis. However, forgiveness should happen after someone is sorry for their actions, has asked for forgiveness and has promised to change their ways, but it is not the asking which is key but the admitting, as in the Sacrament of Reconciliation. The Catechism is clear that forgiveness is linked to a need to ask for forgiveness. *'God created us without us, but he did not will to save us without us. To receive his mercy we must admit our faults.'* (1847) So repentance means saying sorry (contrition), admitting you have done wrong (confession) and promising not to repeat the sin (satisfaction). Not seeking forgiveness has consequences for our eternal life: *'If [mortal sin] is not redeemed by repentance and God's forgiveness, it causes exclusion from Christ's Kingdom and the eternal death of hell, for our freedom has the power to make choices for ever, with no turning back.'* (1861) So the Church teaches that forgiveness is important, but that asking for forgiveness is an important part of that – and we also have to forgive others as Jesus taught in the Our Father.

Retribution

When someone has committed crime, the correct Catholic response is to pray for the person, love the person (though not what they have done) and hope that the person repents of their sins so that they can be forgiven. In common with other Christian groups, the Catholic Church would support the idea that Christians can hate the sin while loving the sinner. Retribution is an act of anger and further wrongdoing and so, in common with other Christian groups, Catholics would be expected to reject retribution as a response to crime. In 2013, Pope Francis said quite clearly: *'Taking retribution is not Christian.'*[9]

Proportionality

In common with other Christian groups, the Church would be likely to support a just response to crime. It argues that while criminals should be punished, the emphasis should be on restorative relations and not be punitive to the crime, and should mean that, others are protected from future possible crimes – but it should also mean that the door is open to the criminal having the opportunity of *'redeeming himself'.* (2267) According to the Church, punishment should be legitimate and seek justice.

Buddhism

Forgiveness

The opposite of forgiveness is resentment, anger and hatred – all of which involve 'holding on' to your negative response to something. This means that you remain attached to negative and destructive thoughts. Therefore forgiveness would seem to be the correct Buddhist response because it allows you to free yourself (and the criminal) from the negative consequences of the crime, as well as practise loving-kindness. In the Dhammapada (a collection of sayings of the Buddha in verse form) it states clearly that: *'Hatred is not brought to an end by more hatred, it is brought to an end by loving-kindness. This is the eternal law.'* (v.5) In Buddhism there is no specific need for a person to ask forgiveness before they are forgiven – because the act of forgiveness is an act of compassion which doesn't come with conditions. This means that forgiveness is a state of mind as well as an action which should be practised for the benefit of all. Importantly too, in some ways forgiveness is irrelevant – a person's actions will have consequences whether they are forgiven or not.

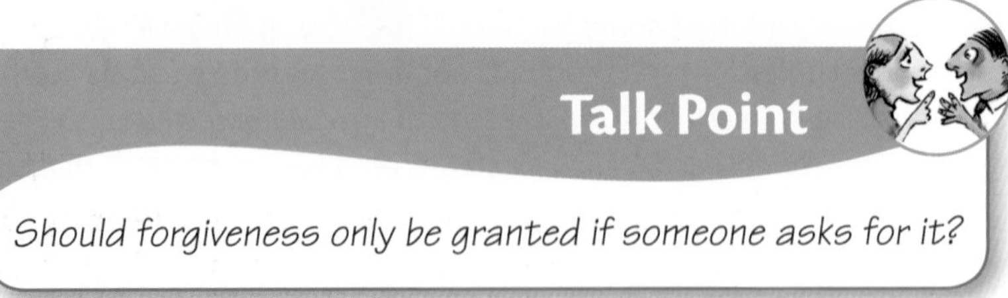

Talk Point

Should forgiveness only be granted if someone asks for it?

Retribution

The Dalai Lama apparently once tweeted: *'While retribution weakens society, forgiveness gives it strength.'* So, if we actually take retribution on a criminal, then, in common with other religious views, we may make ourselves as bad as the criminal. Also, for Buddhists, an act of retribution is unlikely to produce any good kamma (karma) for anyone anywhere – more likely the opposite. So taking retribution would go against Buddhist principles. Even thinking about retribution and holding on to anger is contrary to Buddhism. Elsewhere, the Dalai Lama has written: *'There is a certain irrationality in responding to injustice or harm with hostility. Our hatred has no physical effect on our enemies; it does not harm them. Rather it is we who suffer the ill consequences of such overwhelming bitterness. It eats us from within.'*[10] Holding on to your anger is more likely to mean that you are being punished rather than the criminal.

Proportionality

As Buddhism stresses the importance of the 'middle way' between extremes and is concerned with balance in life, proportionality in punishment would seem to be an appropriate Buddhist response. Punishment is permitted in Buddhism – there are specific punishments which can be given to monks and nuns who break the rules of monastic life. However, these are generally designed to help the guilty person face up to the error of his/her ways and return them to the path towards enlightenment. Therefore in Buddhism, punishment should always allow for the possibility that the criminal might learn from his/her mistakes and turn towards a more productive life. So the punishment should reflect the crime, but should allow for the criminal to change for the better.

Humanism

Forgiveness

There is no one Humanist view on forgiveness or any expected response about it, but as Humanism bases its morality on evidence and reason, it is likely that Humanists would see some value in forgiveness. Firstly, it is obvious that for some, not forgiving means holding on to resentment, anger and hatred. These are potentially very destructive for the person who holds them – and don't necessarily cause any harm to the criminal. Therefore, it probably makes more sense for the victim to give up resentment and have a forgiving attitude – for their own good: of course, that doesn't mean they have to communicate any forgiveness to the criminal. The British Humanist Association states: *'Humanists don't necessarily believe in "turning the other cheek"... this would just increase suffering by encouraging evil actions. But most rational people acknowledge the benefits of eventually forgiving and forgetting even the most terrible of wrongs. The desire for punishment or retribution can dominate the mind of the victim to an unhealthy extent, and retribution can simply perpetuate and multiply wrongs.'*[11]

Retribution

So clearly Humanists would be wary of retribution (although there is no prohibition on it, other than what would be covered in a country's laws). Humanists appreciate that anger and hatred are perfectly reasonable and natural responses to crime – however, whether they are constructive responses is another matter. The problem with retribution is that it is potentially never-ending, as each act of retribution can provoke another. This would not make for a very stable society and would probably increase crime overall rather than reduce it. Thoughts of retribution might harm the person holding them and carrying out retribution would be morally suspect.

Proportionality

The British Humanist Association quotes the Chinese philosopher Confucius, stating that Confucius *'seems to have got it right when asked what he thought of the principle of repaying injury with kindness. He replied, "With what then will you recompense kindness? Recompense injury with justice and kindness with kindness".'* [12] Humanists would accept that punishment has many roles – as a deterrent, as retribution for wrongs, as providing an opportunity for the criminal to make amends, as sending a message out about crime. However, Humanists would be most likely to argue that punishment should match the crime and do no more than is required to respond to the crime appropriately. So for Humanists, justice is important, but justice must be fair and reasonable and allow for the possibility of errors too.

Utilitarianism

Forgiveness

Although there's no kind of requirement for a Utilitarian to forgive anyone for anything – even if they ask for it – the consequences of forgiveness might make it more or less helpful as an approach to punishment. If forgiveness leads to reconciliation and an overall reduction in hatred and anger, then this might eventually lead to reduced crime – beneficial for the majority. So forgiveness might be a good approach, because of its beneficial effects on the individuals concerned as well as the wider benefits for society. However, if forgiveness leads to criminals thinking that they could get away with their crime again, then that might make them more likely to reoffend – which is obviously not good for the happiness of the majority. So, as with many things for Utilitarians, the difficulty is working out the possible consequences of forgiveness. In common with other perspectives, however, Utilitarians could also accept that forgiveness can be in addition to justice – so someone could be forgiven while also being suitably punished, which could mean that any negative consequences of forgiveness (as a 'get out clause' for future crime) would be avoided.

Retribution

Again, there's no specific 'rule' about this for Utilitarians and some modern Utilitarians argue that 'retribution' is 'morally neutral', but once again, the consequences are crucial. If retribution does keep anger and hatred alive and results in an endless cycle of crime, then it's not going to produce the greatest happiness for the majority. Alternatively again, if retribution brings the actions of a criminal to an end (and isn't followed by acts of counter-retribution) then it could be beneficial for society.

Proportionality

It is likely that Utilitarians would support a principle of proportionality, because this is a possible balance between the 'weaker' approaches of retribution and forgiveness. A proportionate response to crime does a number of things: it expresses society's rejection of the crime without automatically rejecting the criminal; it identifies that certain crimes are more serious than others by the match between crime and severity of punishment; it enforces justice and so it might act as a deterrent for further crime. All of this is likely to produce benefits for the majority and so would seem a sensible approach for Utilitarians.

Personal Reflection

- *Is there anything you think is 'unforgivable'?*
- *What are your views on taking retribution?*
- *Can the punishment always fit the crime?*

Active learning

Check your understanding

1. What do the stories at the start of this section teach about forgiveness? Should everyone respond in this way?
2. How far is it possible to forgive *and* to punish?
3. Why might some argue that forgiveness might lead to more crime?
4. Why do some think that retribution is the right response to crime?
5. What is meant by proportionality?

6 Are proportionate sentences effective deterrents?
7 How far do the Church of Scotland and the Roman Catholic Church agree about the importance of forgiveness?
8 What do religions and non-religious belief groups think about retribution?
9 Do Humanists support the idea and practice of forgiveness?
10 How might a Utilitarian support the idea and practice of retribution?

Investigate

1 Use the internet to find stories of forgiveness. In groups, you could each take a story and re-tell this story in a format of your choice (**www.theforgivenessproject.com** is a good starting point).
2 A number of Bible stories link to the idea of forgiveness. Choose one of these stories and consider what it teaches and how this might be applied in the world today.
3 Use one of the three stories at the start of this section. Carry out your own questionnaire research into people's views about this story. Do they agree with the choice of the person? What would they have done? Do you find any patterns in people's responses by age, gender, etc.?
4 Choose two or three countries and investigate the sentences they impose for one or two particular crimes. Are there countries where sentences are more or less proportionate than others?
5 Again, the media often takes a very 'retribution-focused' approach to crime (or certain crimes). Create a collage of newspaper front pages which you think show a retribution-focused approach to crime. Then try to balance this with front pages which take a forgiveness approach to crime.

Analyse and Evaluate

1 How far do the religious perspectives you have studied in this section agree about the right response to crime?
2 'There is more difference than similarity in the response to crime between religious and non-religious perspectives.' What do you think?
3 What are your views on the following statements?
   - Some crimes are unforgivable.
   - Forgiveness should only be given if the criminal asks for it.
   - You can forgive and punish.
   - If criminals knew retribution would be taken, they'd be less likely to commit crime.
   - The only way you can be proportionate in response to some crimes is by killing the criminal.
   - Forgiveness is an attribute of the strong.

Apply

Have a look at your school rules (or school code of conduct). Are the concepts of forgiveness, retribution and proportionality clear in these rules? Could they be rewritten to make these ideas clearer? Produce a revised set of school rules which make clear the role of forgiveness, retribution and proportionality in matching 'crimes and punishments'.

4 Approaches to capital punishment

Some methods of capital punishment past and present ...

(Warning: some not very nice explanations coming up.)

- Boiled alive – sometimes the victim was brought to a boil slowly, other times they were plunged straight into some kind of already boiling liquid.
- Brazen Bull – the victim was put inside a metal chamber and a fire was lit underneath. The victim would be slowly roasted and their screams amplified from within the chamber.
- Slow cutting – the victim is tied to a post and the executioner slowly cuts away pieces of flesh ... one by one ... trying to keep the victim alive for as long as possible.
- Flaying – similar to slow cutting, but the skin is removed from the criminal and an attempt is made to remove the skin in one piece.
- Lethal injection – the victim is strapped to a bed and poison is injected into them.
- Staked in the sun – the victim would be laid on their back and tied to a stake in the desert sun. The sun would do the rest (sometimes they were buried with only their head above the sand).
- The Catherine wheel – the victim was spread out on a wheel and sharp blows broke their bones.
- Crushing – sometimes huge stones were laid on top of the victim until they suffocated – sometimes animals such as elephants were used.
- Hanging – a rope is tied around the victim's neck and they are dropped sharply.
- Beheading – the victim's head is removed with sword, axe, or purpose-built machine such as the guillotine.
- Killed by animals – the victim would be placed in a confined space with an animal which would kill them.
- The Gibbet – the victim is sealed in a cage and suspended in the air – eventually they die.
- Stoning – large rocks are thrown at the victim until they die (sometimes huge blocks are dropped one by one from the feet upwards).
- Buried alive – the victim is buried in a pit and soil completely covers them.
- Electrocution – the victim is strapped to a chair and an electric current is passed through them until they are dead.
- Firing squad – the victim is shot.
- Also ... various forms of drowning, suffocating, burning ...

Capital punishment: the background

Talk Point

Are these descriptions likely to change a person's views on capital punishment?

The 'Yuk Factor'

It would be hard to read these accounts (or look at images of them – best not to) without being revolted and it would be a simple leap from this to arguing that capital punishment is inhumane, horrible and should be a thing of the past (all of which many agree with, of course). However, some argue that we need to be careful not to confuse the 'yuk factor' (the horrible reality of some forms of capital punishment) with the belief that it is a morally acceptable form of punishment. Some societies still carry out capital punishment for some crimes while others reject it totally for any crime. In the UK there are regular calls for the return of capital punishment – usually after some particularly terrible crime has been committed. For some, the response to capital punishment is a simple emotional one – for others, it has to be considered reasonably and sensibly by considering the arguments in detail.

What crimes are linked to capital punishment?

In most countries (NB: in the USA, capital punishment laws vary by state) where capital punishment exists it is applied only when a 'capital crime' has been committed – one which has involved the taking of life by the guilty person. In some countries, however, capital punishment is available as a sentence for a whole range of crimes, including treason, sexual crimes which do not result in murder, economic crimes, adultery, blasphemy, political crimes and drug trafficking. There is debate of course around the world about what counts as a 'crime' – for example, blasphemy is a capital crime in some countries but is regarded as the 'right of free speech' in others.

Capital punishment and the legal process

Capital punishment in most countries usually only happens after a long process of legal debate, discussion and careful review of the evidence proving the person's guilt. When capital punishment has been given as a sentence, the execution often takes place a long time after this, while appeals, reviews and a whole complicated process of challenging the sentence takes place – often involving the country's highest courts. During this time, the guilty person is in prison on what has become known as 'death row' awaiting a final decision about their sentence – and then the execution itself. However, it's important to note that 'in most countries' doesn't necessarily mean all, and in some places the delay between sentencing and execution is very short. Also, some argue it is possible that the legal processes in some countries are less careful than in others – but that's a matter of opinion, of course. If an appeal against the death sentence is successful, the sentence is usually reduced to life in prison. Most countries in the world publicise the number of executions which take place – though not all do. According to Amnesty International, in 2014 at least 22

countries still had the death penalty, and 2466 people were sentenced to death.

Who can be executed?

In most countries where capital punishment exists, certain groups of people cannot receive a death sentence – this includes children and people who are 'insane', or who have 'mental or intellectual disabilities'. However, these exclusions don't apply everywhere and even where they do, the definitions of each of these categories can differ.

What 'rules' apply to capital punishment?

Again, there is wide variation around the world about this. In most countries, capital punishment is carried out in private, or with some witnesses. Some countries still have public executions, though. Also, in most countries, executions are claimed to be 'humane', which means death occurs quickly and as painlessly as possible and the execution respects the dignity of the person being executed. As you might expect, there are differences of opinion about how far any of these are observed during executions, with some claiming that executions are often inhumane, painful and do not respect the person's dignity. (Of course, some supporters of capital punishment might argue that the more inhumane, painful and degrading an execution is, the more likely it will be a good deterrent for others.) The United Nations allows that individual countries can use the death penalty if they think this is the right thing to do, but it states very clearly in the UN Declaration of Human Rights Article 5: *'No one shall be subjected to torture or to cruel, inhuman or degrading treatment or punishment.'* It also states that: *'No one shall be arbitrarily deprived of his life'* which means that the death penalty should only take place after a fair trial. Finally, it states that no one under the age of 18 years should be executed. Countries which are part of the United Nations are expected to agree to these rules – but there is often disagreement about how far they do.

Talk Point

Should there be certain people who cannot be executed?

What forms of capital punishment exist in the world today?

This is difficult to say because some countries do not provide details of capital punishment. However, hanging, electrocution, beheading, shooting, lethal injection, the gas chamber and stoning are still carried out today. Different countries have different reasons for choosing one method rather than another – for example, in some US states, drug companies have made it difficult for authorities to get hold of the chemicals used in lethal injections, so other methods have been considered.

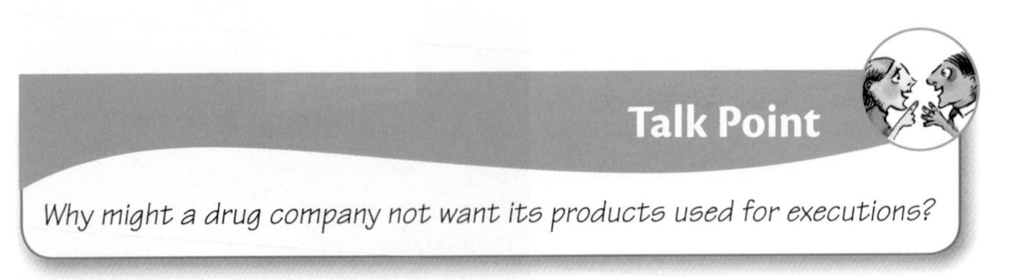

Talk Point

Why might a drug company not want its products used for executions?

What is capital punishment for?

Retribution

Some argue that the main purpose of capital punishment is to 'balance things up'. Society shows that if you do X, then X (or something similar to X) will be done to you. This is society's way of 'getting its own back' on the criminal for a capital crime. Because it is 'the state' doing the execution, this avoids the problem that personal retribution leads to more retribution (although the executed person's family, friends or group may feel more justified in taking retribution against the state for the execution, so this might not apply). Supporters of capital punishment might say that retribution is a perfectly natural and justifiable response to capital crime, while opponents may argue that a society which 'evens up the score' is acting in an immature and irresponsible way.

Deterrence

The deterrence value of a punishment is linked to the view that punishment will 'put people off' doing that crime again, or copying someone who has done so. This is because an example has been made of the criminal which no one will want to happen to them. In the case of capital punishment, this is perhaps the ultimate sentence. If someone knows that a certain crime has and will lead to the death penalty then they will be less likely to carry out that crime. Supporters of capital punishment say that its deterrence value is high – and so 'it works' – however, opponents say that it has little or no deterrence value.

Protection

The argument here is that once the criminal has been executed they can never pose a threat to anyone again. This makes society safer (someone serving a life sentence in prison could still escape or cause harm within the prison). Opponents of capital punishment would agree that society needs to be protected from possible future harm by a criminal, but that capital punishment is not the way to achieve it. In fact, the opposite could happen – capital punishment could turn a criminal into a martyr, whose followers might then feel justified in further acts of crime as a response to the executed person's 'martyrdom' – this makes society more, not less, dangerous.

The existence, reasons for and forms of capital punishment all raise strong opinions – so what are the issues?

What are the arguments for and against capital punishment?

It is the right way for a society to express its rejection of certain crimes

Supporters say that the value of human life is so high that capital punishment is the only appropriate response to someone who has taken a life. This expresses the value of human life. Where capital punishment is used for something other than crimes involving killing, it expresses the importance that society places on such crimes. However, some supporters will argue that it should be reserved for crimes involving killing, while others might extend this to include other crimes. Some argue that capital punishment brings 'closure' to those close to the victims and so is the right thing to do.

It is the wrong way for a society to express its rejection of certain crimes

If a society values human life, it values all human life – even criminals who have killed. It makes no sense to say that further killing shows that killing is wrong. Also, state executions mean the state becomes a killer too (or more precisely, the executioner). As for crimes which do not involve killing, many opponents will argue that capital punishment is a disproportionate response to such crimes. Opponents of capital punishment are likely to argue that it is the wrong response to any crime. They are also likely to argue that capital punishment does not bring any 'closure' to those close to victims – how can another killing put anything right?

It is a good deterrent

It is argued that capital punishment does reduce crime and that this is a result of the knowledge that potential criminals have that execution may be the end result of their actions. This is likely to make them avoid crime and so makes society safer. Even just the threat of it is enough to deter crime. This also includes the 'once a criminal' argument, where supporters say that criminals do not mend their ways (and they will point to examples of repeat offenders) and so execution is the best way to remove them from society.

It is not a good deterrent

Opponents argue that places where there is capital punishment have the same levels of crime as places where there is no capital punishment. Also, some capital crimes are cold and calculated and others are carried out in the heat of the moment. In many cases, criminals simply don't think about the possible consequences of their actions (and some think they will never be caught) – so it has no deterrent value. Opponents may argue that criminals do indeed 'mend their ways' in prison (and they will point to examples of reformed offenders) and, in fact, might become helpful in the fight against crime – executing them will rob them and society of this opportunity to take advantage of their change of heart.

It is a humane way to deal with a criminal

Supporters say that it is a merciful way to punish someone – perhaps even better than a life sentence because at least it's over quickly. They also argue that in the right form it can be painless.

It is inhumane

Opponents repeat many stories of 'botched' executions which seemed to be slow and painful. Even if the execution is somehow quick and painless, the whole process of execution – no matter how it is carried out – does not respect the dignity of the person being executed.

It is the right response to the due process of law

Supporters say that where capital punishment is the end result of a fair legal process, then the accused has been given all the chances they deserve (certainly more than their victim/s). Society doesn't take capital punishment lightly and, where it is used, there are many safeguards in place to make sure the courts get it right. Also, in most places where capital punishment exists, the state is generally fair and well balanced in its use of capital punishment – where this does not happen does not mean that capital punishment is wrong, it means that the state's way of doing things is wrong. Capital punishment punishes criminals and there's no more to it than that.

The due process of law is often flawed

Courts should convict on the basis of evidence alone – but do they? Opponents argue that evidence is often complex and that guilty verdicts can be the result of a very complicated process which can involve bias, interpretation, lack of understanding and a whole range of other factors – in fact, it might also reflect the skill of the lawyer as much as the guilt of the accused. No verdict is a simple conclusion and execution is the wrong end result of a very complicated process. Opponents might also add that becoming a 'criminal' is often a complex series of events and processes – which are often more likely to apply to the more vulnerable members of society. Is capital punishment therefore just a quick way of brushing social inequalities under the carpet?

It is final and irreversible

Opponents of capital punishment will argue that because it is so final, it means that mistakes made cannot be put right (you can free someone from a life sentence, but not un-execute them). Opponents point to the many cases where guilty verdicts have been overturned later because of new evidence, doubts about the original evidence, or some other reason. Perhaps even if one person is wrongly found guilty and executed, this should be enough to bring into doubt the whole business of capital punishment. Mistakes happen and it should be possible to put this right: capital punishment makes this impossible. Opponents also argue that some states use capital punishment to silence political opponents and to enforce the view of a minority about what is right and wrong. This misuse of power is a further argument against capital punishment as an option.

Talk Point

Which of these arguments do you find most and least convincing?

Some religious and philosophical perspectives

Christianity

While Christians support justice and punishment as part of justice, there are mixed views about capital punishment. Some Christian groups support it based on the 'eye for an eye' principle in the Bible, while others reject it because of the 'turn the other cheek' principle in the Bible. Some argue for it because it is a just punishment for certain crimes, while others argue against it because it is just another form of killing, which is wrong. Some argue that it doesn't work as a deterrent and offers the criminal no chance for redeeming themself, others argue that it does work as a deterrent and God will choose whether the executed person can redeem themself after their death. Most Christians would be likely to oppose the execution of children and those unfit for trial for some other reason, such as insanity. Christians would also be likely to oppose capital punishment for political crimes and probably also for 'religious crimes' such as blasphemy.

The Church of Scotland

In 2008, the Church and Society Council produced a report: 'The Death Penalty'. This report explored in detail ethical, historical and theological thinking about the death penalty. Although it recognises that there are different views within the

Churches about capital punishment, it reaches a very clear conclusion: *'This study has led to the conviction that judgement is God's prerogative. While humans, acting under his authority, are called upon to judge, human judgement must always be understood as provisional ... No human is omniscient and therefore mistakes can be made. The irrevocable nature of death makes such mistakes extremely grave ... we know that God is compassionate. He calls us to be likewise ... the death penalty has manifestly failed to deter murder, war crimes and genocide ... Therefore the Church of Scotland affirms that capital punishment is always and wholly unacceptable and does not provide an answer to even the most heinous of crimes; and commits itself to ... oppose death sentences and executions and promote the cause of abolition of the death penalty worldwide.'* [13] So the Church's view is clear: capital punishment doesn't work, is not an act of compassion, can lead to terrible mistakes and should no longer exist – no matter what the crime.

The Roman Catholic Church

Like many Christian groups, the Catholic Church supported capital punishment for certain crimes. However, the Catechism of the Catholic Church (2267) states: *'Assuming that the guilty party's identity and responsibility have been fully determined, the traditional teaching of the Church does not exclude recourse to the death penalty, if this is the only possible way of effectively defending lives against the unjust aggressor. If, however, non-lethal means are sufficient to defend and protect people's safety from the aggressor, authority will limit itself to such means ... Today, in fact, as a consequence of the possibilities which the state has for effectively preventing crime, by rendering one who has committed an offense incapable of doing harm – without definitely taking away the possibility of redeeming himself – the cases in which the execution of the offender is an absolute necessity "are very rare, if not practically non-existent".'* So, *in principle* it teaches that where there's no doubt about guilt and where there seems to be no other way to protect society, capital punishment is an option. However, *in practice* there is almost always another way to punish appropriately. In March 2015, Pope Francis went beyond this teaching and said quite clearly: *'Nowadays the death penalty is inadmissible, no matter how serious the crime committed ... It is an offence against the inviolability of life and the dignity of the human person ...it does not render justice to the victims, but rather fosters vengeance.'* [14] This is not new teaching, however. In 1999 Pope John Paul II asked for an end to the death penalty because he regarded it as cruel and unnecessary.

Buddhism

The first precept states: *'Abstain from taking life.'* This would seem to suggest that Buddhism rejects capital punishment, although many religions do have a version of the 'You shall not kill' rule which is followed – or not – according to the situation. In Buddhism, too, this is the case, because some Buddhist countries do not have the death penalty and some do. In fact, it is sometimes claimed that some Buddhist teachers argue for the death penalty because it is a form of compassion by stopping the criminal building further bad kamma through repeat offending. However, most Buddhists argue that killing in response to crime can never be an act of compassion and instead fuels the flames of suffering by causing more suffering – it is also considered very hard to kill anyone in any circumstance without experiencing a negative mental state. Also, because capital punishment is final, it does not allow the criminal a chance to change, become more compassionate and continue towards improving their spiritual life. Being born as a human is considered a rare and precious thing, because it is a great opportunity to make spiritual progress: killing a fellow-human being robs them of this opportunity.

Are these three religious perspectives in agreement about capital punishment?

Humanism

There is no one view on capital punishment within Humanism. Some Humanists accept it as a justifiable response to certain crimes, although they are also likely to agree that it should be humane and respect the criminal's dignity as a human being. Some think it is a perfectly understandable and justifiable response to the suffering caused by certain crimes and that it may have some deterrent value. However, others take the opposite approach, arguing that it is never the right response to crime and that it doesn't work as a deterrent. Many Humanists also argue that because the causes of crime are very complex, 'simple' responses such as capital punishment are wrong. For example, the British Humanist Association publication, 'A Humanist discussion of … crime and punishment' suggests that capital punishment *'does not seem to deter murder'*, but it also states that *'prison doesn't work very well'*. It also points out that in the developed world, *'most criminals are young men from the lower socio-economic groups'* which implies that crime has a link to social circumstances which have to be understood and put right. Many Humanists also suggest that the possibility of making mistakes has such serious consequences (you cannot reverse an execution) that this alone is a good enough argument for rejecting it. Humanists base their moral choices on evidence and reason, and for most Humanists, their view is that both evidence and reason lead to rejecting capital punishment. Humanist Society Scotland supports human rights which are opposed to the death penalty.

Utilitarianism

Utilitarians could take completely opposite views on capital punishment, depending on their assessment of its consequences. If capital punishment does effectively deter further crime, then that would benefit the majority and so capital punishment would be right. If it does not, then capital punishment would be pointless, other than for retribution – and it might be difficult to see how retribution benefits the majority. So a Utilitarian would want to know what the evidence was for the deterrent value of capital punishment. The Utilitarian philosopher Jeremy Bentham amended his views on the death penalty throughout his life. He argued against it because it was not an effective deterrent, it was unequally used – because mostly the poor suffered it – and because it can never be put right after an error. Early in his life he argued that it should be retained for some murders and for treason – because the punishment would serve as a deterrent to others in these cases. However, by 1809 he argued that the death penalty should be abolished in all cases. His successor, J. S. Mill disagreed – arguing that capital punishment was an effective deterrent. He agreed that courts could make mistakes, but that the job was to make sure they didn't – not to abolish the death penalty just in case they did. Mill also argued that the suffering for the guilty person was less having been executed than it would be in serving a pointless life sentence in prison.

Personal Reflection

* *What are your views on capital punishment?*
* *Which of the religious/philosophical perspectives on capital punishment do you think are most effective in making their case?*
* *Should decisions about capital punishment be made 'with your heart or with your head'?*

Active learning

Check your understanding

1. Why might some argue that some forms of capital punishment are more acceptable than others – and how far would you agree?
2. Which groups of people are usually excluded from being able to be sentenced to death and why?
3. There are other 'rules' which usually apply when a person is executed for crime. What kinds of rules are there?
4. How far is capital punishment an effective deterrent?
5. Explain two arguments in favour of capital punishment and two against.
6. How far are religions agreed about capital punishment?
7. What does the British Humanist Association think of capital punishment?

8 What different views could be held about capital punishment by a Utilitarian?
9 Why might someone argue that capital punishment is better than life in prison?
10 What kinds of actions have prompted calls for a return of capital punishment in the UK in recent history?

Investigate

(Beware: lots of internet sites linked to capital punishment are not pleasant.)

1 At any one time there are likely to be individual cases that raise issues about capital punishment. Choose one of these cases and produce your own report/presentation about this case. Amnesty International's website is a good place to start in sourcing out such cases, but be aware that Amnesty International is opposed to the death penalty. Perhaps in groups in class you could each focus on a different 'type' of case – for example, someone sentenced to death for an offence which did not involve killing, a child sentenced to death, someone with mental health issues, etc.
2 Carry out your own research into views about capital punishment in your school community. Display your findings in a format of your choice.
3 Using one of the case studies in activity 1 above, produce your own speech/drama/campaign poster about this case.
4 You have looked at the responses to capital punishment from two branches of Christianity and from Buddhism. Choose one other religious perspective and find out about its views on capital punishment. How similar/different are these to the religions you have examined in this section?
5 Produce your own annotated world map showing where capital punishment exists in the world today, and what methods are used. What patterns are there – if any – about where and how capital punishment is carried out?

Analyse and Evaluate

1 In pairs, use one or more of the following statements – one person in each pair should write an argument in support of the statement (expanding the argument) and the other an argument against. You should then compare and discuss your responses.
   - Capital punishment is right in certain situations.
   - Capital punishment is an effective deterrent.
   - A society should have the right to take retribution for murder.
   - Only killing should be punishable by death.
   - The possibility of error should be enough to abolish capital punishment everywhere.
   - Capital punishment is a choice that different cultures have to make for themselves.
2 How similar are religious and non-religious views on capital punishment?
3 Based on your own view of capital punishment, produce an extended piece of writing which supports your view with evidence and opinion.

Apply

Either write a script for a TV programme which explores capital punishment, or produce your own presentation on capital punishment. This should be aimed at a specific target group of your choice. You should be conscious about the images you use, however, and ensure that these are sensitive to a range of different people's possible responses to such images.

5 Sentencing in the UK

Karen and Sharon live in a pretty run-down area of Scotland and there has been some major vandalism in the area lately. The police have finally caught the culprits – a teenage gang where the average age is 12 years old. Karen and Sharon have very different views about how these junior criminals should be dealt with by the law ...

Karen: I see they've caught they wee yobs who've been tearing the place up round here.

Sharon: Aye, twelve years old most of them.

Karen: So I heard. Lock them up and throw away the key I say.

Sharon: And what good would that do?

Karen: It'll keep them off the streets, teach them a very hard lesson about their behaviour and put other wee yobs off being copycats.

Sharon: Ye canny seriously think that a twelve-year-old should be banged up in Barlinnie, can ye?

Karen: I sure do. They've committed a crime, just like anyone else, so they should go to the jail just like anyone else.

Sharon: For spray-painting and smashing windows?

Karen: Spray-painting and window-smashing today, but what'll be next – it'll be robbery, assault and probably murder if they're not stopped in their tiny tracks now.

Sharon: Come on, all they'll learn in the jail is how to be better yobs – there are master criminals in there only too happy to share their skills with the next generation of hoodlums. →

Karen: So put them in solitary for a few years, then when they come out they'll no really want to go back to the jail again, that's for sure.

Sharon: *Ye really think having a horrible time in the jail is going to make them come out all squeaky clean and ready to say sorry to the world – no very likely I think – they'll only be angrier at the big bad world. There's got to be a better way.*

Karen: Well, what do ye suggest?

Sharon: *They could do some community service and pay people back for what they've done.*

Karen: Aye right, painting some poor old woman's house … just wait for her stuff to go walkies as those wee yobs nick anything she has of value and hot foot it down to the pawn shop.

Sharon: *Och, that wouldn't happen, they get supervised and educated.*

Karen: Aye, by some harassed social worker with a caseload of thousands who hasn't really got the time to do much more than tick boxes and say what good boys and girls they are now – and education – they have that chance at the school – they just don't go and get it.

Sharon: *Maybe their parents could be fined.*

Karen: Aye, great idea, because their parents are all having three holidays a year, have two cars and have financial advisers to guide them in how to manage their millions. Their parents are skint – where would they find money to pay a fine?

Sharon: *Fair enough – what about probation, or tagging, or something like that?*

Karen: Soft – they'll just take that to mean they've got off with it and they'll just be worse next time. No, the only way is lock them up – doesn't matter what age they are, a crime's a crime, and it'll only get worse if they're not stopped now. The jail for them, and I don't mean a cushy life with three square meals and your own TV and washing done for you …

Talk Point

What should happen to the teenage gang?

Sentencing in Scotland

Like other countries, Scotland has a set of sentences which the courts can pass for crimes. In general how severe these sentences are is linked to how serious the crime has been. The purposes of sentencing those who have been found guilty are:

- **Punishment** It seems obvious of course, but sentences are there to punish people for the wrong things they have done. A sentence has to be some kind of penalty for wrongdoing. It has to involve the person sentenced 'paying back' for their wrongdoing. This evens up the score between the punished person, any victims of the wrongs they have done and society generally.
- **Retribution** This is the payback part of the punishment and involves the guilty person being 'got back at' by society for their wrongdoing.
- **Protection** Some sentences – specifically 'custodial sentences' – are designed to protect society from further crimes committed by the guilty person. The idea is that as the person is safely locked up in jail they can't commit the crime which got them there in the first place and so society is protected from them for the duration of their prison sentence. The kinds of crimes which usually result in prison sentences are where the courts think that the person is likely to reoffend if they are not in jail.

- **Rehabilitation/Reform** Some sentences are designed to help the guilty person learn the error of their ways. They might be asked to do community service or follow a programme of anger management in prison, for example. Also, some sentences recognise that some crimes may be the result of behavioural issues, which require treatment rather than punishment – and so there might be some medical and/or psychological treatment involved in the sentence.
- **Deterrence** All sentences are designed to have a deterrent effect. This means that they will put other people off doing the crime which resulted in the sentence. The sentence should also deter the person sentenced from repeating their crime. Again, the more serious society thinks the crime is, the more serious the punishment is, and so on.

Sentences available to the courts in Scotland

There are various types of court in Scotland, each of which deals with different levels of seriousness of offence. Each court can pass a range of sentences and the higher the court, the greater the sentence that can be passed. There are two main types – custodial (prison) and non-custodial (something other than prison). In Scotland, sentences can take various forms – each with its own possible benefits and drawbacks, and each might be more clearly linked to one purpose of punishment rather than another: the courts system is very costly all in all – and even small fines can involve large costs to society through paying for the courts system.

Probation orders/Community Payback

Definition

These involve an offender[i] agreeing to a certain set of conditions rather than going to prison. This might involve taking part in counselling or other services aimed at ensuring that the issue which led to the crime is addressed in some way. For example, if the offender has a drug addiction then they might have to undergo treatment for this as part of their probation (drug treatment and testing order). The offender might also have certain restrictions placed on their movements – through electronic tagging for example – and may have to do some kind of community service or follow a programme of some kind (supervised attendance orders). If the offender does not follow the rules of the probation/ Community Payback Order s/he will return to court and may end up in prison.

Purpose

The aim here is to rehabilitate the offender so they do not reoffend. There is also an element of paying back to society through, for example, Community Payback or even compensation being paid to victims.

Advantages

This saves society the cost of prison. It also gives something back to society through the offender's possible community work. It places restrictions on the offender which are severe enough to cause inconvenience and, perhaps most importantly, it allows offenders to do something positive as a result of their crime – which helps society and might give the offender a sense of purpose (and even lead to a job). This might help them to reform and avoid crime in the future.

Disadvantages

Some argue that this has little deterrence value. If you know that your crime will lead to a very 'light' sentence such as probation/Community Payback, then it won't put you off doing it in the first place. Some also say that it offers little protection to society, because the offender will remain in the community and so will still be able to carry out further crimes.

---

[i] Note: the term 'offender' is used to refer to someone found guilty of an offence whether this results in a prison sentence or not. In prisons, the phrase 'person in custody' tends to be used rather than offender (and rather than 'prisoner' in some cases).

Fines

Definition

Fines are usually applied when the crime is relatively low level and is 'victimless' – for example, road traffic offences not involving injury, drug- and alcohol-related crimes, antisocial behaviour crimes, some crimes against property and crimes such as fraud. In general the fine matches the crime and the offender has to pay back a sum of money to make up for their crime. If you do not pay your fine, then action can be taken to get the money from you in some other way and ultimately you can be sent to prison for not paying a fine.

Purpose

Fines should act as a deterrent – if you know that an action (say parking on a double yellow line) will lead to a fine then you might avoid doing so. Fines also pay something back to society – the fine you pay will go to the government to be used as it sees fit – this pays society back for your crime.

Advantages

This avoids the high costs of sending someone to prison and some argue that where a crime is victimless, prison is not the correct sentence because there is no real need to protect society from the criminal. It is also financially beneficial for society as it receives money – it is often claimed that some local councils (which take money for parking fines) make a considerable amount of money out of this. It may also have a deterrent value because people don't want to have to give away their hard-earned money because of their criminal behaviour and it might also lead to reform – because if you have been heavily fined for something once, you might change your ways so that you are not fined again.

Disadvantages

One major argument is that fines are more of a problem for those with low/no income than those who are wealthy. Fines match the crime, not the person, so for example, a fine of £100 might mean something very different to someone whose monthly income is £6000 than to someone whose monthly income is £1000. So perhaps wealthy people are less deterred by fines than people who are poorer, which is unfair. Also, if a crime is partly motivated by financial circumstances, being fined is going to make the situation worse and so perhaps lead to more crime.

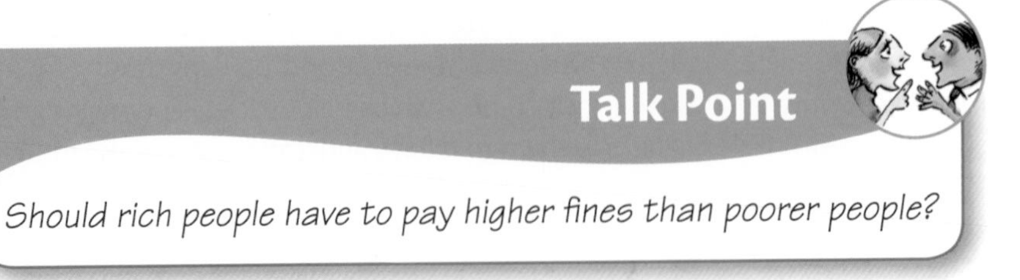

Talk Point

Should rich people have to pay higher fines than poorer people?

Prison

Definition

Prison is considered to be the final sanction a society can impose for crime. Sentences vary greatly from days to life in prison (which can mean different things in practice) according to the seriousness of the crime. Prison can be the first option in sentencing – especially where the crime has victims and is very serious. It can also be the last resort – for example, where someone has failed to meet the conditions of lower, non-custodial sentences. Once in prison, you can be eligible for parole after a certain time, which can ultimately mean you are released from prison early. However, very strict conditions have to be in place before parole is granted and while on parole you must obey strict conditions or you will be returned to prison (you can also be returned if it is considered that you pose any danger to society).

There are three categories of prison sentence in Scotland: high supervision – where all offender activities and movements are monitored; medium supervision – where the offender has some restrictions on their movement and activities; and low supervision – where there are minimum restrictions on movement and activities. Categories are regularly reviewed by prison governors. The category an offender is placed in is linked to the danger they present to society if they escaped (and within prison presumably even if they don't escape). This means that the security levels for high supervision are much stricter than for low supervision. People in prison generally have to follow certain rules and will be allocated tasks to do as part of their sentence.

Purpose

For many the main purpose of prison is retribution – your freedom is taken away as a result of your crime. This pays society back for what you have done and means you have to sacrifice your freedom for your wrongdoing. Prison should also act as a powerful deterrent – if you know a crime will lead to prison, then you should be more likely to avoid carrying out such a crime. Prison also exists to protect society. If you have carried out violent crime/murder then being in prison will mean that society is protected from you doing the same again. Some also see prison as having an important role in rehabilitation – in fact, the Scottish Prison Service motto is 'Unlocking potential – transforming lives' which suggests that it thinks of prison as a method of rehabilitating offenders.

Advantages

Some argue that prison sentences deter crime – and the longer the sentence the greater the deterrent. People will think twice about committing crime if they know it will lead to them ending up in prison – especially if prison is unpleasant. Of course, locking someone up means that they cannot commit their offence again out in society, so there is an element of protection provided by prison. Some argue that the seriousness of prison sentencing is just punishment for certain crimes and expresses society's view of the seriousness of these crimes. Some argue that prisons do rehabilitate offenders – programmes can be put in place in prison which help offenders to adjust back into society on release – for example, educational programmes, learning skills and so on which the offender can use when back in society to avoid repeating their crime.

Talk Point

Do you think prison should only be for those who have committed violent crime or crimes which have involved killing?

Disadvantages

Prisons are very expensive to run. It costs a considerable amount of money to house every offender and even inspecting prisons is costly. In 2011–12 inspecting prisons cost a total of £358,425.06, and in 2013–14 the Scottish Government reported that the Scottish Prison Service cost £264.1 million. Some feel that prisons do not deter criminal actions. Some criminals just think of it as an 'occupational hazard' which just goes with their 'job'. Others don't think about the consequences of their actions and so ending up in prison is not something that ever crosses their mind. Some, of course, probably think that they will never be caught – so prison is not a deterrent. For some criminals, prison may not be seen as much of a punishment anyway – especially if their sentence is a low supervision type.

Many argue that prisons should be horrible experiences to act as deterrents, while others say this would not help in rehabilitating offenders, which is their main point. Some also believe that prisons don't work because they are ways for criminals to learn new techniques and approaches to crime – from other criminals. There is also an argument which says that prisons just give offenders a long time to get angry at society – which will make them more likely to reoffend when released – so prison protects while the offender is in prison but will make them more likely to offend when released. Also, while being in prison protects society from further crime, it does not necessarily protect other persons in custody, or prison staff – so it does not work as a form of protection for all. Some also argue that prison is just a convenient way to deal with social problems: prisons generally have a high proportion of offenders who have had difficult life circumstances in one way or another and their crime was the end result of all that – further punishment isn't the answer, not to mention the view of some that certain crimes should never result in prison. In addition, no matter how well you have been rehabilitated in prison, when you come out, you will have a criminal record, which might deter some from employing you – so your rehabilitation might not be as valuable as you think. Finally, many argue that prison doesn't just affect the offender, but their family too. Families of persons in custody may find life much more difficult because of the reduction in their income and other support the offender may have provided for them. This can be very serious for some families and means that not only is the offender punished but their family is too.

Talk Point

Should children who commit crimes be treated any differently to adults?

Youth sentencing in Scotland

In May 2014, it was reported that in the previous two years, 40,000 offences were committed by children – this included 25 three- and four-year-olds who were involved in shoplifting and vandalism. One other dimension to sentencing in Scotland is how younger criminals are treated. In Scotland the age of criminal responsibility is eight years old (though this is under review) and you can be prosecuted for crime from 12 years old. You cannot be sent to prison under the age of 12. Between 12 and 18 you're probably likely to end up in the Children's Hearings System, though you could end up in the ordinary courts too. The Children's Hearings System generally focuses on addressing the behaviours of the child and ensuring the welfare of the child. If you are aged between 16 and 21 and receive a custodial sentence you may end up in one of Scotland's Young Offenders Institutions and you can also be fined, put on probation and serve Community Payback Orders.

There's quite a lot of debate and discussion about how society should sentence and deal with children who commit crimes. The general approach taken in Scotland is one where the legal system tries to act in a way which understands the different needs for support for children who commit crimes compared with adults. However, this is a very difficult area because some might argue that it is the crime which should be punished no matter who carries it out, while others might say that we have to take the individual's circumstances into account – and age is an important circumstance. Generally speaking, it is probably fair to say that the criminal justice system in Scotland takes an approach to child crime which is a mixture of appropriate punishment and protection for society, but with a great emphasis on the rehabilitation of offenders.

Some religious and philosophical perspectives

Christianity

Within Christianity there are a range of viewpoints about the link between crime and sentencing. Some Christian traditions have very strong views about the punishment aspect of any sentence and the need to pay back to society for wrongs done. However, it is arguable that most Christians would support sentencing which had the aim of rehabilitating offenders. Apart from the view that this demonstrates compassion towards the offender, it might well be the best way to ensure that the offender doesn't reoffend. It is also likely to help the offender contribute to society after their punishment rather than just continue to offend, which is obviously better for everyone. Many prisons have Christian chaplains and the Kainos ('new beginnings') Christian community has been directly involved in prison work to support the rehabilitation of offenders.

The Church of Scotland

In a document entitled 'What's the alternative?' (2005), the Church of Scotland says of prison: '*... the facts show that prison is an ineffective method of reducing crime and re-offending although it has an important role in protecting society from the most violent offenders. Why do we keep sending people there? Is it time to approach the problem from another angle – that of putting right the harm done, assisting the victim to recover and attempting to reintegrate the offender into society?*'[15] The Church recognises that there is a need for prison, as protection for society, but also that it should have a key role in rehabilitating offenders. It supports alternatives to prison which aim to help the offender avoid reoffending and it supports approaches to victim support and also support for the families of offenders. Its 'Crossreach' service is involved in a number of actions to support those who come into contact with the criminal justice system in Scotland. The Church of Scotland supports a constructive alternative to prison where this is possible – so would support Community Payback and other non-custodial approaches. The Church of Scotland would also support fines as punishment for some crimes. It uses the story of Zacchaeus the corrupt tax collector to show the importance of giving back to the community – even if this is only financially – claiming that Zacchaeus 'restores that he might be restored'. However, it is likely that the Church would also question the value of fining those who are already experiencing poverty because this might just make their situation worse and potentially lead to more crime.

The Roman Catholic Church

For the Catholic Church, human dignity must be respected in all aspects of the criminal justice system – for victim, offenders and the families of offenders – as well as those involved in the various stages of criminal justice. It supports sentencing which protects the public from further harm, but such sentences should also permit the offender to be rehabilitated. The United States Conference of Catholic Bishops states: '*We cannot and will not tolerate behaviour that threatens the lives and violates the rights of others ... the community has a right to establish and enforce laws to protect people and advance the common good. At the same time a Catholic approach does not give up on those who violate those laws. We believe that both victims and offenders are children of God ... their lives and dignity should be protected and respected.*'[16] This teaching is clear and stressed continually throughout this document. There is a place for punishment – and all forms of punishment considered in this section are options, but the aim should be support for victims, protection of society and rehabilitation of offenders. The Church recognises that the causes of crime are complex, so sentencing has to avoid being simplistic. In relation to fines, the Church is likely to support this in some cases, but again, would be concerned if fining those already poor is of much value, since it might lead to making the situation worse.

Buddhism

The Angulimala Sutta tells the tale of a ruthless murderer who mends his ways after an encounter with the Buddha. He becomes a monk and although the local people and the authorities want him punished the Buddha says that his life as a monk is more valuable now than any punishment might be. This is a clear indication that for the Buddha, reform is the best way to deal with crime and that offenders should be supported to mend their ways so as not to reoffend. In fact, in the UK, one Buddhist prison chaplaincy organisation is named after Angulimala and has Buddhist chaplains in many of Scotland's prisons. The Ven Ajahn Khemadhammo of the Angulimala organisation says that the key in prisons is to help offenders *'salvage something positive from their predicament'*, and that's why there are Buddhist chaplains there. None of this is to say that Buddhism rejects punishment – around the world, countries where Buddhism is central generally use the same kinds of punishments available anywhere and for the same reasons. Buddhists, too, would wish to demonstrate compassion towards the victims of crime, the families of offenders and offenders themselves and so any sentencing would need to take that into account. No matter what the punishment is, in Buddhism it should always have the potential to allow the offender to turn things around for the better and it should always allow the opportunity to show compassion to all involved in the crime.

Talk Point

In the story of Angulimala, was the murderer 'let off' for his crimes by the Buddha? Was this the right thing to do?

Humanism

Humanists prefer to make moral decisions based on the best available evidence. It would therefore need to be clear that specific sentences lead to specific consequences. For example, there would be little point in harsh sentences which were meant to deter further crime if they in fact led to further crime on release (or even increased the likelihood of further crime!). Humanists would be unlikely to disagree with any of the sentences considered in this section, though they would probably want sentences to be fair and proportionate. As the causes of crime are complex, so too are the ways of responding to it. Humanists would want to gather all the available evidence linked to the possible causes of crime and also the possible effects of a range of sentences. Humanists would want to be sure that any sentence would be likely to deter further crime and not be likely to lead to any increase in crime (and, where possible, reduce it, of course).

Utilitarianism

In Utilitarianism, any form of sentencing is acceptable if it leads to benefits for the majority. The difficulty is in predicting the likely outcomes of sentences. If prison leads to a build-up of resentment in an offender and so more chance of them reoffending then perhaps it is of little value; on the other hand, it might give offenders time to think about what they have done and change their ways on release. Obviously it protects the majority from further harm which is of value – but how long-term this is might be questionable depending upon what the prison experience is like for the offender. For a Utilitarian, sentencing can have value as punishment and as a deterrent (if it is clear that it is an effective deterrent), but Utilitarians would also be open to sentences which allow for rehabilitation of offenders because a rehabilitated offender is much less likely to reoffend on release from prison, which is beneficial for the majority. Utilitarians would be likely to support any alternative to a custodial sentence – again, if it was clear that such an approach gave something useful back to society and had a good chance of reducing the likelihood of an offender reoffending. The greatest happiness is, perhaps, more likely to come from sentencing which aims to get something positive out of the situation rather than just punish for the sake of punishing.

Personal Reflection

* *How should offenders be treated? Should it depend on their crime? Their circumstances?*
* *Should children be sent to prison if they have committed crime?*
* *Should prisons be harsh environments for offenders so as to deter crime, or easier so as to rehabilitate criminals?*

Active learning

Check your understanding

1. What are the major purposes of different kinds of sentence in the UK?
2. What kinds of sentences are available to the courts in Scotland and for which crimes?
3. For which crimes are custodial sentences usually passed – and are these always appropriate?
4. What are the benefits and drawbacks of fines?
5. Why might someone argue that prison only makes things worse?
6. How far should youth crime be treated in the same way as crimes committed by adults?
7. In what ways do religions support alternatives to prison – and why?
8. Explain why religions think that not only the victims of crime should be society's concern.
9. What evidence might a Humanist want to gather before supporting a particular kind of sentence?
10. Would a Utilitarian support harsh sentences?

Investigate

1. The Children's Hearings and Panel System is used in Scotland to approach issues where children are involved in crime. Find out what the various parts of this system do and how it generally responds to children caught up in crime. You could create a short report of your findings or a website page to help people understand the Children's Hearings System.
2. The special unit at Barlinnie prison in Glasgow was set up as a new way to deal with criminals, though it took quite a controversial approach. What did it do and why? Was this a successful approach to crime? What issues did some people have with it and were these justified?
3. What do prison chaplains do? Find out, and create a job advert for a prison chaplain from a religion/denomination of your choice.
4. Some who have been involved in crime have turned their lives around through religion. Find out about one such person, how they changed their life and what the consequences of this were for them and for others. Prepare a magazine item about this person.

Analyse and Evaluate

1. Discuss each of the following statements and reach your own conclusions:
   - A crime is a crime no matter what age the offender.
   - Prison is punishment – so it should be very unpleasant.
   - Prison doesn't work.
   - Once a criminal, always a criminal.
   - Too much time is spent on criminals and not enough on their victims.
   - Religious views about punishment are too soft.
   - Life in prison should mean life.
2. 'There are more similarities between religious and non-religious views about sentencing than there are differences.' Critically evaluate this statement.
3. How far do you think punishment and rehabilitation are equally important?

Apply

In the USA, some prison wings have been run by religious groups and some experimental work like this has taken place in England. Imagine that a religious or non-religious group has been asked to put forward plans for it to run a wing of a low supervision prison in Scotland. Draw up some plans for this. Your plans could include:

- an explanation of the 'philosophy' of your group's prison wing
- some rules which would apply in your prison wing
- any special activities you would expect prisoners in this wing to follow
- some ideas about the physical design of your wing.

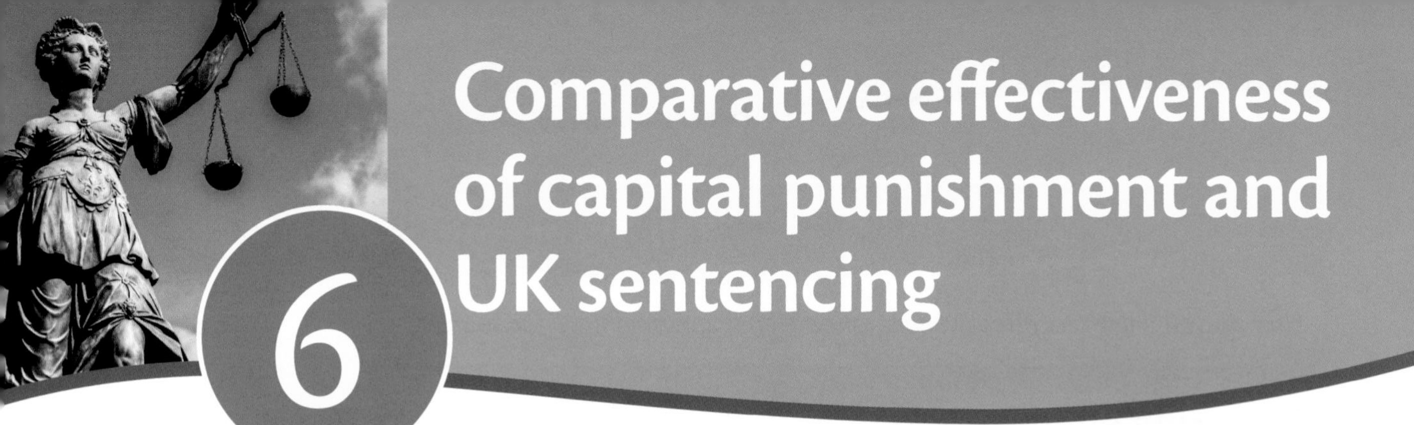

6 Comparative effectiveness of capital punishment and UK sentencing

Shona has been in and out of prison since she was a teenager, starting with a young offenders institution. She says: 'Prison doesn't really bother me. I know the drill. I know how it works. It's not tough at all. You get a room, your food cooked and actually, although some of the other women in the prison aren't always too friendly, in general you end up with a wee group who become quite good friends. Your day is planned for you and you don't have to worry about paying the bills. You can learn stuff in the prison if you want to and mostly people mind their own business. Yes, you don't have your freedom, but then you don't have all the other stuff that goes with your freedom either – having to shop, cook, clean your house … blah blah. In this kind of prison you get to go outside anyway so no … the thought of going to prison again after I get out of this one doesn't bother me too much.'

Alan has just come out of prison after a short sentence. He says: 'I hope I never go back in there again. It's not humane. Every bit of your life is controlled by someone else, there's no privacy … ever. You live in constant threat of someone belting you one, and you know that sometimes the prison staff might just turn a blind eye to it, and that'll be you in the hospital. You have to watch everything you say or do – some of the other prisoners are just waiting to be offended for nothing and when they have big pals, they'll be knocking at your door – and you can't choose not to answer it. Your life is on hold in prison – and you count the moments until you can get your life back. Those who say they don't mind it – I think there must be something very wrong with them. I wouldn't wish it on my worst enemy.'

What does effectiveness mean?

Both capital punishment and sentencing have a range of purposes, which you looked at in the previous chapter. They both aim to deter, to take something from you in return for something you have taken from someone (or something) else. They aim to make you pay for your crime and in the case of sentences, the aim can be to persuade you not to reoffend – and in some cases to help you become rehabilitated so you do not offend again. The difficulty with effectiveness as an idea is that – in relation to crime – there is no sure way of agreeing about what it means and so whether a particular sentence does the job society means it to (and of course 'society' isn't always agreed about what a sentence is intended to do!). Some people argue that effectiveness is such a difficult idea to pin down that it is very difficult to work out if one sentence is more effective than another – or if any sentence works at all. Effectiveness of sentencing is something that probably concerns the legal system/governments and authorities most of all – because it's legal systems/governments and authorities which decide what sentences are and which will then try to work out if the sentences passed are effective.

Talk Point

How do you think the effectiveness of sentencing is/might be measured?

Measuring effectiveness

Reoffending

One way of measuring effectiveness is linked to the likelihood that an offender will repeat their crime after their sentence has been completed. This is known as 'recidivism' and there are very different views and statistics about how likely offenders are to reoffend after particular sentences. Also, although sentences are matched to certain crimes, perhaps some people are more likely to reoffend after a particular sentence than others – this would be very difficult to analyse because it might be unique to each person. Obviously, in the case of capital punishment, the offender cannot reoffend as they are dead. However, between sentencing and execution perhaps they could reoffend while in prison and, some might argue, there's no real incentive not to kill another person in prison because if they have been sentenced to death already then that sentence can hardly be increased. (Although perhaps the hope that they might not be executed still acts to keep them from further killing while in prison, which would be one way to make sure their execution goes ahead.) As for other sentences, a variety of factors might affect the effectiveness of the sentence, so before having a look at some data, let's think about the link between sentencing and reoffending more generally:

- If the sentence is thought of as 'light' then it might not deter reoffending (e.g. a short prison sentence in a low supervision prison, which might not bother some people).
- If the sentence isn't much of a concern for the person then it might not deter reoffending – for example, a fine for speeding might be a lot less serious for someone very wealthy than for someone who is on a tight budget.
- If a person thinks they are not likely to get caught then no matter what the sentence, it might not deter reoffending. Sometimes people think that they'll get away with it, so sentences are not really all that important because they think they'll never have to worry about it.
- Perhaps the most obvious difficulty with the possible effectiveness of any sentence on rates of reoffending is this: many crimes are committed in the 'heat of the moment', with no thought given to the consequences. Even if someone has been sentenced for a crime previously, they may still reoffend because they simply don't think about what might happen after they have offended. This can also be complicated where any offence is committed while under the influence of drugs, alcohol, or in any kind of altered mental state.

Public confidence

This means how confident the public are that sentences deter people from criminal behaviour in the first place, and/or that they deter reoffending. This is a very difficult idea to measure too because it can only really be done through asking a sample of the public – and getting a very balanced sample can be difficult. Also, researchers then need to generalise from the sample to the whole population – and this is affected by how well the sample represented the whole population. So, other than these statistical and research difficulties, what other issues are there with 'public confidence'?

- The whole idea of 'confidence' is difficult to measure. If it means how 'safe' a person feels, this can be defined in many ways – and is a feeling after all which will vary between individuals. If it means how confident a person is that they won't be the victim of a crime, how do they know this? The media is full of reports about crime, but has fewer stories about nice people who live ordinary lives and never cause any harm to anyone. This could mean that 'public confidence' in being safe from crime is always a little shaky.
- 'The public's' sources of information may be unreliable. Most people don't spend a lot of time analysing the relationship between sentencing and crime. They depend on, for example, the media to report this for them. Of course, someone reoffending after serving a sentence is newsworthy, while first offences perhaps are less so. This means that 'the failures' of sentences are more often in the news than the successes. This could mean that the public's confidence in sentencing is biased by this.
- As well as the media, individual experience will be another source of information. If you have been the victim of a crime, then it is easy to make a simple leap to blaming a 'weak' criminal justice system and concluding that sentences aren't tough enough to deter crime/reoffending. Also, being a victim of crime can be so traumatic that no matter what the sentences available, you might never be confident about your safety in the future.
- 'Public confidence' can vary according to who you are, where you live and what's happening in the world. For example, some minority groups may be less confident in the criminal justice system than the general public. At certain points in time, this confidence may decrease (or increase, of course) – for example, where minority groups become victims of hate crimes in response to events in the news. Confidence may be different according to your postcode, your socio-economic group, or a range of other factors.
- In Scotland, some of the measures of public confidence in the criminal justice system rely on volunteers. People might volunteer for all sorts of reasons, but it is possible that they will do so because they have a particular view about the criminal justice system which might affect their responses.

One final issue here is a concern that governments might be persuaded to link sentencing to its probable outcome on public confidence. This could mean that sentences would be made harsher to 'send out a message' to the public that a particular government was not 'soft on crime'. While this might increase public confidence in sentencing (or not), would it be right or fair? You have thought about the reasons behind some sentences and their possible effects on crime – should sentences be used by governments to make examples of people, or should 'public confidence' not be taken into account when sentencing?

In relation to capital punishment, as this no longer takes place in the UK there is no evidence about its effect on public confidence. Some argue that the public might be more confident about the criminal justice system if execution was available as a response to crime. On the other hand, perhaps public confidence would be harmed by any reintroduction of capital punishment, because there's always the possibility that it could be you who is wrongly accused, found guilty and executed.

Talk Point

Should governments use sentences for crime to 'send out a message to the public'?

Early release

This links specifically to custodial sentences. In many sentences, early release is possible where an offender has met certain conditions. They may be supervised in some way on release, or subject to some conditions, such as curfews and/or electronic tagging. The key issue about early release from custody is how far the parole board thinks the offender is likely to be a risk to the public once released and how well their life when released can be 'managed' by the authorities. The parole board for Scotland states that parole is *'not a reward for good behaviour in prison'* but does take into account what the offender may have done in prison to rehabilitate themselves and so be unlikely to reoffend. If the released offender breaks any of the rules of their licence to be released then they will go straight back to prison. The effectiveness of early release is also quite difficult to measure:

- Obviously if an offender reoffends shortly after early release then its effectiveness might be questioned. But then an offender might reoffend shortly after being released having served the full term of their sentence – this would mean that it was not the time of release which was at issue, but other factors.
- Reoffending after early release is probably more likely to be reported by the media than other timescales for reoffending. Perhaps because some people feel that early release is being 'soft' on crime, any reoffending afterwards is likely to make the news. Also, early release is a statement by the authorities that the offender is not likely to reoffend. If they do, then it suggests that the authorities have got it badly wrong and that's newsworthy.
- Offenders who do not reoffend after early release (or any timescale for release) are unlikely to make the news and so be brought to public attention.
- Release from prison at any time can make it difficult for offenders to reintegrate into society. Having a criminal record may put employers off giving you a job and may make others wary of you in all sorts of ways. This could lead to difficulties on release and an increased likelihood of returning to crime.

Qualitative and quantitative measures explained

So, to try to summarise, there are two main ways in which the effectiveness of sentencing might be measured:

Qualitative measures

This involves gathering data about thoughts, views, feelings and so on. This might be about the public's view of sentencing and its effectiveness in deterring/punishing crime and making reoffending less likely. It might also take into account the thoughts/views/feelings of offenders and victims.

Benefits

This tells us in detail what people think and feel and so gives us good information about people's views. They can explain what they think and why they think it.

Drawbacks

It is difficult to analyse qualitative data. Because it is about people's thoughts and feelings, it may have no link at all to the evidence. For example, people might believe that reintroducing capital punishment will reduce crime, but people can also believe that they have been abducted by aliens – in both cases the relationship between belief and evidence is complicated. Also, no matter how big the sample is, it may not be representative.

Quantitative data

These are data in the form of numbers, percentages and so on.

Benefits

This is easier to analyse and gives a helpful picture of overall trends – perhaps across a great number of people.

Drawbacks

This kind of data might show trends, but it doesn't always explain what they mean. For example, in relation to reoffending we can easily see what percentage of offenders reoffend after fulfilling their sentence. However, this statistic does not tell us much about *why* they reoffend and so may hide the very complex nature of reoffending. It also does not necessarily tell us about the relationship between the sentence and reoffending: perhaps the reoffending had nothing to do with the sentence no matter how severe or 'light' it was. Also, in relation to people's views, a questionnaire might reveal that 95 per cent of those surveyed want capital punishment brought back in the UK. This tells us little about the pros and cons of doing so.

Some data

The trouble with data is that it is often very complex to analyse and draw conclusions from. Sometimes there are conflicting data with one set showing one thing and another showing the opposite. This makes it hard to decide what to do with it – especially when the stakes are as high as they are when deciding on sentences for crimes.

Capital punishment

Reoffending

Obviously once executed an offender cannot reoffend. So the key issue here is does the presence of capital punishment deter offences in the first place? Amnesty International[17] – which opposes the death penalty – cites the Death Penalty Information Center. This claims that in the USA, the murder rate has remained consistently higher in those states which have the death penalty compared to those which do not. This could suggest that the death penalty is not an effective deterrent. However, every murder is a unique act and how far a murderer takes into account the existence of the death penalty is very hard to judge. Also, supporters of the death penalty argue that where the death penalty exists, murderers cannot reoffend and so the murder rate is actually much lower than it would be if they were free to reoffend – although obviously there's no direct data to support this. However, they say that murderers are more likely to murder again, compared with people who have never murdered, so removing this opportunity from them through execution is the right thing to do to save lives.

Public confidence

Public views about capital punishment vary greatly. In March 2015, the BBC reported that *'Support for the death penalty falls below 50 per cent for the first time'.* It referred to the NatCen British Social Attitudes Report which surveyed 2878 people. In all, 48 per cent of these supported the reintroduction of the death penalty (compared with 75 per cent in 1983). Also in 2014, a YouGov poll found that 55 per cent of those surveyed thought the death penalty was an effective deterrent for possible murders. So it looks like, in the UK, the death penalty is becoming less popular among the public.

Talk Point

What do you think might happen to public attitudes towards the reintroduction of the death penalty after high-profile murders or acts of terrorism which are heavily covered by the media?

UK sentencing

Reoffending

Again, this would require very complex data across all crimes: the UK Ministry of Justice provides 'proven reoffending statistics' in England and Wales (see **www.gov.uk**). The 43-page report provides a very complicated picture. Reoffending rates for all offenders fell by 2.5 percentage points from 2002–13, but increased by 0.4 percentage points from 2012–13. From 2002–13, the number of reoffences decreased by 34.4 per cent, while from 2012–13 they decreased by 20.9 per cent. However, for the 12 months ending in September 2013 there were still 420,764 reoffences. In Scotland, from 1997–98 to 2012–2013, the average number of reconvictions per offender decreased by nearly 6 per cent. From 2012–13 the reconviction rate has fallen by 1 percentage point and the average number of reconvictions per offender has fallen by 0.03 convictions (6 per cent – **www.gov.scot**). Wading through these statistics is a complex process, but what does it tell us? It does seem as if reoffending rates are decreasing, though how large this effect is remains a matter for discussion. Like capital punishment, it is still very difficult to link the sentence to its deterrent effect. Offenders do reoffend, although the rates are falling – so the deterrent effect of sentencing isn't 100 per cent successful. Also, it might be the case that some offenders who reoffend are not caught and sentenced and so their reoffence doesn't show up in the statistics. This makes using statistics like this very tricky in deciding how effective sentences are in the first place.

Talk Point

How much do you know about what sentences are given for different crimes in Scotland?

Public confidence

The British Crime Survey (which covers England and Wales) has existed since 1982. It is carried out through interviews and for the report in 2010 around 47,000 adults (aged 16+) were used as a sample. The survey asks a number of questions about the Criminal Justice System (CJS). Seven of the most important questions are:

1. How confident are you that the CJS is effective in bringing people who commit crimes to justice?
2. How confident are you that the CJS respects the rights of those accused of committing a crime and treats them fairly?
3. How effective do you think the CJS as a whole is in reducing crime?
4. How confident are you that the CJS deals with cases promptly and efficiently?
5. How confident are you that the CJS meets the needs of victims of crime?
6. How confident are you that the CJS is effective at dealing with young people accused of crime?
7. How confident are you that people who come forward as witnesses are treated well by the CJS?

Talk Point

How many of these questions do you think you could usefully answer? What answers would you give and what would your answers be based on?

The Scottish Crime and Justice Survey (SCJS)[18] measures public confidence in the CJS in Scotland: around 12,000 people voluntarily complete this survey each year. In 2013 this resulted in a 146-page summary! This asks a huge range of questions which cover – for Scotland:

1 The extent of crime
2 Risk and characteristics of crime
3 Impact and perceptions of crime
4 Reporting crime and support for victims
5 Public perceptions of crime
6 The Scottish Justice system and organisations

In this report, 76 per cent of adults surveyed thought the crime rate in their local area had stayed the same or reduced in the past two years. Twenty per cent thought it had increased. Interestingly, this report stated that adults were more likely *'to think that they were likely to experience crime'* than they actually were. For example, 7 per cent of adults thought their home would be burgled, while in fact there was only a 1.2 per cent risk of this occurring. Also, perhaps importantly, 61 per cent of adults said they didn't know much about the CJS in Scotland, and 15 per cent said they knew nothing at all. These statistics suggest that there are many different public perceptions of crime, with the effectiveness of sentencing only one part of that. The situation is very complex and so it is very difficult to draw any clear conclusions on the relationship between sentences and crime and its effect on public confidence. Given the figure that 76 per cent of adults know little or nothing about the CJS in Scotland it would be hard to draw any conclusions about the effectiveness of sentences in affecting public attitudes to crime.

Early release

From July 2006 to March 2010, 21 per cent of offenders released on a 'home detention curfew' were recalled.[19] This shows that those recalled broke the terms of their release (it doesn't necessarily mean they reoffended); however, it does suggest that almost a quarter of those who got early release were perhaps not really ready for it, but then it also shows that three-quarters were (unless they reoffended and/or broke the terms of their release and were not caught, of course). So again, the data are complex and make it difficult to draw firm conclusions about the effectiveness of early release and its effect on crime in the first place.

Some religious and philosophical perspectives

Christianity

Much of what has been said in this section so far has explored different Christian views about the effectiveness of sentencing and its relationship to crime. However, some general principles are likely to apply across Christian traditions, linked to Christian beliefs about the dignity of all human beings and the need to protect the innocent from harm, punish those guilty of crime, but make sure that punishments are proportionate and respect the dignity of offenders and victims.

The Church of Scotland

Effect of sentencing on reoffending

The Church of Scotland supports prison sentencing, but also alternatives to custody. Its desire to treat victims and offenders with humanity means that it would be likely to support sentences which would reduce rates of reoffending (but not the death penalty). However, sentencing has to be proportionate and clearly effective so, like the rest of the public, the Church of Scotland would want to look very carefully at the data linking sentencing to reoffending rates.

Public confidence

While the Church of Scotland would obviously want the public to be confident that sentences matched and deterred crime it would be unlikely to support any sentences which were mostly designed to 'make an example' of an offender or to show that a government was 'tough on crime'. The sentence should punish the offender, protect the public and deter crime, but should also be fair and appropriate. Any attempt to make a sentence harsher than it needs to be would not respect the dignity of the offender.

Early release

The Church of Scotland would be likely to support early release where the CJS decided it was justified – as long as the public are likely to remain protected from reoffending by those given early release. The Church has a strong tradition of supporting the rehabilitation of offenders and of exploring alternatives to custody – so it would be likely to support properly supervised early release.

The Roman Catholic Church

Effect of sentencing on reoffending

Similarly, the Catholic Church stresses the dignity of all in the eyes of God – so sentences must be proportionate and respect victims and offenders while protecting the innocent from further crime. The Church understands that crime is complex and so sentencing is not straightforward. However, any sentence should ideally have the effect of reducing reoffending (though capital punishment is, in practice, rejected).

Public confidence

Again, the Church would not be likely to support sentencing which made an example of offenders just to satisfy the public. People should be confident in the CJS, but it should not be unnecessarily harsh on offenders just to satisfy that – nor should it be used as a 'political tool' by a government.

Early release

The Church would be likely to support early release if proper conditions were attached to it – and provided it did not increase reoffending rates, of course. Sentencing should respect the dignity of the offender and if early release can do this (while protecting others) it should be an option to be considered. The Church would be interested in ensuring that there had been proper process and assessment of the offender prior to release, and many of its members work with offenders to support these processes and support the offender's rehabilitation.

Buddhism

Effect of sentencing on reoffending

Buddhists too would be likely to support proportionate sentencing which reduced reoffending rates. While sentences should be appropriate to the crime, they should also allow society to demonstrate compassion to all involved – even where this may involve some conflict between compassion for victim and offender.

Public confidence

The CJS should not make an example of offenders because this is not an act of compassion. Similarly, it would be wrong for a government to make sentences harsh just to keep the public happy.

Early release

This could be seen as an act of compassion towards the offender. However, a Buddhist would also want to make sure that it continued to protect the public from reoffending and that it did not lead to increases in offences because people saw it as a 'light' sentence.

Humanism

Effect of sentencing on reoffending

Humanists base their beliefs on evidence. This means that they would want to carefully examine the evidence about the relationship between sentencing and reoffending to ensure that sentences were unlikely to lead to reoffending. This could mean that sentences which were too harsh – or too lenient – could equally well lead to reoffending. Like other belief groups and perspectives, Humanists want to reduce offending and reoffending, but know that both are complex processes. The more we understand them, the more likely we are to be able to reduce them.

Public confidence

Humanists too would be likely to reject sentences imposed just to keep the public happy. The complexities of measuring public confidence and how important it is in the first place are both difficult ideas to get hold of. Humanists would want sentences to match crimes, protect others from crime, but also treat offenders with humanity. They should not be used as propaganda tools, nor should offenders be used as examples to others.

Early release

Humanists would accept this principle provided it was carefully regulated and understood. Humanists also support alternatives to custody where this is possible and so would be likely to support early release schemes.

Utilitarianism

Effect of sentencing on reoffending

Obviously what is important to a Utilitarian here – as for many other perspectives – is the relationship between sentencing and reoffending. For a Utilitarian, there would also be a focus on victim and offender – as how both are treated by the CJS could have all sorts of implications for them individually and for society. Again, the difficulty would be predicting the outcome of a range of options on overall happiness. If harsh sentences reduced the likelihood of reoffending then they would be supported, but if they increased the likelihood of reoffending then they would not. While Utilitarians are concerned about the majority (possible victims of crime) they do not ignore the minority (offenders), and so balancing up the interests of the two groups is the difficulty. For a Utilitarian, therefore, the relationship is mostly about cause and effect – and they would want to be clear about the actual and possible effects of certain sentences on reoffending rates.

Public confidence

This would matter to a Utilitarian because society's happiness is likely to be affected by its confidence in the CJS. However, it would still be unlikely for Utilitarians to support overly harsh sentencing for crimes just to keep people 'happy'. This could be a false happiness and would be at the expense of the minority (offenders) which would not generally be acceptable.

Early release

Again this could be accepted or rejected by Utilitarians depending upon its effect on reoffending and on the deterrent value of sentences. If it leads to increases in crime then it would be rejected, though if it had no effect or reduced crime then it would be accepted.

Personal Reflection

* *Do you think capital punishment is an effective deterrent?*
* *Should sentences 'make an example' of offenders?*
* *How complicated do you think the relationship between sentencing and crime actually is?*

Active learning

Check your understanding

1. How might society judge how 'effective' a sentence is?
2. What do reoffending rates in Scotland tell us about the effectiveness of sentencing?
3. What is meant by 'public confidence' and how is it measured?
4. What are the benefits and drawbacks of early release schemes – and who do these affect most?
5. How far should 'public confidence in the CJS' be taken into account when deciding about the rights and wrongs of capital punishment?
6. How far do the Church of Scotland and the Roman Catholic Church agree about the relationship between sentencing and reoffending?
7. In relation to crime, who would a Buddhist want to show compassion for and why?
8. What alternatives to custody are there and what are the claims for their effectiveness?
9. Should religions and other belief groups be allowed to run prisons according to their own beliefs?
10. Explain why governments might not want to be thought of as 'soft on crime'. What are your views about their taking this into account when making laws and policies?

Investigate

1. A number of documents have been referred to in this chapter. In groups, choose one of these and make a more detailed study of it. You should then report back to the rest of the class.
2. Speed challenge: For each of the following crimes find out what sentence is possible in Scotland (and even if one is) and in one other country. The group that completes all fastest wins.
   - Impersonating a police officer
   - Providing false information on a job application
   - Buying alcohol for an underage person
   - Being drunk in public
   - Threatening your next-door neighbour
   - Shoplifting
   - Not paying a parking fine
3. Using the SCJS you learned about in this section, come up with one question to ask people based on each of the six sections of this survey. Now ask those questions of a range of people in and out of school. How closely do your findings match those of the SCJS? Perhaps you could team up with another school doing RMPS and compare your findings.
4. Create a graffiti wall in your classroom (or school) where people can put sticky notes around the statement: 'What is most likely to bring an end to crime is ...'

Analyse and Evaluate

1. Choose one of the crimes you have investigated and in pairs do the following: One of you should argue that the sentence available for this in Scotland should be hugely increased. The other person should argue that it should be hugely decreased (or should not be an offence at all). You should now have a mini debate.
2. Create a table for the religious and philosophical perspectives you have examined in this section. Select a number of points from this section (e.g. 'sentences should respect the dignity of the offender'). Now mark your table showing where the different perspectives agree/disagree.
3. For each of the following statements discuss your views in class:
   - The main purpose of a prison sentence is protecting the public.
   - Governments should not be 'soft on crime'.
   - Religions pay too much attention to the needs of the offender.
   - Reporting of crime by the media makes more crime likely.

Apply

You have been asked to write a speech for the First Minister of Scotland. This speech is about reoffending rates in Scotland and is entitled 'Reoffending in Scotland – why the Scottish Criminal Justice System works'. You should write the main bullet points for this speech (or the whole speech if you have time).

RELIGION AND RELATIONSHIPS

7 Religious, moral and legal aspects of marriage

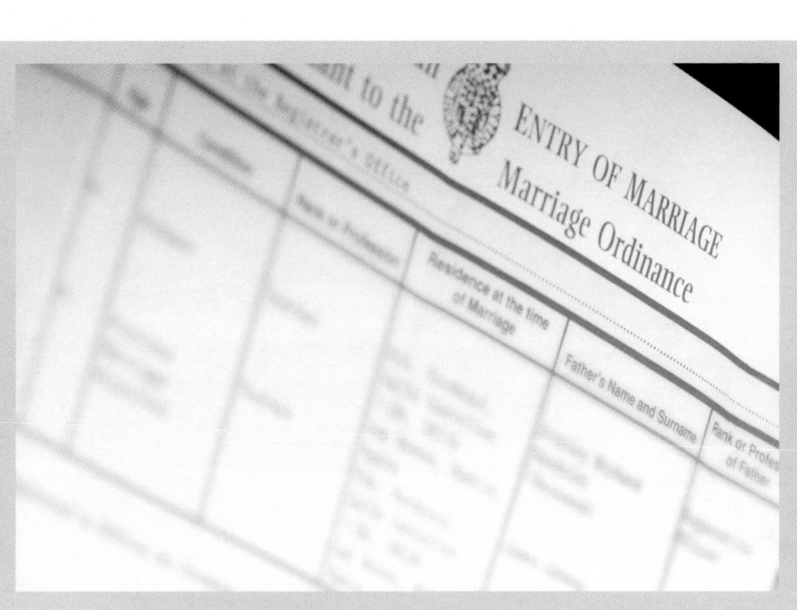

A man, a woman, only two
Should tie the knot and say 'I do'
All other kinds are just pretence (some say)
And marriage is a word not a sentence
If deep in love are four or three
That cannot lead to matrimony
For when all is said and done
Marriage happens when two become one
Nothing is allowed to detract
From marriage's solemn contract
For both, it lasts for life:
That is, for husband and wife
Unless of course
There are grounds for divorce
But 'why,' say others 'was it banned*,
To bring together man and husband?
Or two in love who are both ladies

→

Janets, Carols, or maybe Sadies?
Why, if it's love and it's consensual
Must it still be heterosexual?'
'Because,' say others 'that's nature's way
And nature really isn't gay
Besides if it means just any two
You could marry your dog or your cockatoo'
'Now you're being silly,' others say
'Two humans is the only way
To get it right on your special day
All would laugh, frown and deride
If you went down the aisle with a gerbil as your bride'
'But why the need for ceremonies,
White dress, bow ties and kilted knees
And bridesmaids dressed all pink and frilly
And hats and shoes which are often silly?
Why in a church in front of God?
Which is sometimes strange and sometimes odd
They speak their vows, then kiss and leave
While in God they simply don't believe'
Perhaps it's all a silly caper
Just for a bit of paper

* same-sex marriage became legal in Scotland in 2014

What is marriage?

Talk Point

What moral issues might marriage raise?

Marriage as an idea seems quite simple really, but ...

Marriage is the joining together of a couple who are making a public declaration of their love for each other (or at least their intention to stay together). It is a legally binding contract between two people which ensures that they both have certain rights as part of the relationship – for example, shared property. For some it is a fitting public declaration of two people's feelings for each other – for others it's an out-of-date practice which is unnecessary in the twenty-first century. For some, it involves a religious dimension and for others it does not. At the moment, in the UK, marriage can only take place between two people, but there are places in the world where marriage can take place between more than two people at the same time (or where you can have many wives or husbands). In most places in the world, marriage is the end result of falling in love – though in some places it is arranged for two individuals by two families. In some places, such arranged marriages allow the two individuals to have a say about the marriage – in other places this does not happen and these are referred to as forced marriages. In some cultures there are strict customs (and sometimes laws) about sex before marriage and whether or not married couples can engage in sexual activity with people they are not married to. Some think of marriage just as a piece of paper and others think differently. Some think you need to have a marriage ceremony and others do not. Some think that living together is just as meaningful as being married, others disagree. Some think that marriage is for life and so you can never divorce, others disagree. There are cultures where you can temporarily marry someone for a few days (or hours) and then divorce them. There are places in the world where you can legally marry at 12, in other places you need to be 21, in some places you need your parents' consent, in others you don't.

Marriage ... for or against?

The arguments in support of marriage usually go something like this:

- Marriage is a public commitment of two people to each other. This public commitment means that community/society is more likely to support the marriage.
- Because marriage is a formal (and legal) agreement, the couple will bring a greater level of commitment to it and so it is less likely to break down – this is better for them and for society generally.
- This means that a married relationship is a more stable one – and a stable relationship is much better for bringing up children.

Those who don't feel that marriage is necessary might say:

- A long-term relationship doesn't need 'a bit of paper' to make it strong – many couples go through life perfectly happy without ever being married.
- Marriages break down just like any relationships can – marriage is no guarantee that the relationship will survive.
- Relationships are not just about bringing up children, and even where couples choose to have children, the stability of their upbringing isn't really affected by whether the couple is formally married or not.

Some legal aspects of marriage

In Scotland[20], you can have a 'civil, religious or belief' marriage. Both people involved (opposite or same-sex couples) must give notice to a registrar at least 29 days in advance of the marriage (unless there are 'exceptional circumstances' which make this impossible). Both involved must:

- be at least 16 years old on the day of their marriage
- not be related to each other in any way (there are 17 degrees of relationship which are not allowed to be married)
- be unmarried or not in a civil partnership
- be able to understand marriage and able to consent to it.

Also:

- The marriage would have to be valid in the country where you normally live.
- You can be married by anyone approved to do so by the Marriage (Scotland) Act 1977, for example, minister/priest/celebrant/registrar.
- The marriage can take place anywhere provided it is done in the presence of someone authorised by the Registrar General for that purpose.
- You will have to provide proof of your identity, nationality and where you normally live, as well as proof that any previous marriage or civil partnership has been legally ended (annulled or dissolved).
- There must be two people aged 16 or over present at your marriage to act as witnesses.

Talk Point

Are there any of the legal restrictions on marriage that you would question?

Once married, both people have specific legal protection which is different to any other couple. The Scottish Government states: *'The law is very clear: couples living together do not have the same rights as married couples and civil partners.'*[21] These rights relate mostly to what happens if the marriage 'breaks down' or one partner dies, and cover things such as joint ownership of property and financial responsibility for children which are summed up in the Family Law (Scotland) Act 2006. So the legal aspects of marriage in Scotland are very clear – but, of course, laws can be understood in different ways by different people and that's partly why there are courts and lawyers. For example, once married, couples have certain rights to support them in bringing up their children, but their children have rights too. Once they are over 12 children can *'increasingly take responsibility for things that affect them'*, and even under 12, their views should be listened to.

Also, the ability of those being married 'to understand marriage' can be a complex issue. What, for example, if one or both people who want to get married have learning difficulties? At what point (if any) could it be claimed that someone with learning difficulties could not understand marriage? Finally, there is the issue of consent. This is designed to ensure that both partners are making a completely free choice about getting married. There could be all sorts of reasons why someone might feel pressurised into marriage – how can we know when it is their free choice, and how might we prove that there was any pressure involved?

In Scots law, a marriage can be legally ended by the courts if it has *'broken down irretrievably'* or if one partner has an 'interim gender recognition certificate' (i.e. you are transgender and have *'decided to live permanently in your acquired gender'*). Divorce can be very straightforward (known as a DIY Divorce) if both partners agree about all aspects of the divorce, but it can also be very complex where there are disagreements – in which case the courts have to make decisions about it. Disagreements are most likely about financial matters or over any children from the marriage.

Some moral aspects of marriage

There are many possible moral issues linked to marriage, all of which could of course involve a wide variety of viewpoints:

Age-related issues

The age of consent for marriage is 16 years old in Scotland. Is this too young, too old, just right? What about big age differences? It's perfectly legal for someone who is 100 years old to marry a 16-year-old, but would people have different views about the morality of this? Should the age of consent be the same for everyone, or are some people not mature enough at 16, or mature enough at 15, and anyway, who would decide what 'mature' meant?

Consent-related issues

How can we be sure that both partners have freely chosen to marry? One or both may be under pressure which no one is aware of, or which looks like a 'cultural practice', but is in fact coercion. Who would decide about that? Some arranged marriages allow both partners some freedom to reject their families' choices; it is sometimes claimed that others don't – so when might an arranged marriage become a forced marriage?

Understanding-related issues

How can we be sure that one or both partners fully understand marriage? People's ability to understand things can be linked to their mental state, their upbringing, temporary illness and many other factors.

Degree of kinship

In Scotland it is illegal, for example, for siblings to marry, or for you to marry your aunt or uncle – but is it immoral? It is often argued that this is because of the fact that the closer you are to your partner in family relationships the more likely it is that any children you have will have genetically inherited difficulties; but what if a married couple who were genetically close chose not to have children (or not even to engage in a sexual relationship) – would that be immoral?

Multiple-partner marriages

In Scotland, marriage is only legal between two people. But is having many wives or many husbands immoral? If everyone involved is happy with the arrangement, then what would make it wrong?

Same-sex marriage

In Scotland this is now legal and both partners have all the same rights as those in opposite-sex marriage. However, there remain people who think same-sex marriage is immoral.

Divorce

Divorces and separations are of course perfectly legal in Scotland, but there are still some who argue that marriage is for life and so divorce is immoral. This would also mean that anyone remarrying after divorce might be considered by such people as committing adultery.

Behaviour during marriage

The law does not set out how people should behave when married – other than where behaviour of any partner in a marriage is in some way abusive. However, there are many different moral positions on behaviour during marriage. This can range from 'power' in a marriage – for example, are both partners equal or is one the 'head of the house' – to sexual activity in marriage – for example, whether sex outside marriage is accepted by one or both partners. Some 'open marriages' allow one or both partners to have sex with other people, while others think such marriages are immoral.

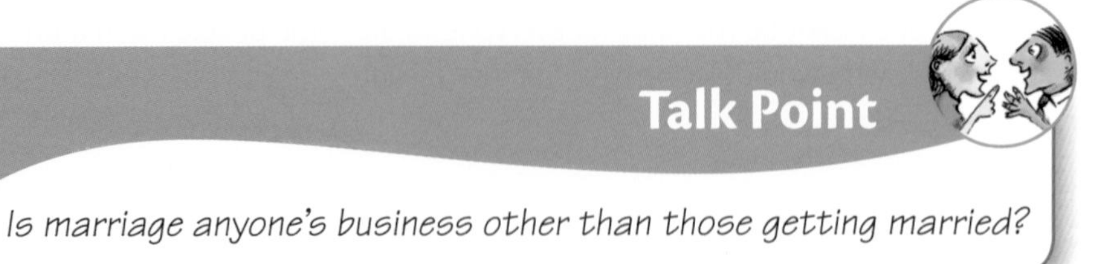

Some religious and philosophical aspects of marriage

Marriage in Christianity

It would take a separate book to explore fully Christian responses to all the legal and moral aspects of marriage we have thought about so far – so the best thing to do is to set out what two denominations within Christianity teach about marriage.

The Church of Scotland

Generally speaking, the Church of Scotland accepts the legal position on marriage in Scotland in relation to age, consent and other legal matters. It is prepared to provide church weddings for anyone in a parish, even if they don't go to church – although it is up to individual ministers to discuss this with the couple and decide if it is the right thing for them. However, currently, Church of Scotland Ministers are not permitted to carry out same-sex marriages because this is prohibited by Church of Scotland Law[22]. Marriage in the Church of Scotland means between a man and a woman. Divorced people can be married in the Church of Scotland because marriage is not thought of as a sacrament.

The Roman Catholic Church

For Catholics marriage is a sacrament between an adult man and a woman and should take place in church. Both partners should ideally be baptised Catholics. However, the Church does accept that Catholics can marry other Christians – though it points out the potential difficulties which might follow because of the couple's different beliefs. It also accepts Catholics marrying those who are not baptised – though expresses the view that the marriage *'can prepare the non-believing spouse to accept the grace of conversion.'*[23] (1637) So you don't marry someone who is not baptised in order to convert them – you simply witness to your faith throughout the marriage. It is important to stress that the Church expresses joy at married love. Its view is that the ideal is marriage between two baptised Catholics because marriage can be something you sometimes have to work at and this is much easier if you both share the same beliefs: it is not, therefore, a 'grudging' acceptance of marriage between Catholics and those of other beliefs, but an awareness of the helpfulness in a couple sharing beliefs. Both partners must give full consent (no legal barriers to marriage and no one under any form of constraint) to the marriage and there must be no *'natural or ecclesiastical (Church) law which prohibits it.'* Married couples are expected to be completely faithful to each other. Marriage is also for life and *'cannot be dissolved by any human power or for any reason other than death.'* (2382) However, the Church accepts that civil divorces may be required in some circumstances, and that people may even remarry, but they will not be allowed to receive communion. The Church also allows marriages to be annulled. This is a complicated process which means that the Church states that the marriage *as defined by the Church*, never really existed. For the Church, marriage has three key characteristics: faithfulness, indissolubility and fertility – and these are used to define marriage and respond to any 'attacks' on the concept of marriage.

Buddhism

In general, Buddhists follow the customs and laws around marriage in the countries where they live. At the time of Buddha, marriage would have been between a man and a woman – though there were polygamous marriages too. Marriage is not any kind of religious duty, but a matter for personal choice. Once married, the couple should follow the five precepts of Buddhism in relation to how they behave towards each other. There is no need for any specific marriage ceremony, although in practice many Buddhists choose to have one according to the customs of the country in which they live and even to have this 'blessed' by Buddhist monks in a ceremony. The Buddha advised that people should not commit adultery and should show respect to each other. Divorce and remarriage are nobody's business but those involved – but, of course, in many cases this is more closely linked to local and national customs than to Buddhist teaching.

Humanism

The Humanist Society Scotland[24] states: *'We believe that marriage and civil partnerships are based on mutual love and respect. We also know that every couple is different and that is why our ceremonies are unique and personal.'* Humanists believe that marriage, civil partnerships and long-term relationships are all equally valid and it is for individuals to decide what kind of relationships they have. Humanists think it is equally appropriate for opposite-sex and same-sex couples to be in a relationship. In fact, Humanist Society Scotland was very outspoken in its support for the legalisation of gay marriage in Scotland. In relation to the other moral aspects of marriage mentioned before, Humanists would generally follow the law of the country they lived in – unless that law discriminated against a group (as, for example where same-sex marriage/relationships are illegal).

Talk Point

Is marriage 'the best form' of long-term relationship?

Utilitarianism

For a Utilitarian, to be married or not is linked to the overall happiness this would bring to society. If marriage is 'more stable' than other forms of relationship then a Utilitarian would support it as opposed to other forms of relationship, but there would have to be good evidence that it was more stable. Utilitarians would also judge each of the moral aspects of marriage in relation to the likelihood that they produced the greatest good for the greatest number. For example, polygamy (one man, many wives) and polyandry (one woman, many husbands) could be accepted if everyone involved in such a relationship understands and accepts this form of relationship. To prohibit it might reduce overall happiness for those involved and if there are no effects beyond those involved then it will not take away from overall happiness in society.

Personal Reflection

* *What are your views on marriage?*
* *Do you think attitudes to marriage are changing?*
* *Is marriage 'just a piece of paper'?*

Active learning

Check your understanding

1 Describe the key rules, laws and principles which apply to marriage in Scotland.
2 Describe two arguments for and against getting married – and explain your own view.
3 What rights does marriage/civil partnership provide to couples in Scotland?
4 Explain your own views about the legal age of consent for marriage/civil partnership in Scotland.
5 What arguments might there be for and against 'multiple-partner' marriages/civil partnerships?
6 What are the key similarities and differences in views of marriage between the Church of Scotland and the Roman Catholic Church?
7 What views are held in religions about same-sex marriage?
8 What views do Humanists have on marriage and in what ways are these similar to/different from religious views?
9 In your view, is marriage preferable to any other kind of relationship?
10 What different views are there about divorce?

Investigate

1 Gather information from online surveys about attitudes to marriage around the world. You can then present these data graphically with your own comments added. You could aim to answer all or some of the following:
   - What views are there around the world about marriage?
   - How do views about marriage differ between men and women/different social groups/occupations, etc.?
   - What different views are held about marrying 'for love' and 'arranged marriage'?
   - How 'popular' is marriage across the world? Is it more popular in some places than others?
   - Is marriage more or less common now than in the past?
   - What is the balance around the world of religious marriages/non-religious marriages and civil partnerships?
   - Where in the world is same-sex marriage legal?

2 What are the main similarities and differences between religious and non-religious marriage ceremonies?

3 During a marriage ceremony the couple usually recite vows to each other. Find out about a range of different vows which are commonly made during marriage. What kind of vows might you use if you were going to be married?

4 What are the requirements for a divorce in Scotland and how do these compare with other countries around the world?

5 There are many rules and laws around the world about who can be married (e.g. age, family relationship and so on). How do these rules and laws differ around the world?

Analyse and Evaluate

1 Choose one religious or non-religious perspective you have studied in this section. For each of the following statements, suggest how someone who holds the perspective might respond. You can also suggest different responses to the same statement which might be given by those who follow your chosen perspective.
   - Marriage is out of date.
   - No one under 18 should be allowed to marry.
   - Marriage should always be 'for love'.
   - You should only be allowed to marry if you fully understand what marriage means.
   - Same-sex marriage is no different to opposite-sex marriage.
   - Marrying more than one person is morally reasonable in all/some circumstances.

2 Choose one of the perspectives you have studied in this chapter. Explain the strengths and weaknesses of this perspective's view on marriage.

3 Compare one religious and one non-religious perspective on one aspect of marriage you have examined in this chapter.

Apply

Your task is to create a leaflet (or presentation) for a religious organisation which explores same-sex marriage in Scotland. Your aim is to ensure that followers of this religious organisation understand the law in Scotland about same-sex marriage and think about the religious and moral issues this raises. You should explore different views about same-sex marriage from this religious perspective and leave it up to the followers to make their own minds up about any issues you raise.

8 Nature of relationships: sexuality

I was born bisexual, just like I was born with blue eyes.

Some people are gay … get over it!

Transgender? That's just unnatural.

LGBT people are still persecuted, bullied and badly treated – and it's worse in some places than others. Why does anyone think they have the right to do this?

I think being gay is something God is unhappy about, but I should still show compassion to people no matter who or what they are.

God loves everyone, no matter who or what they are – and duh – that includes LGBT people – and while we're at it, why would God be unhappy about two people loving each other whatever their gender is?

Lesbian, gay, bisexual, transgender, intersex – I mean, in what way is any of this an issue? If you're not causing harm to anyone or anything, who cares about your sexuality?

You can't believe how terrified I was of telling my parents that I'm gay. I thought they'd throw me out of the house, send me to a psychiatrist, never speak to me again. When I did tell them, they said, 'Yes, we thought you probably were. We love you, now what would you like for dinner?' and our relationship went on just like it had before.

Love brings good kamma – LGBT love or any other kind …

No, I don't think you can 'control' being LGBT. But I think you do need help about it – maybe counselling or something.

We live in a world where everyone is scared to say that something is wrong. I think being LGBT is wrong.

Sexuality: born, made or chosen?

LGBT refers to people who are lesbian, gay, bisexual or transgender and is about your sexuality. There are lots of different views about the origins of your sexuality. Some typical theories are:

- You are born LGBT– it's in your genes and is biological – just like the colour of your eyes; or maybe something about your time in the womb led to you being LGBT – no matter, it's in your biological 'programming' (the nature argument).
- You learn to be LGBT – as you develop in life, a load of very complicated circumstances in your environment – powerful role models for example – lead to you being LGBT (the nurture argument).
- Being LGBT is a result of a combination of nature and nurture factors (the interactionist argument).
- Being LGBT is a choice you make – there's no 'cause' or 'reason' for it – any more than there's much of a cause or reason for you preferring chips to boiled potatoes (this raises the whole concept of 'free will' which is another issue altogether ...).

Evolutionary biologists, psychologists, sociologists and many other groups and individuals suggest a whole range of explanations for human behaviour and actions – including being LGBT. The most likely explanation for any human behaviour (and non-human animals too, where same-sex and bisexual 'relationships' are claimed to have been observed) is that it is a complicated mixture of nature and nurture.

A brief history of LGBT

Some would say that people who are LGBT have been around throughout human history. Artwork from ancient civilisations sometimes shows LGBT activities. Responses to LGBT around the world have been different in different times and places – from serious and terrible persecution and lack of interest to times and places where LGBT people have been celebrated. Today, it's no different. In some cultures, LGBT people are very badly treated and must keep their sexuality hidden and in others, they are celebrated and treated like movie stars. In some countries, you can still be imprisoned (or executed) for being LGBT, while in others you can marry and are likely to be treated as a valued member of society. In fact, male homosexual activities in the UK only stopped being a criminal offence in 1982. In India, male homosexual activities stopped being a criminal offence in 2009 and were then made a criminal offence again in 2013[25]. In Scotland, same-sex marriage was made legal in 2014. Oddly, in some countries it is illegal to be a male but not a female homosexual – in fact, in the UK lesbian sex has never been illegal. People who identify themselves as transgender (meaning they don't accept they are the gender they were born into) are accepted in some countries, offered what some think of as medical treatment in others, and punished in others.

What's the issue?

Of course, for many people, there's no 'issue' at all because being LGBT is just something that is part of the variety and diversity of life on Earth and for them there's no real difference whether you simply are LGBT or actively engage in an LGBT lifestyle. However, sexuality remains a topic of debate which can stir up some heated viewpoints for two main reasons:

- **Issue A** Some people think that being LGBT as opposed to heterosexual is wrong. This might be based on religious or other kinds of belief but is often based on a belief that it is 'unnatural' so in some way a 'threat' to the way human society works. Sometimes people think that *being* LGBT is not wrong but any sexual *activity* which is not heterosexual *is* wrong – they think you could *be* LGBT but should not *act* upon it.

- **Issue B** For others, the issue is not whether any kind of sexuality or sexual practice is right or wrong, but is about how society treats people – whatever their sexuality. People still suffer discrimination and persecution if they are not heterosexual and so how LGBT people are treated is the issue.

Responses to issues of sexuality: Issue A

Christianity

Like all responses from Christianity, it's important to remember that there's no one agreed view. Different Christian Churches and groups hold very different – sometimes completely opposite – views about sexuality. Also, individual Christians might not always share the 'official' view of the denomination of Christianity they are part of. Some Christian denominations issue teachings which all members of that denomination are expected to support, while others leave it up to individual members to decide through their own prayer, Bible study and learning. Here are two specific examples of different approaches to sexuality.

The Roman Catholic Church

In discussing the sixth commandment (You shall not commit adultery) the Catechism of the Roman Catholic Church (2357) sets out its views on homosexuality: '... *Basing itself on Sacred Scripture, which presents homosexual acts as acts of grave depravity, tradition has always declared that "homosexual acts are intrinsically disordered". They are contrary to the natural law. They close the sexual act to the gift of life. They do not proceed from a genuine affective and sexual complementarity. Under no circumstances can they be approved.*'[26]

The Roman Catholic Church recognises that homosexuality exists, but that the practice of homosexuality goes against God's laws. This means that: '*Homosexual persons are called to chastity*' (2359), meaning that homosexuals should not engage in homosexual acts. Pope Francis recently emphasised the Church's teaching that being homosexual is not a sin, but homosexual acts are by saying, '*If a person is gay and seeks God and has good will, who am I to judge?*' The Roman Catholic Church's view of people who identify themselves as transgender and intersex is covered by its view that humans were created male and female. It says: '*Everyone, man and woman, should acknowledge and accept his sexual identity*' (2333), by which the Roman Catholic Church means the gender you are born into – so this would make living as the opposite gender to the one you were born as wrong, as would any kind of gender reassignment procedures (sex change). The Church stresses that human dignity is deserved not earned, and that a person is body and soul.

The Church of Scotland

In its document of May 2013, *Theological commission on same-sex relationships and the ministry* the Church of Scotland sets out the variety of views which exist about homosexuality. This commission (a group of experts looking into an issue) states[27]: '*We are aware that some have argued that the Church has not taken a formal position on homosexual practice. While this may be so, we are of the view that the Church has never formally departed from the traditional teaching of the wider church on homosexuality and our debates have proceeded on that basis.*' So the Church of Scotland's view is that homosexual acts do not fit with Christian belief and so is similar to Roman Catholic teaching. However, the Church of Scotland accepts civil partnerships and is also about to consider recognising *actively* homosexual ministers – this could mean that while in theory the Church of Scotland opposes homosexuality, in practice it accepts it.

Buddhism

In Buddhism, the third precept states that Buddhists should 'avoid sexual misconduct'. But what is meant by misconduct is understood differently by different Buddhist traditions and individuals. Buddhist monks are prohibited from sexual activity, but lay Buddhists are not. The difficulty is that what counts as 'sexual misconduct' is understood in different ways. Most Buddhists would accept that any sexual activity which causes harm to you or anyone else is wrong, but of course that would apply equally to heterosexual sex, as well as any other kind. Buddhism also has no one agreed view about people who identify themselves as transgender or intersex. Buddhists do believe that everything is in a constant state of change – nothing stays the same – so perhaps how 'we' think of 'our' gender doesn't really apply in the same way in Buddhism. As Buddhists believe there is no 'self', then Buddhists can think of 'themselves' any way they like.

Humanism

Humanist Society Scotland was one of the key campaigners in favour of legalising same-sex marriage. For Humanists, sexuality is no one's concern but the individual's and they state: *'Humanist Society Scotland (HSS) consider both civil partnership and marriage ought to be available to any couple, same or mixed sex ... all the people of Scotland deserve to be able to choose a ceremony that will reflect their lives and their beliefs, as well as their love for one another. The overriding reason for this position is that the personal motivations for, and the social benefits of, marriage are universal, irrespective of the gender and sexuality of the couple.'*[28] Humanism is based on the belief that we have only one life and it is ours to do with as we please – provided we don't harm others in the process of course. Our sexuality is our own business.

Utilitarianism

As Utilitarianism is based on the principle of the greatest good for the greatest number, it could take a number of positions on sexuality. As the LGBT community is in a minority, any 'consequences' of LGBT practices (whatever those might be) would only be wrong if they are likely to harm the majority. So, for example, imagine almost everyone was LGBT – this could obviously have an impact on the number of children produced (though not necessarily, as many same-sex couples have children through IVF and other arrangements). This could harm the majority – there might not be enough people around to look after you in your old age, for example! So, for Utilitarians being LGBT or actively engaging in an LGBT lifestyle could be considered wrong if it 'imbalances' society in some way. However, this is projecting into an unknown future – for now, the Utilitarian Peter Singer sums up one Utilitarian view: *'If a form of sexual activity brings satisfaction to those who take part in it, and harms no one, what can be immoral about it?'*[29]

Responses to issues of sexuality: Issue B

Christianity

Again, there is no one accepted view about how people who are LGBT should be 'treated' by society. However, there is probably more agreement within Christianity about how society should behave towards people who are LGBT. In fact, most Christians are likely to take a compassionate view of anyone's sexual identity – as Christianity is based on the idea of 'treat others as you would like to be treated'.

The Roman Catholic Church

The Catechism states quite clearly: '*The number of men and women who have deep-seated homosexual tendencies is not negligible. This inclination, which is objectively disordered, constitutes for most of them a trial. They must be accepted with respect, compassion, and sensitivity. Every sign of unjust discrimination in their regard should be avoided.*' (2358) So, the Church teaches compassion towards those who are LGBT while still considering the active practices of lesbian, gay and bisexual relationships unacceptable. In fact, Church teaching refers not just to compassion but to respect – that all Christians have an obligation to treat others in accordance with their dignity as human beings.

The Church of Scotland

In 2015, the Church of Scotland was still debating the role of same-sex clergy, but its acceptance of same-sex marriage suggests that it would also support a compassionate approach to people who are LGBT. The Church teaches that all are made in the image of God, and that this does not refer to our physical self, but to our reason and spirit. This would imply that people who are LGBT should be treated with love, understanding, consideration and compassion.

Buddhism

The principle of karuna (compassion) is central to Buddhism. The Dalai Lama has famously said: '*Be compassionate whenever possible. It is always possible.*' So Buddhists would be unlikely to accept any discrimination or unkind treatment of people who are LGBT – and this would extend not only to unkind actions, but also unkind thoughts. It is important to remember, however, that local and national customs around the world will play an important part in how individual Buddhists address LGBT issues.

Humanism

Humanist Society Scotland in its vision statement includes: '*The worth, dignity and autonomy of every person is respected and individual freedom is balanced with social responsibility and a duty of care for future generations; ethical and moral problems are addressed with compassion, knowledge and reason.*'[30] So clearly for Humanists, no matter who you are, no matter how you think of or express your sexuality, you are a valued person. Therefore any kind of discrimination based on sexuality would be hard to justify from a Humanist perspective.

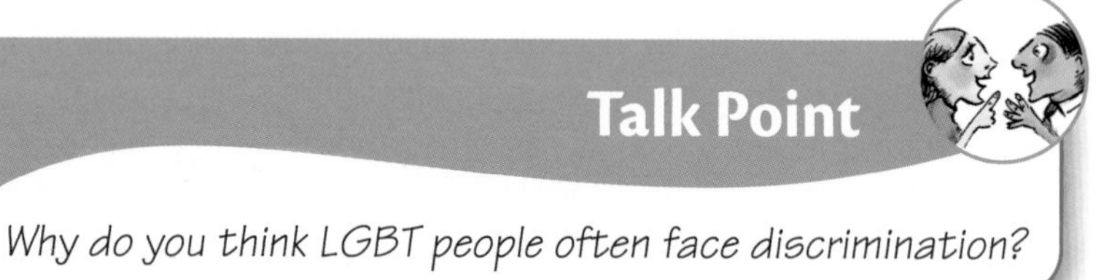

Utilitarianism

Here, the picture is fairly straightforward. It would be hard to imagine any form of discrimination against the LGBT community bringing the greatest happiness to the greatest number – as discrimination doesn't generally lead to happiness. However, the Utilitarian J. S. Mill did suggest that individual freedoms could sometimes be challenged if they led to harm to others. In *On Liberty* he said: '*… the only purpose for which power can be rightfully exercised over any member of a civilized community, against his will, is to prevent harm to others.*' So, perhaps if you thought that being LGBT or living an LGBT lifestyle caused some kind of harm, then you might think that opposing it in some way was acceptable – though for a Utilitarian this would probably mean some kind of legislation, not unkind discrimination. However, again, you would need to be able to show that being LGBT or living a LGBT lifestyle was in some way harmful to others.

Personal Reflection

- *What issues – if any – are raised for you by the topic of sexuality/sexual identity?*
- *What do you think of the various viewpoints considered in this chapter?*
- *Are attitudes towards LGBT people changing?*

Active learning

Check your understanding

1. In your opinion, is a person 'born LGBT'?
2. In what different ways are LGBT people treated in different cultures of the world?
3. What arguments are given by those who think that being anything other than heterosexual is wrong?
4. What different views are held within and between religious groups about the 'right and wrong' of being LGBT?
5. Why do some consider there is a difference between *being* LGBT and *acting on* being LGBT?
6. What views are held by non-religious perspectives and groups on LGBT issues?
7. How important is the principle of compassion across religions in considering LGBT issues?
8. What might be the causes of discrimination towards LGBT people and how should these be addressed?
9. How far do you agree that sexual identity is no one else's business other than the person involved?
10. Some religions make homosexuality something which prohibits a person from holding a role in the religion (like minister, priest, etc.). What reasons are given for this and how do those who disagree explain their opposition to this?

Investigate

1. What are the main organisations which campaign for LGBT rights? What are the main issues they deal with and in what different ways do they do so?
2. What laws in Scotland protect people who are LGBT and what laws cover the right of people who want to express their views about LGBT issues?
3. Some 'explanations' for being LGBT are below. For each one, find out what the main argument being suggested is:
   - It is genetically inherited.
   - It is linked to your time in the womb.
   - It is linked to birth order.
   - It is learned through observation of role models.
   - It is learned by association.
   - It is linked to cultural norms in a society.
   - It is a simple matter of choice.
4. The way that LGBT people and issues have been portrayed in the media has changed over the years. Investigate how LGBT people have been portrayed over time. You might want to choose a specific aspect of the media to investigate – for example, the portrayal of LGBT people in TV soaps, or in literature, etc.
5. People who are LGBT can be treated very differently according to the country they live in. In what different ways are LGBT people treated around the world?

Analyse and Evaluate

1 One of the main arguments against looking for any 'cause' of being LGBT is what happens if any 'cause' is 'discovered'. Choose one of the possible 'causes' of being LGBT you have examined in this chapter (or found out about). Now express a range of views about what, if anything, should be 'done' if such a cause was discovered.
2 Script a conversation between the following four people about LGBT issues:
   - A religious person who thinks LGBT activities are wrong and a religious person who disagrees.
   - A non-religious person who thinks LGBT activities are wrong and one who disagrees.
3 Imagine that a gene was 'discovered' which 'makes you gay'. What different views might religious people have about testing for this gene in the early stages of a pregnancy?

Apply

Although there are disagreements within religions and between religious people and non-religious people about a number of LGBT issues, most agree that the LGBT community should be treated with care and compassion. Although this is already covered by a number of laws in Scotland, produce a poster which states ten things which people should do to show care and compassion towards people who identify themselves as LGBT.

9 Nature of relationships: love and intimacy

Rab and Donnie have just returned from a Halloween party and Rab has fallen in love ...

Donnie: Rab, will ye get that look aff yer face, yer givin' me the creeps.

Rab: *Ah'm meant tae give ye the heebie-jeebies, it's Halloween.*

Donnie: Aye but Rab, ye've taken aff yer mask and yer costume ... it's yer pure cheesy look that's giving me the frighteners.

Rab: *Ma look, Donnie, simply announces tae a' the world that ah'm in love.*

Donnie: Love is it? Whit unfortunate lassie is aboot tae be on yer stalkin' list and taking oot a court order against ye bein' in the same country as her?

Rab: *That lassie that was done up as a troll fae Lord o' the Rings.*

Donnie: She wisnae a troll fae Lord o' the Rings, she wis dressed up as a lollipop lady.

Rab: *Wis she? That wis a good mask though!*

Donnie: Rab, she wisnae wearin' a mask.

Rab: *Aw well, she wis really nice-lookin anyway, and ah'm in love.*

Donnie: How can ye be in love, ye know nothing aboot her.

Rab: *Ah don't need tae know anything, it wis love at first sight.*

Donnie: If she ever finds oot aboot it, it'll be love at first fright merr like.

Rab: *Naw, it's true, ma heart's been stolen.*

Donnie: Aw well, that's good then, it'll be able tae keep yer brain company.

Rab: *Naw Donnie, Cupid has shot his arrow.*

Donnie: And it's obviously hit yoo in both yer eyes at exactly the same moment. Anyway, ye canny be in love just efter seein' somebody at a party – ye need tae talk tae her, get tae know her, find oot if ye have anythin' in common, see if ye bond.

Rab: *C'mon Donnie, where's yer romantic side – is it no' just possible that she's the wan, ma spiritual soul mate, that me and her are destined tae be together for a' eternity.*

Donnie: Naw, it's no possible – it'll be the scariest Halloween that lassie has ever had if you go down on one knee oot of the blue efter spyin' her from afar and mistakin' her for Shrek.

Rab: *Ah'm no gonnie propose tae her, just ask her oot oan a date.*

Donnie: Whit, like, just approach her in the street and ask nicely if she will be make so bold as tae accompany you tae the nearest sit-in chippy for a fish supper and a deep-fried Creme Egg?

Rab: *Naw, ah'll just ask her if she'll go oot wi' me.*

Donnie: Yoor call Rab, but I sure hope she doesny have her lollipop stick wi' her when ye ask.

What is love?

According to the Christian Bible, love is 'patient, kind, keeps no record of wrongs ...' but this tells us about the qualities of love, not how it comes about, or what it actually means. Love has emotional qualities – people in love talk about how many opposite emotions it brings about, such as happiness, pain, reward, disappointment. There are also physical consequences of being in love – sleeplessness, heartache, feverishness, which sound like symptoms of an illness – and maybe that's what love is ...

In 1986, psychologist Robert Sternberg[31] came up with three types of love: Liking (intimacy alone); Empty Love (Commitment alone); and Infatuation (Passion alone). Combining these in various ways leads to seven kinds of love: Romantic love; companionate love and fatuous love – with the 'best' kind of love being a combination of intimacy + passion + commitment = Consummate love. In fact, there's even a formula for love! Byrne (1971)[32] said love is:

$$Y = \left[\frac{(\Sigma PR)}{(\Sigma PR + \Sigma NR)}\right] + k$$

(Y= attraction, *PR* = positive reinforcement, *NR* = negative reinforcement and *k* is a constant ...)

This gives us an idea of what love might – or might not – be, but not how people 'fall in love'. Does love start with physical and emotional attraction – do 'opposites attract', or are we more likely to fall in love the more we have in common with someone? What factors lead to us 'falling in love'? Falling in love is probably a very complicated mixture of physical factors, chemistry, psychology, situational factors, social factors and probably a whole load of other things too. It has been shown that people are more likely to find other people attractive if they are asked to stare into their eyes, play footsie under the table, sit in the dark together, and share exciting experiences together, such as walking over a scary rope bridge![33] According to all of these pieces of research, attraction is possible 'at first sight', but is love? That's a trickier one to answer.

Is 'love at first sight' possible?

What is intimacy?

Basically this links to 'how far you can go' in a relationship (or even if you are not in a relationship). Some argue that there is a kind of unspoken set of rules about this which we do (or should) follow. So, for example, this might mean not having sex until: you are married; or you are in a long-term relationship; or you have been seeing each other for a specific time period; or not on a first date. Of course, there are disagreements about this and in Scotland there are no laws about it in relation to two adults freely consenting to a relationship. The concept of intimacy might also link to what counts as physical intimacy not including sexual intercourse – so, for example, types of kissing, physical touching and so on. Again, there are different views about this with some cultures frowning even on couples holding hands. For some, there are no rules about intimacy – everyone makes their own choices about this – for others there are social customs which they choose to follow – and these might be based on religious beliefs, for example.

The importance of love and intimacy for religion and beliefs

Most religions stress that love is an important part of any close relationship. For some, love comes first and the relationship develops after that, though others accept that relationships can begin and love can develop afterwards. The relationship between love, sex, intimacy and marriage is very complicated across religions and belief groups. Most religions teach that sex, intimacy and marriage should involve love between those involved, though there are some differences here in how strictly followers are expected to comply with that. In general, most religions would oppose sex without love, while non-religious belief groups would leave this up to individuals. However, the degree of physical intimacy in any relationship ('how far you can go') varies across religious groups. Importantly, there is often some difference between what religions teach in this respect and what their followers actually do, with surveys sometimes showing a gap between religious teachings and the practices of the followers of those religions. For example, Cochran and Beeghley (1991) showed that in a survey of Christian attitudes to sex before marriage, 25 per cent of Roman Catholics, 44 per cent of Protestants and 39 per cent of Baptists stated that sex before marriage was 'always wrong'[34]. As you've seen too, some religions accept that there can be love between same-sex couples and others take the opposite view.

For non-religious groups there is usually less of an emphasis on being in love before reaching a certain level of intimacy, having sex or being married, though there is variation here too with some non-religious individuals regarding sex/intimacy as something which requires no love and others thinking the opposite. For non-religious groups, love is usually equally likely in a same-sex relationship as in a heterosexual one. Also, most religions generally argue that you can only be 'in love' with one person at a time (or at least in a loving relationship with one person at a time), though there are religions which accept polygamy and polyandry.

Christianity

Love is a central theme in Christianity, and in relationships this includes romantic love. The differences within Christianity and between Christianity and other religions are usually related to how important love is for other aspects of a relationship. In particular, there are differences within Christianity about how much two people need to be in love before increasing their levels of physical intimacy and having sex. However, Christianity clearly teaches that in any relationship, care, consideration and respect for each other is central and it's probably true to say that a married Christian couple (or a Christian couple in a long-term relationship) should fall into the *consummate love* category which Sternberg identified.

The Church of Scotland

In 2001, guidelines[35] were produced by the Scottish Executive (now Government) which included a range of 'faith perspectives' on sexual health and relationships. The Church of Scotland stated: *'Our sexuality is both a divine gift and a human responsibility. The Church of Scotland accepts that sexual intercourse is not solely or even primarily for the purpose of procreation but serves to enrich relationships and believes that our sexuality can be expressed in a variety of loving relationships that offer mutual joy and pleasure.'* Now at first sight, this looks like anything goes, but the Church then makes clear its view that it considers marriage as the *'best and securest foundation for a long and happy relationship',* and that marriage means that sex will be *'in the context of trust and security'*. So for the Church of Scotland, marriage is considered the proper place for sexual intimacy, but it does not state outright that it is the only place.

The Roman Catholic Church

The Catholic Catechism states: *'Sexuality, by means of which man and woman give themselves to one another through the acts which are proper and exclusive to spouses, is not something simply biological, but concerns the innermost being of the human person as such. It is realized in a truly human way only if it is an integral part of the love by which a man and woman commit themselves totally to one another until death.'* (2361) So this teaching is quite clear. Sex remains something which is for husbands and wives in the context of a loving relationship and this loving relationship is for life. In other places the Catholic Church has stated that all sexual activity should involve love and that a sexual act is only moral if it is 'unitive and procreative' – which means that it is carried out in a loving marriage relationship and is open to the possibility of creating new life. The level of intimacy between husband and wife should also always respect each other's dignity. Love between a married couple isn't only physical, it is spiritual too, and the Church is clear that even looking with desire at someone you're not married to is sinful. As for intimacy, the Catholic Catechism (2348) states that all baptised Catholics are called to chastity.

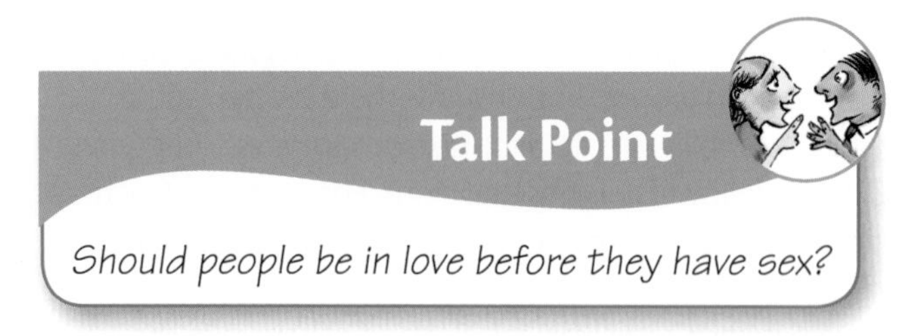

Buddhism

Ordained Buddhists are expected to avoid intimacy and sexual activity, though lay Buddhists are not, although both groups must accept the third precept which states: *'I undertake to refrain from sensual (kama) misconduct.'* This could obviously be understood as being linked to sexual intercourse, but could also apply to levels of sexual intimacy which are not full sexual intercourse. It could also cover a whole range of activities which are related to sex and sexual pleasure because the word *kama* in Pali means 'sensual desire' and does not simply mean sex. The key here is avoiding harm to self and others – and anything related to sex or sexual intimacy which might cause harm would be unacceptable to Buddhists. Buddhism stresses control over our senses, and particularly over our desires. Sexual intimacy can produce strong desire, so Buddhists need to be aware of that. In the Dhammapada it is said: *'Don't give way to heedlessness/or to intimacy/with a sensual delight-/for a heedful person, absorbed in jhana, attains an abundance of ease.'* In short, Buddhists should control their desires, and practise detachment from the driving force of sexual intimacy. A Buddhist accepts that love is important in any relationship, but even love is something which, like everything, is constantly changing.

Humanism

According to the American Humanist Association[36]: *'Sex has no inherent meaning ... no inherent goal or purpose. The social norms that govern sexuality ... are a product of their unique time and place.'* It also adds: *'Short of harming others or compelling them to do likewise, individuals should be permitted to express their sexual proclivities and pursue their lifestyles as they desire. We also wish to cultivate the development of a responsible attitude towards sexuality, in which humans are not exploited as sexual objects, and in which intimacy, sensitivity, respect and honesty in interpersonal relationships are encouraged.'* So for humanism, sexual intimacy does not need to be in the context of love, does not need to be husband and wife and is open to individual choice between consenting adults[37]. So it is really up to consenting adults to decide on their level of intimacy and their sexual activities, as long as in doing so they demonstrate sensitivity, honesty and respect.

Utilitarianism

Utilitarians would consider that love is a matter of personal expression and that sexual intimacy is also likely to be a matter of personal choice. Anything in a relationship would be wrong only if it led to harm for the majority. Clearly, if everyone treated everyone else just to satisfy their own desires, then that might not lead to a very happy society (but then if everyone understood and agreed to this, then perhaps it might). How far love is required in a relationship and how far it needs to be present in any acts of sexual intimacy is hard to judge in relation to Utilitarianism because it would be difficult to predict the outcome for the majority of different approaches to sexual behaviour, intimacy and the place of love in relationships.

So for a Utilitarian, judging the likely impact on the majority of a range of matters linked to love, sex and intimacy will probably be a personal choice, and as long as the principle of achieving the 'greatest good for the greatest number' is followed then that would be enough.

Talk Point

Should people always follow the customs about love and intimacy of the culture in which they live?

Personal Reflection

- *How important is it to be 'in love' in a long-term relationship?*
- *Should people only be sexually intimate when they are in love?*
- *Do you think love can be summed up in a mathematical formula?*

Active learning

Check your understanding

1 How would you describe and explain 'love'?
2 Do you think that levels of intimacy should reflect how much in love people are?
3 What views are there in religions about the role of intimacy in a relationship?
4 Could love be described mathematically?
5 Is sex 'acceptable' before/outside marriage?
6 What different views might there be about the claim that 'sex has no inherent meaning'?
7 The Roman Catholic Church describes marriage as a 'sacrament'. What is meant by this?
8 What might a Buddhist mean by 'sensual misconduct'?
9 What different rules are there about intimacy for lay and ordained Buddhists?
10 Does the relationship between sex and love have any implications for the happiness of the majority?

Investigate

1 What online advice is 'out there' for young people who are asking questions about love and intimacy? As a class you could do a survey of the sites which are available for young people and you could review these for teenagers. You could give them stars for helpfulness, accuracy, honesty, realism and any other category you can think of.
2 Many online dating services work on the idea that if you can match up a range of likes and dislikes between people, then eventually you can find a 'match' which is more likely to lead to love. What different methods of matching are used across a range of websites (or other matchmaking activities/groups)?
3 What do different Christian denominations say about how far there can be love between homosexuals/lesbians, bisexuals and people who are transgender? How far is there 'a Christian view' and how far is this different from the views of other religions and non-religious perspectives such as Humanism?
4 Within religions, there are many different definitions of 'love'. Investigate the many different meanings of this word and create your own information sheet about this in the form of a dictionary-type series of pages.

Analyse and Evaluate

1 Here is a series of statements relating to love and intimacy. For each one, explain your own view and suggest how someone who had the opposite view to you might respond:
   - There is no such thing as love.
   - You cannot love someone 'at first sight'; that's just attraction.
   - Love can be scientifically researched, analysed and explained.
   - Sex without love is meaningless.

- Sex should never happen before a couple are a proper couple.
- 'How far you can go' in relation to sexual intimacy is no one's business but the people involved.
- It is better to remain a virgin until you are married.
- Love must be present for a marriage to mean anything.

2 'As far as love and intimacy are concerned, religious and non-religious people agree more often than they disagree.' What are your views about this statement?

3 In relation to helping young people understand the importance of love and what intimacy means, how helpful do you think religious and non-religious views are about these aspects of life?

Apply

Create your own 'agony aunt/uncle' column for a teenage magazine or web page. This should include letters you have made up which ask questions about love, relationships and intimacy. This column or web page will have 'regular agony aunts/uncles' who respond to the 'letters written in'. There should be three of these answering each problem: a religious person from a religion of your choice; a Humanist; and someone else from a perspective of your choice. You could do this as a class activity where some groups write the 'letters' and others write the responses.

10 Perspectives on the roles of men and women

Jan and Jen are two Edinburgh ladies sitting at Craiglockhart Tennis Centre watching the men's singles final, enjoying strawberries and cream ...

Jan: I can't believe they have a female umpire.

Jen: *Quite so dear, I simply can't imagine how she will be able to call out the scores and overrule line judges.*

Jan: Absolutely – you would think they would have thought about that.

Jen: *Oh not these days, dear – anything goes I think, not like the old days.*

Jan: No, sadly not ...

Two weeks later Jen and Jan are at Tollcross Swimming Pool watching the world Championships, enjoying chips and a burger ...

Jan: Oh good heavens, another female referee. There was one this morning.

Jen: *Oh my, I do hope she has kept up to date with the new rules about backstroke turns.*

Jan: I suspect not.

Jen: *Quite so – it is rather complex.*

Jan: Perhaps she'll have put some extra effort into reading up about it – just in case.

Jen: *Oh I do hope so ...*

One week later Jen and Jan are at an athletics competition in the Grangemouth stadium enjoying some nice ice cream ...

Jan: Is that a woman there judging at the pole vault?

Jen: *Certainly looks that way.*

Jan: Won't she have some trouble judging if the vaulter gets over the bar?

Jen: *Might be tricky for her. I hope the poor athlete isn't disadvantaged.*

Jan: Yes, I suppose you can sometimes be quite fortunate with your judge, and then again ...

... Now, what would have the conversation been like if Jen and Jan had managed to get tickets for the (men's) Champions League (football) final to discover a female referee in charge?

Fair play ...?

Here's a challenge. Over the next week watch as much sport on TV as you can (you can explain that this is homework). Every time you watch make a note of how many times you see female officials (referees, umpires, judges and so on). How did you get on with tennis, swimming, men's football, women's rugby? Of course, you might have discovered that finding televised women's sport was a bit trickier than men's televised sport (for some sports anyway, perhaps).

When we think of the roles of men and women in society, it is easy to begin with some of the more 'traditional' roles which are given to them (or thought by some to apply more to men than women or the other way round). Sport is an interesting example of where more 'traditional' (or some would simply say 'biased') views of the roles of men and women are still around. For example, there was considerable interest when Kylie McMullan became the first woman assistant referee in Scottish Premier League (men's) football – in May 2014. In August 2014, Shelley Kerr became British male football's first female manager at Lowland League club Stirling University. Former Celtic scout Helena Costa became the world's first 'top' female football manager of second division French side Clermont Foot 63, but walked out after 49 days in her job claiming that the club had a lack of respect for women – although days later the club hired a new coach to replace her ... Ms Corinne Diacre. So, are some sports the last 'hiding places' for traditional views of men and women in the UK?

Talk Point

Are some jobs more suited to men than women or women than men?

'Traditional' roles of men and women

These vary greatly but can be summarised in the following ways:

- **Jobs** There are some jobs which are considered as 'men's jobs' and some which are not.
- **Relationships** Men and women are often thought to have different roles in relationships, for example, provider, nurturer, etc.
- **Individual characteristics** For example, some emotions and behaviours are considered 'feminine' and others are 'masculine'.
- **Social status** Some think men and women are equal, others disagree.
- **Social activities** Some think that social activities should be different for men and women.
- **Appearance** Some think that men should look and dress in certain ways and women should look and dress differently (e.g. is your school uniform the same for boys and girls?).

And there are probably many other perspectives about the 'traditional roles of men and women'.

In some cultures of the world, there are very clear roles for men and women in society. Some of these are contained in laws, and others are just social customs which people stick to because they are used to doing so – or because there is social pressure to do so. It is hard to know sometimes whether these 'traditional' views of men and women are because of our upbringing, or are something we are born with – or both. In some cultures, men are the 'breadwinners' and women remain at home to raise children; in others these roles are not so clear-cut. In some cultures there is pressure on men and women to behave in ways which 'match their gender'; in others this is not the case. Gender roles have also changed with time and whether there are male and female 'roles' depends as much on when you live(d) as where you live(d).

The idea of 'gender stereotypes' is where we link certain qualities with certain genders. This can lead to us behaving differently towards genders, and perhaps for people of different genders to think differently about themselves, for example, the 'pink and blue' issue. If you saw a baby dressed in pink would you be more likely to think it was a boy or a girl? In 2011, psychologists LoBlue and DeLoache[38] asked boys and girls in a range of ages to choose objects of particular colours. They found that before two years old there was no colour preference for boys or girls, by two years old girls chose pink more than boys, and by two and a half, girls showed a clear preference for pink and boys for blue. Some research has also shown that adults behave differently towards babies depending on whether the babies are dressed in pink or blue (no matter what the gender of the babies is – and this is unknown by the adults). However, whether we 'learn' gender stereotypes or they are 'inborn' (or, more likely, a complex combination of both) is still debated in psychology.

What is the key issue?

Perhaps whether we learn our gender or whether it is inborn is not as important as the *effect gender roles have on our life*. The key issue with traditional roles of men and women is probably how far these 'traditional roles' stop men or women from living the life they choose to live. If social customs, laws and 'accepted practices' stop you from being who you want to be, then perhaps that is the issue. For example, let's say you are a man who wants to stay at home and raise your children. Your female partner is happy to go out to work. What if you live in a place where that is socially unacceptable (or at least frowned upon)? Why should any rule, law or custom in society prevent you from doing that without any social disapproval? Why should anyone feel any pressure to 'conform to the norm for their gender' (especially if those 'norms' are just things our society has made up)? There is evidence that people do feel under pressure to conform to social expectations (discrimination?) about their gender – and of course, some might argue that social expectations about gender roles are there for good reasons. However, there are many laws which try to put an end to gender discrimination:

- **The Equality Act (2010)** This Law brings together laws about equal pay, race relations, sex discrimination, disability discrimination and all forms of possible discrimination based on who you are. In short, it makes a whole range of activities where people are discriminated against based on their gender (and many other things) illegal. In Scotland, these laws are summed up in a clear statement:
  'No one shall be denied opportunities because of their race or ethnicity, their disability, their gender or sexual orientation, their age or religion. This principle underpins all the work of the Scottish Government.'[39]
- **The United Nations Universal Declaration on Human Rights** This declaration (the UK is a signatory, so should uphold all its articles) includes 30 Articles expressing the United Nations' position on a number of human rights. Its very first sentence states:
  'All human beings are born free and equal in dignity and rights.'

  It then goes on to say: *'Everyone is entitled to all the rights and freedoms set forth in this Declaration, without distinction of any kind, such as race, colour, sex, language, religion, political or other opinion.'*[40]

So it is clear that the law in Scotland and the UK rejects any kind of different treatment according to your gender – so why do different perspectives on the roles of men and women remain?

Social customs and expectations

If you have been brought up to believe that men and women are different and so should have different roles in life, then that might be difficult to shake yourself free from (though not impossible, of course). Going against social customs can see you shunned by society, or a group in society you want to remain part of.

Social pressure

Social pressures can be overt (open and obvious) or covert (unspoken and less obvious). Resisting social pressure is a complicated and sometimes difficult process and perhaps people end up accepting gender roles because it's easier than trying to fight against them.

Individual beliefs

Some people simply think that it's more 'natural' for men and women to have different roles in society. They may believe that this is a result of biology or some other cause. They may also be concerned when they think things are 'unnatural' or 'inappropriate' in relation to gender.

Teachings and other beliefs

Many people live their lives according to religions, other belief systems and philosophies. Some of these are clear in their view that men and women are different and should have different roles in life. If you want to remain part of these religions/belief systems/philosophies, then you might have to accept some or all of their teachings (although some teachings are clearer than others).

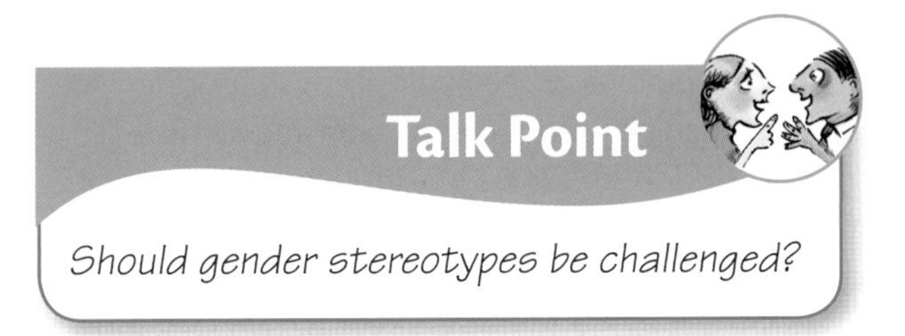

Some religious and philosophical perspectives

Christianity

Within Christianity, discrimination, unfair treatment and anything which harms a person should obviously be rejected. However, the problem is in defining what these terms mean. One Christian might think that a belief such as 'the man is head of the household' (see 1 Corinthians 11:3) is perfectly normal and acceptable, and another might think this is just thinly disguised gender discrimination – not to be accepted even if it is in the Bible. One key issue here, as in all the issues you study in this course, is how far Christianity should (and can) 'move with the times'. Should Christians have views about the roles of men and women which are timeless, or should they adapt their beliefs to changing circumstances? That's not an easy one to answer for any issue.

The Church of Scotland

There is no specific teaching within the Church of Scotland about the roles of men and women. Individual Christians can develop their own perspective on this aspect of life through their study, prayer and Christian life. However, the Church of Scotland was one of the first Christian Churches in the UK to ordain women as ministers (in 1969) and there have also been women Moderators of the General Assembly (effectively leaders of the Church of Scotland for a year) which suggests that the Church accepts equality in the kinds of roles men and women can have in the Church. During a campaign in Scotland about violence against women called 'Speak Out!', the Church of Scotland Moderator said that *'some unhealthy stereotypes still haunt the corridors of church and society'*[41], but he also stated his view that *'Jesus challenged the order of his day and as a result we saw him make a place for women in society which was not the common practice. There is still much work to be done in following his example.'* This suggests that the Church of Scotland invites its members to consider how women and men are treated in society and not to accept traditional roles simply because things have 'always been that way'.

The Roman Catholic Church

The Catechism of the Catholic Church states clearly: *'Man and woman have been created ... by God, in perfect equality as human persons.'* (369) The Catholic document *Guadium et Spes* also made it clear that any kind of discrimination is *'contrary to God's intent'*[42]. However, in Catholicism, as in the Church of Scotland, there are differing views on the roles of men and women in society and Catholics in different cultures may have very different views about this. Regardless of the culture, the Church teaches that men and women are equals. However, people can be equal but different. One issue within Catholicism is that it has very clearly defined roles for men and women in the Church. In particular, women cannot be ordained as priests in the Catholic Church: *'Only a baptized man validly receives sacred ordination.'* (1577) The Church position on this is that it upholds this because Jesus chose only men as his disciples and so it is 'bound' by his choice. However, the Church recognises a range of other roles for women in the Church and in society.

Buddhism

In countries where Buddhism is the main religion, there are still likely to be cultural differences in the roles of men and women. At the time of the Buddha, women in his culture sometimes had very traditional roles as mothers and home-makers, but had wider roles in society too. Perhaps most importantly, the Buddha accepted that women could achieve enlightenment just as men could. He also accepted women as Buddhist monks (though he wasn't too sure about this at first in case the women 'distracted' the men). The Buddha would have been unlikely to support any discrimination against women because this would go against all of his teachings about compassion and kamma. However, there remain some differences in views about women within Buddhism, with some groups accepting that women can become bodhisattvas and others not so sure about that. Also, in some forms of Buddhism, there remain differences in authority between Buddhist monks and nuns and even whether women can become ordained at all. However, generally speaking, the roles of men and women in Buddhism are, in theory, mostly similar, although often different in practice according to local and national customs. Even where there are differences in practices in Buddhist countries, Buddhist teachings would generally oppose any discrimination based on gender.

Talk Point

Do these perspectives support women or make life difficult for them?

Humanism

The British Humanist Association states: *'Humanists support personal freedom. This must involve allowing everyone opportunities and choices in the worlds of education, employment and home. Girls and women should not have restricted roles imposed upon them, but neither should they feel they have to do everything ... within Humanist organisations, men and women are treated equally.'*[43] So, for Humanists, gender roles are each individual's free choice. If you choose the 'traditional' role for a man or woman or a less traditional role, that is for you to decide. The key point here is that this should not be enforced in any way either on purpose or in any more subtle way by social pressure. Humanists would oppose all forms of discrimination.

Utilitarianism

If particular gender roles led to unhappiness for the majority, then obviously a Utilitarian would have to consider this carefully. Where gender roles are enforced in a culture (officially or just through cultural norms) then this could lead to unhappiness for a great many people – and so lead to an unhappy society overall. However, if these gender roles are freely chosen by those involved and they are happy with this choice, then this would probably contribute to overall happiness and so be acceptable to Utilitarians. So really, for Utilitarians, the issue is likely to come down to individual choice and the importance of any pressures on people to choose something which doesn't suit them. The consequences of having fixed gender roles in society (which people may or may not be free to opt out of) is therefore important – but of course predicting future consequences is usually difficult and so it would be hard to make decisions now based on what might happen once those decisions have been taken. Generally speaking, Utilitarians consider freedom as a key feature of all aspects of life – so being free to choose the gender role you adopt would be important. In 1869, in the opening lines to his book *On Liberty*, the Utilitarian J. S. Mill stated that *'the legal subordination of one sex to the other – is wrong in itself, and now one of the chief hindrances to human improvement; and that it ought to be replaced by a principle of perfect equality, admitting no power or privilege on one side, nor disability on the other'.* These were very strong words for 1869, and some would say equally applicable today.

Talk Point

What things do women experience today which people in the future might be shocked by?

Personal Reflection

* *'Men and women are equal but different.' What do you think?*
* *Should all jobs be equally open to men and women?*
* *In what ways do your actions support/challenge gender stereotyping?*

Active learning

Check your understanding

1 In what ways does sport display gender equality/inequality?
2 What is meant by 'the traditional roles of men and women' and how 'traditional' are these roles in the twenty-first century?
3 What is a gender stereotype and what are the possible causes and effects of such stereotypes?
4 What laws cover gender discrimination in the UK?
5 What international laws and agreements exist about gender discrimination?
6 Why might 'traditional' views about the roles of men and women still be around?
7 Does Christianity consider men and women fully equal?
8 How far do religions oppose gender discrimination?
9 What are the views of Humanists on gender discrimination?
10 In 1869, what views were stated by J. S. Mill on the subordination of women?

Investigate

1 Investigate a range of sports where you will try to answer the following questions. In how many and in which sports:
  - Do men compete against women?
  - Are there male and female officials?
  - Do female officials officiate in male sporting events?
  - Do male officials officiate in female sporting events?
  - Are male and female athletes paid the same prize money?
  - Is there equal TV coverage of male and female sporting events?
  - Are there male coaches?
  - Are there female coaches?
  - Do males coach in female sports contexts and females in male?
  - Are male and female sporting events exactly the same (e.g. sets played in tennis)?
  - Are there different rules for men and women playing the same sport?

2 Carry out an internet search for the following people and try to find out the balance between men and women in these roles in society.
  - Primary teachers
  - Secondary teachers
  - Heads of police forces
  - Chancellors of universities
  - MSPs, MPs, MEPs
  - Local councillors
  - World leaders
  - Engineers
  - Joiners
  - General Practitioners
  - Any other categories you can think of

3 Look up the UN Universal Declaration on Human Rights. Identify which of the articles link to gender equality issues. How might someone who wanted to challenge the 'traditional' roles of men and women use the articles to support their challenge?

4 Collect a range of newspapers or magazines. Now work through them and identify stories, articles, images and so on which portray men/women in 'traditional roles' (or express 'traditional' views about men and women). You could create a display of your findings.

Analyse and Evaluate

1 Compare Christian and Buddhist teachings about the roles of women. What are the similarities and differences?

2 Now do the same for a range of non-religious views. How consistent are they and how do they compare with religious views?

3 Some argue that having specific gender roles protects men and women; others say that can lead to men and women feeling they have to behave in ways they might not want to. Think about the religious and non-religious views you have studied. Which of them might provide freedom for men and women to behave as they want to, which might protect men and women and which might 'force' men and women to adopt roles they'd rather not?

Apply

You're now going to apply your learning to your own school. Think about the roles of males and females in your own school (pupils and staff). In what ways does your school support 'traditional' roles for males and females and in what ways does (or should) it challenge such roles? Your task should be summed up in a report or presentation which you might like to present to your school leaders/staff, or anyone else you think might benefit from it. Perhaps if you have another school nearby you could compare your findings with theirs, or do your own study alongside pupils from that school.

11 Gender inequality and exploitation

Gender inequality

- Approximately 70 per cent of people in national minimum wage jobs are women.
- Up to 30,000 women are sacked each year for simply being pregnant.
- Women with or without children, who work, spend 15 hours a week doing household chores while men spend only 5.
- 23 per cent of reporters on national daily newspapers in the UK are women.
- Men outnumber women by 4 to 1 as 'experts' on major TV and news channels.
- Women make up 17 per cent of the boards of directors of major UK businesses.[44]

What is gender inequality?

Gender inequality is where people are treated differently because they are men/boys or women/girls. Sometimes such inequalities are because a society has rules and laws which allow it to happen (or promote it), and sometimes it is because of customs and traditions in society. Sometimes, of course, it is just because of different 'expectations' of the genders which can lead to people conforming to what is expected of them, or feeling pressured to conform. In one way the issue is very simple – it is about both genders being treated equally in all respects. In another way it is more complex because, some would say, men and women are different and these differences can lead to different expectations and practices.

Talk Point

Why do you think men and women are still treated differently in the world today?

Where are gender inequalities likely to be found?

Home life

The 'traditional roles' of men and women may still lead to differences in what is expected of both genders at home. Many women still cook and clean and look after children, probably far more than men. This seems to be the case even when women are working too. In some families this will be agreed, in others perhaps it just happens and in some there might be pressure on men or women to follow this model. This might also lead to differences in the treatment of boys and girls and over what is expected of them.

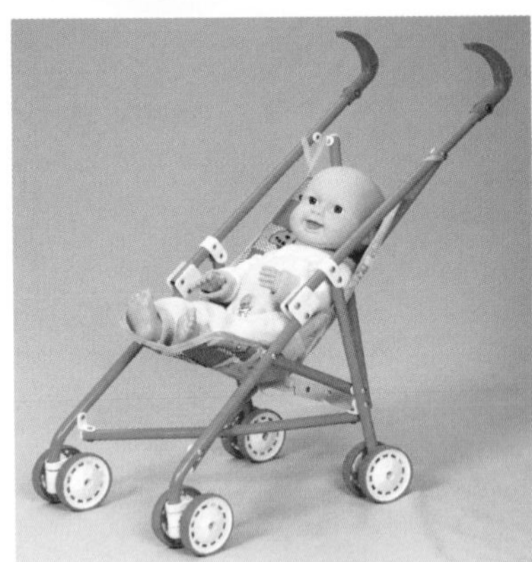

Working life

It is still the case that women are likely to be in lower-paid jobs than men. It is also still true that women are far less likely to be in senior positions in the workplace. There are still occupations which seem to have inbuilt gender imbalance – there are, for example, relatively few female construction workers, but also relatively few men working in early learning and childcare. Many argue that most workplaces are still run by and for men and that gender inequality is at its most obvious in the workplace.

The media

It is argued that there are still clear differences in the roles of men and women in the media and in how they are portrayed. Many gender stereotypes are still found in the media and some argue that inequalities are promoted by the media (or at least uncritically accepted by them).

Power in society

It is claimed that most of the powerful roles in society are still held by men. This includes politics at all levels, business and 'top jobs' in almost every field of life and work.

Education

It is claimed that in the UK there are still gender inequalities in education. For example, some subjects are still mostly studied by men and others by women. Around the world the position is much more serious, however, because there are still many places where education for girls is not seen as important at all. Here, many ways are found to withhold education from girls, some of which are very serious indeed.

There are many other ways in which gender inequalities are present in society, and some major differences around the world in how men and women are treated. Although it remains mostly women who are on the receiving end of unequal treatment, some men's groups argue that some of the ways men are treated and portrayed in society are becoming quite negative.

The possible *causes* of gender inequalities are probably very complex. Unequal treatment based on gender is most likely linked to ideas people have about the roles of men and women, about power generally in society, as well as many other factors at an individual and a social level.

The *effects* of the unequal treatment of genders can also be very varied and very complicated: there are direct effects of course, such as economic inequalities. There are also effects on how you see yourself and on your self-esteem and self-worth. There are consequences of not being free to be who you feel you are or do what you want in life if you're having to conform to specific gender roles. There are also very serious issues – for example, violence in the home and in society is still far more likely to be experienced by women than by men. Also, the treatment of some women and girls worldwide still includes forced marriages, sexual violence, female genital mutilation and many more examples of negative treatment based on gender.

The issue of opportunity

Apart from these very serious abuses, some argue that the key issue in relation to gender inequality is linked to opportunity. Put quite simply the argument is that everyone should have the same opportunities in life no matter who or what they are. This means that no matter what views you hold about the 'roles of men and women', both genders should be provided with the same opportunities to live their life as they choose to. This means that there should be no pressure (subtle or obvious) to conform to 'what is expected' of one gender or another and there should be no differences between how men/boys and women/girls are treated. Everyone should be due the same rights and respect regardless of which gender they are. This sounds very simple of course, so the question might be why this is still an issue in the twenty-first century.

Gender exploitation

Exploitation means treating people unfairly to benefit from their work. Of course, anyone anywhere can suffer from exploitation, and exploitation can be based on race, social status, age and a whole range of other factors. Exploitation means that those with 'power' make use of those who are 'powerless'. This can take place in the home, the workplace, or anywhere else in society.

Again, the amount of *control* someone is able to exert over how they are treated and its effects on them, and how far others benefit from this, is an important issue. For example, in most jobs people 'sell' their labour. This means that 'the boss' can make a profit from your work and does not need to pass any of that profit on to you, other than your wage. When this is just normal working practice and when it is exploitation is a matter for discussion. If 'the boss' is making lots of money from your work, are you being exploited? So exploitation is more complicated than it seems at first, but a reasonable definition is where you are treated *unfairly* for someone else's benefit. If you are being treated in an unfair way based on your gender, then this is gender exploitation.

People are likely to experience gender exploitation in different ways:

- **Labour exploitation** Women (and girls) very often receive much lower pay for work than men doing the same job.
- **Sexual exploitation** This is a very serious and complex issue. It can involve prostitution, pornography, human trafficking and a range of other ways in which someone makes money out of sex-related activities. While commercial sexual exploitation can and does affect males and females, it is much more likely to apply to women and girls. It is argued that such exploitation is harmful in itself, because it turns women and girls into 'objects of entertainment' and makes certain behaviours towards women and girls seem acceptable. It is also claimed that there is a strong link between sexual exploitation and violence against women as well as a range of other criminal acts. As well as more formal and organised methods of sexual exploitation, many argue that any treatment of women which aims to

benefit unfairly from them is exploitation. For example, using women to sell products in ways which involved them being sexualised, or the role of women in videos which accompany popular music.

- **Domestic exploitation** In many places, women and girls remain likely to be the ones who work in the home (even if they have jobs outside the home). In some cultures this can be very serious – with girls and women being denied any education because they are expected to stay at home and look after the family (and this can often be accompanied by different levels of violence against women/girls). It can also involve slavery – which affects more women/girls than men/boys.

It is important in all of these situations to be aware that gender exploitation can apply to women/girls and to men/boys. However, it remains true that females are far more likely to suffer from a variety of forms of gender exploitation than men. For some, one of the major factors in gender exploitation is that it can build to very serious consequences from what might look like very simple beginnings. For example, they might argue, if a popular female pop singer turns herself into an 'object', this might make people think that treating women as objects is acceptable – which could then lead to people overlooking gender exploitation or even thinking that it is in some way acceptable.

The *causes* of gender exploitation are also very complex. For many they are an issue of power – with those who have the power simply making use of those who do not. As much of the power in the world is held by men, then this perhaps explains at least in part why gender exploitation is more likely to be linked to women – though this is only part of the exploitation, of course.

The *effects* of gender exploitation can be very individual or very wide-ranging. It can lead to individuals suffering seriously physically and/or mentally and doing a range of things to help them cope. It might also lead to an uncaring and perhaps more violent society – where exploitation is ignored or simply accepted as 'something that happens, but is nothing to do with me'.

Gender inequality and gender exploitation are both, like all of the moral issues you will study, closely linked to a range of factors including social customs and practices and individual beliefs. However, it is important to point out that gender inequalities and exploitation can be affected by our own choices and behaviours – they are not problems 'out there' but have the potential to affect everyone everywhere. Perhaps even in your own school there are examples of gender inequalities and gender exploitation – perhaps something you do contributes to that …

Some religious and philosophical perspectives

Christianity

There is likely to be widespread agreement within Christianity that all are equal regardless of gender. Some Christians might argue that men and women have different roles in society, but that they remain equal as persons. It is also likely that Christians in all contexts will reject any kind of exploitation of anyone anywhere – and so gender exploitation will be rejected. However, as in all moral issues, differences in practices may be present around the world even in countries which are Christian and also within Christian communities themselves.

The Church of Scotland

In a report on human trafficking[45], the Church says: '*Human beings have been created by God and are loved equally by God. Therefore no man, woman or child can ever be treated as a commodity or a possession.*' It adds that Christians should work to secure justice for everyone and to protect the most vulnerable in society through compassionate action. In 2015, the Church of Scotland called on the Scottish Government to make the buying of sex illegal, because it considered that this would reduce human trafficking. However, it came in for some criticism over this because some said that making buying sex illegal would actually lead to sex workers being in even more danger from exploitation – because, it was argued, the whole industry would become even more secretive and so less able to be regulated by laws. How it is best tackled might be for debate, but the Church of Scotland is clear about its opposition to all forms of exploitation.

The Roman Catholic Church

In 1988, Pope John Paul II wrote an Apostolic Letter called *Mulieris Dignitatem*. In this he said: '*In all of Jesus' teaching, as well as in his behaviour, one can find nothing which reflects the discrimination against women prevalent in his day. On the contrary, his words and works always express the honour and respect due to women.*' The Roman Catholic Church has always been active in challenging exploitation. Liberation Theology developed as a way of applying Christian belief to attacking all forms of exploitation. In 2015, Pope Francis said: '*Whenever sin corrupts the human heart and distances us from our Creator and our neighbours, the latter are no longer regarded as beings of equal dignity, as brothers or sisters sharing a common humanity, but rather as objects.*'[46] The Roman Catholic charity CAFOD adds: '*CAFOD's Vision, Mission and Values state that we believe in the intrinsic dignity of every person, celebrate difference and aim to create relationships of mutual respect wherein the rights and dignity of every person are respected.*' SCIAF, the Church's official aid agency in Scotland, states that it has always been committed to protecting the poorest and most vulnerable in society from all forms of discrimination and exploitation.[47]

Buddhism

The five precepts of Buddhism are all based on the idea that you should not exploit anyone else – or yourself. In particular the second precept states that you should '*undertake not to take what is not given*'. This means that you should avoid anything which is not freely given – so clearly anything which is the product of any form of exploitation could be seen as something which is 'not given'. The eightfold path also states that Buddhists should engage in '*right livelihood*'. This could mean two things in relation to exploitation: firstly, making money out of someone else's misfortune or through exploiting them could not be thought of as right livelihood. Secondly, someone being forced to do degrading and exploitative work would not be able to have a right livelihood.

The whole point of living a Buddhist life is to avoid causing harm to anything. In fact, Buddhism would go further in saying it's not about avoiding harmful actions, it's about promoting helpful ones. Compassion is central to Buddhism so treating someone unfairly for any reason at all would not be an act of compassion. The Buddha said that how we treat others has consequences for them and for us: '*When watching after yourself, you watch after others. When watching after others, you watch after yourself.*' So, for Buddhists not treating people as equals and exploiting others has negative kammic consequences, while doing the opposite has the opposite effect.

Humanism

When the Equalities Act (2010) was being put together, the British Humanist Association (BHA) campaigned to ensure that religious organisations could not 'ignore' some aspects of equalities law based on religious belief. For Humanists, equality should extend to everyone, everywhere, regardless of their gender, or any other aspect of their life. The values of the BHA state that: '*In all our work, we strive to embody our values by: recognising the dignity of individuals and treating them with respect; respecting and promoting freedom, democracy, human rights, and the rule of law.'*[48] Clearly, this would mean that any kind of exploitation would not be accepted by a Humanist and actively campaigned against because Humanists value the dignity of all people and their right to choose their own lifestyle and not have it enforced upon them by anyone.

Utilitarianism

Although Utilitarianism supports the benefit of the majority, this does not mean that it ignores the plight of the minority and it has always championed the rights of those exploited in society. In 1869, J. S. Mill wrote a document called 'On the Subjection of Women'. In this he expressed very radical views for his time. He challenged the low status of women at the time, and argued that no reason for it could be supported. He specifically challenged the use of women as prostitutes – who in Mill's day were 'blamed' for being prostitutes while the men who used them were not blamed. In fact, Mill thought that prostitution was a *'great social evil'* because of the way it made women into objects where men had power over them. Even in family relationships, Mill suggested that women's place in society relative to men was similar to slavery and that the status of women was something left over from the past when strength and power were more important than reason. Mill argued that the greatest happiness in society would only come when there was meaningful balance between the rights of men and women.

Talk Point

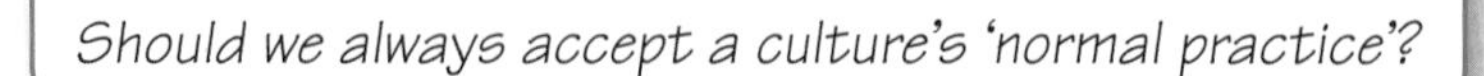

Should we always accept a culture's 'normal practice'?

Personal Reflection

* *'Exploitation means different things to different people.' What do you think?*
* *Some people argue that because power is always distributed unequally in any society, there will always be exploitation. Do you agree?*
* *In what ways do you/could you act to oppose exploitation?*

Active learning

Check your understanding

1. Describe some of the evidence which shows that gender inequalities are still present in the UK today.
2. How might gender inequalities be present in home life?
3. In what ways can gender inequality be present in education systems?
4. Describe ways in which people might experience exploitation based on their gender.
5. Does gender exploitation affect one gender more than another? What evidence is there for your answer?
6. What evidence does the Catholic Church present to support its view that Jesus opposed gender discrimination?
7. In what ways are Buddhist views similar to Christian views on gender exploitation?
8. In what ways are the views of Humanists about gender exploitation similar to those of religions?
9. What were J. S. Mill's views on prostitution and why was this unusual in his day?
10. What, in your opinion, are the most effective ways to deal with gender exploitation?

Investigate

1 Do a search online to find out about the various campaigns against exploitation at work. What claims are made about exploitation and who does it affect? What is the balance between exploitation of men and women? What do the campaigns urge people to do in response?
2 Look through a series of typical daily newspapers and magazines and create your own collage of images which you think involve the sexual exploitation of men/women. How common is this and how available are these images? How often is this exploitation carried out by ordinary high street shops/shopping chains and other 'everyday' organisations?
3 Some people remain surprised that slavery still takes place in the twenty-first century. Carry out your own research into slavery in the twenty-first century and produce a FAQs leaflet informing people about the extent of slavery in the twenty-first century.
4 The music industry has been the subject of criticism in relation to the sexual exploitation of women (and less often, but occasionally, men). In groups, create a video montage of clips from music popular with your age group which you think are exploitative. You could create some questions about each montage inviting those watching to analyse what they see.

Analyse and Evaluate

1 According to some perspectives, what counts as exploitation can be different in different cultures and societies. Do you agree? Is there anything which you would consider to be exploitation no matter where or when it takes place? You could run this as a class debate.
2 The Prohibition of Female Genital Mutilation (Scotland) Act 2005 makes it a criminal offence (up to 14 years in prison) to 'aid, abet, counsel, procure or incite' female genital mutilation anywhere in the world. Does any country have the right to say what should take place in another culture – or, perhaps, does it have the responsibility to do so?
3 'Religious people often claim that all are equal regardless of gender, but in practice they don't act that way.' What do you think? Try to use sources from religious views in putting together your answer as an extended piece of writing.
4 How far do you think non-religious perspectives and philosophies can be used to oppose gender exploitation?

Apply

Choose one of the forms of gender exploitation you have studied in this chapter. Create your own short TV commercial which explains what the issues are, what you think should be done about them and how people might help out.

RELIGION,
ENVIRONMENT
AND GLOBAL
ISSUES

12 Perspectives on humans' stewardship of the environment

We have a tiny planet, it sparkles blue and green
For those of us who live on it, it's all we've ever seen (in person anyway)
Venus, it is boiling hot, and full of CO_2
And if you tried to breathe on it, you'd quickly turn all blue
Now Pluto we have newly viewed – a planet, yes or no?
But it's 4 million miles away, so there you cannot go
No, Earth is all you have.

And Mars is way too cold for us – minus 80 degrees
On landing there without a suit you'd quickly, horribly, freeze
Saturn has such pretty rings – a halo full of class
But on its surface could you stand – on a planet, made of gas?
One day perhaps we just might reach our fellows in the sky
But getting there, we may well ask – smart, but really, why?
No, Earth is all you have.

What of other systems, stars, one day we'll make the trip?
Not unless we work out how to build a real space ship
Perhaps there's other life on these, with whom we could be mates
Or maybe they won't welcome us and tell us 'on your skates!'
Maybe they'll be fully booked – a planet overstuffed
And humans searching for new homes won't make them very chuffed
No, Earth is all you have.

So heating up our planet, chopping down our woods
Using up resources to make pointless, silly goods
Eating up our fossil fuels, polluting all our seas
Slicing through our ozone layer and burning down our trees
Using all our energy to power our PCs
Or using dodgy chemicals, then running out of bees
No, Earth is all you have.

→

But wait! Our planet can defend itself from anything we do
It will adjust and sort itself so safely it comes through
No need for fear or worry, why make a pointless fuss?
Our planet might just sort it all by getting rid of us
Yes, humans – we're so very wise, so clever and so smart
But maybe our wise planet will simply press 'restart'
And all the humans will be gone, no shops, no cars, no school
But many insects may survive and our planet they will rule
But there must be something we can do to stop this horrid end
Reach for the stars and colonise, our hopes to space we'll send
No, Earth is all you have.

Stewardship

Many of those who are concerned about the environment use the concept of 'stewardship' to support their views about the *power* and *responsibility* humans have over the natural world. They argue that the human species is the only one on the planet which has the power to understand nature and affect it based on this understanding in positive and negative ways. We can research, analyse, investigate, test, draw conclusions and communicate with each other about how we should respond to what we find. This is a unique set of abilities which only humans have on this scale. We are in a position to affect things on a global scale, to be aware of the consequences of our actions and to change our ways if we conclude that our actions are unhelpful. Again, this is all unique to humans on a global scale.

As well as this incredible power, we also understand what it means to be responsible for our actions. Humans can link causes and effects, predict future possibilities and make changes now which are likely to lead to improvements. Humans can be *forward thinking* in ways which other species do not seem to be (at least to anything like the extent we are), and so we can make reasonable judgements now about what the consequences of our current actions might be in the future.

All of this leads many to the conclusion that humans are uniquely placed to act as stewards of the natural world. A steward is someone who looks after things – like a caretaker – so being stewards of the planet would mean that it's our job as a species to look after the planet.

Talk Point

How can – and do – humans care for (and harm) the planet?

The concept of stewardship has both religious and non-religious origins.

Religious origins of stewardship

In Judaism, Christianity and Islam the creation story outlines the relationship between humans and the natural world. Initially, everything was perfect and all human needs were met by nature in a paradise known as Eden. Humans were given 'dominion' over the natural world by the creator – and lived in perfect harmony with all living things. There is disagreement within these three faiths about what dominion means: some think it means mastery – that humans rule over nature, nature is there to serve human needs and humans can treat nature in any way they like. Others think dominion is all about being responsible for nature on behalf of the creator – humans have a unique power and responsibility which means that they must care for nature. These two very different understandings of dominion have led to very different ways of seeing the relationship between humanity and the natural world and so two very different ways in which humans have treated the natural world. Those who think of dominion as lordship, mastery and nature being there for human use can easily exploit nature with no thought to any harm it may cause – or to any consequences which may follow. Those who think of it as caring stewardship are more likely to preserve, look after and work with nature.

So there could have been a difficulty with understanding dominion even if the original paradise state had remained – but it didn't: the relationship between humans and the creator broke down and things changed drastically. This event, known as 'The Fall', was where humans rejected the creator and decided to go their own way – against the creator's wishes. According to these three faiths, one consequence of this was that humans would now have to struggle for survival in the natural world – they would have to work hard to get what they needed to survive from nature. After The Fall the formerly harmonious relationship between humanity and nature changed to one where they were pitted against each other. However, many from these three faiths still take the view that humans have dominion over nature, but there are still different understandings of what this 'dominion' means. All three of these faiths, however, stress the importance of demonstrating compassion and care for all life – which is likely to lead to a caring approach to the natural world. Also, as these faiths believe that nature belongs to the creator – it is a human duty to care for anything which belongs to that creator.

In faiths such as Buddhism and Hinduism, the relationship between humans and nature is a little different. In these faiths, humans have no role as lords over nature. Humans, like all forms of life, are part of nature and subject to the laws of cause and effect known as kamma (karma). However, this can lead to followers of those faiths acting in ways to protect nature, because if they don't then the negative effects of this might cause them difficulties (and do the same for other living things): so human relationships with the natural world are governed by the laws of kamma. This is likely to lead to humans caring for nature. In Hinduism too, there is a strong tradition of environmental concern. In many stories of the Hindu gods, they take on the form of living things other than humans – and so in some ways, it is true to say that all living things have something of the divine in them and so are worthy of protection.

Non-religious origins of stewardship

Across many non-religious groups and philosophies there are of course many different views about the relationship between humans and nature. There is no belief here that any god granted power to humans over nature – or that any supernatural laws are involved in our relationship with nature and how we should treat it. However, non-religious viewpoints can still support the idea that humans have a role as stewards of the environment. Humans have evolved to be uniquely powerful parts of the natural world. This power brings responsibility as we can uniquely harm or help nature so our (current) place at the top of the evolutionary tree gives us a unique responsibility to behave towards nature in ways which aren't likely to harm our role as the most highly evolved species (or, for many, harm anything else). Of course, many non-religious people view nature as something worthy of protection in itself – an emotional response with no need for any logic behind it. Others take a more instrumental view – arguing that if we harm nature now, then we may have to pay for it now – or our descendants might. So we are stewards in the sense that we protect nature to protect ourselves and future generations. It is therefore perfectly possible to be non-religious and still think of humans as being able to exercise stewardship over the natural world.

Some perspectives on stewardship

They key question really is this: given that humans are the only species which have the power to act as stewards of the natural world on a global scale, why should we do so? There are a range of answers to this – from 'why bother?' to 'we must' – and it is also possible that each of these answers could come equally from religious and non-religious standpoints.

Why bother?

For some this can simply be an approach based on laziness. Perhaps they recognise that humans have power over and so responsibility for the natural world, but they just don't care. Acting in environmentally friendly ways can be time-consuming, complicated and sometimes costly – so some might simply think that they can't be bothered doing so. For some, this might be because they don't really see the point. They might feel that it's someone else's job (like the government), or that little things they do are not going to make any real difference. Some governments might even act this way – they might make excuses for their own actions, or leave it up to other countries to do the job for them while they 'look after their own'. For others – governments included perhaps – the 'why bother?' approach is about costs and benefits. Some argue that the benefits of acting like responsible stewards of nature won't come for a long time – so why should we put effort in now when we're not going to get the results of it? It is also possible that governments weigh up the benefits now with the costs now and find it hard to reach a conclusion (although as governments they have to). For example, let's say that your country is a relatively poor one and the country next to you is much wealthier. Also, the country next to you is acting aggressively towards you. As a government, do you spend your money on looking after nature or on building up your military defences?

Of course, there are also some who might argue that the reason for not bothering to act as good stewards of nature is because there actually isn't any problem. Many who oppose environmentalists' claims say that there is no environmental crisis – just natural cycles of life on Earth. So we do not need to 'look out for nature' in any way, or change our lifestyle, because there is no problem to be fixed.

Finally in the 'why bother?' camp there is an argument which says that it might look as if humans have great power over the environment, but we really don't. Nature can sort itself out without our help. There may well be environmental issues to be fixed, but humans either don't know how to do them, or even if they did, there's nothing they could do on a big enough scale to make any difference – besides, nature will put itself right without any help from us puny humans. For some, this is a scientific conclusion about the ways in which nature balances itself out over time with or without human 'help' – for others this could be a religious conclusion which might lead them to think that their God/god/gods/kamma might put it all right without any need for human action.

'We need to do something, but it's difficult to know what'

Many people may argue that there are environmental issues to be addressed and that we should act as good stewards of the natural world – but it's not clear what we should do. Environmental science can be very complex and there are many different views about whether there is an 'environmental crisis' or not, what might be causing it and how best we might put it right if it does exist. For ordinary people, being able to make sense of all the claims and counter-claims about environmental issues is far too complex – and this can lead to them doing little or nothing because they genuinely don't know what to do. So you might want to demonstrate good stewardship of the Earth – but what does this mean in practice? This can even apply to governments, because of how complicated it is to know what the problem is (and if it exists), what might have caused it and how we might put it right.

One example is in relation to energy creation. There are many ways to create energy, three of which are: fossil fuels, renewable energy sources and nuclear energy. Even with these three, there are differences of opinion – *even between those who are environmental activists and think it is vital that we address environmental issues*. This kind of thing makes it very difficult for individuals to know how best they can help the environment, because even the experts disagree. So, although many people do think they should live a more environmentally friendly life, many do not know how to do so for the best. It's fine to be a steward of nature but how do you do so for the best?

'We must do something'

Many reach the conclusion that there is some kind of 'environmental crisis' and that we should each take action to put this right. Again here, knowing what the problem is and how to put it right is the big issue. Also, responding to environmental issues takes action by individual governments, but also across the world's governments – and this is complex. Other than that, knowing how you can individually make the biggest difference is sometimes difficult too. For example, should you use glass bottles or plastic bottles? Each has an environmental cost – but using which is 'better' for the environment? This viewpoint stresses the fact that humans are stewards of the Earth and that this responsibility is an important one and perhaps one which we can put into action. Often this stewardship is linked to looking after nature now on behalf of future generations (even though we might never see any benefits in our lifetime). This might also involve making sacrifices now so that others benefit in future. For example, while some environmentalists argue that nuclear power is a cleaner, more efficient and more or less limitless source of energy compared to burning fossil fuels, others argue that it is very dangerous and leaves behind toxic waste which our descendants will have to deal with – so we benefit now and they pay the price for thousands of years to come (although some also argue that future generations will work out how to safely dispose of the waste we have left behind).

Modern environmentalist viewpoints

The relationship between humans and the natural world has varied over time. It is often claimed that humans in the past were much more 'in tune' with the natural world than we are today – living with the seasons and according to the cycles of nature rather than the clock, taking only what they needed and so on. However, there are different opinions about just how true this is and some claim that humans in the past also exploited the natural world just as happens today – though perhaps on a smaller scale. Those who are active in protecting the environment today come from a variety of backgrounds and philosophical perspectives. The origins of environmentalist movements today vary. Some trace their origins back to the 'romantic' period – where, it is argued, humans began to see the natural world as something to be cherished and protected rather than exploited for short-term gain. Some suggest that key figures, such as John Muir, changed our thinking about nature from something we had to fight against and 'tame' in order to survive to something we should work with, in harmony, for our mutual benefit. Some point to the first pictures of Earth from space – suggesting that this was an important moment when we first realised how delicate and fragile our planet is – and so how important it is to look after it. There is no one point of origin of the modern environmental movement, or even one definition of what a 'modern environmentalist' is (although it's reasonable to assume that it means individuals and groups who value and want to care for nature).

Talk Point

Why do you think some people care about the natural world (and some people don't)?

Whatever the origins and meanings of environmentalism, there are different reasons why people value nature:

- **Nature has intrinsic value** This is based on the idea that nature is valuable for itself – no other reason is needed. The argument is that there is something about nature which is worthy of protection and concern. This needs no further argument, because we either accept this or not. Someone taking this view protects the natural world because it simply deserves to be protected.
- **Nature has extrinsic value** This suggests that nature is of value because it is useful to us. It's sometimes referred to as *instrumental value* – and means that nature should be protected because of its use to us. Sometimes this is positive – we should protect nature because it sustains us, we need the natural world in order to survive so we need to look after it. This can also have a negative dimension – if we don't look after nature, perhaps the negative consequences for us will be very serious.

Of course, the reasons why environmentalists are concerned about our treatment of the natural world vary a great deal and might involve elements of intrinsic and extrinsic value. We can add to this that environmentalism may be based on a particular philosophy, life-stance, religious belief system, political views, scientific perspectives, personal experience and so on. Whatever the motivation, environmentalists are likely to agree on the key issue: humans are a uniquely powerful species – the most powerful species on our planet today. This power gives them the ability to protect or harm nature in ways which no other species can. Along with this power comes the responsibility of being the only species which can have a significant effect on nature – good or bad – and the only species which can protect and preserve it. It is also important to remember that for many modern environmentalists, humans are only a part of the complicated ecosystem of our planet – nature isn't something 'out there'; we are part of it and bound up in whatever happens to it.

So environmentalists agree that humans have the responsibility of looking after nature both now and for future generations – we can be stewards of the Earth – but how we do this in practice varies even within environmental movements:

- **Individual lifestyles** Most environmentalists would agree that each individual needs to consider their impact on nature. It is everyone's responsibility to live a life which has as little negative impact on nature as possible. Whether this is reducing your carbon footprint or a range of specific environmental actions in your everyday life, it is something we must all do. Environmentalists put this into practice by advising the public through education, for example.

- **Political policy and practice** Some environmentalists argue that governments must take the lead in stewardship of the environment. Policies and ways of governing must recognise the need to protect nature. Many environmentalists campaign to persuade governments to look after nature and to put into place policies and practices which care for the natural world. They might do this through campaigning, advising governments and so on.
- **Scientific research and interventions** Many environmentalists agree that the relationship between humans and nature is complex – and that nature itself is a complex system. We need to understand what the problems are, what the possible threats are and what we might best do to put them right. This involves scientific research and interventions (plans of action) which we then put into action to protect nature. Many environmentalists are involved in scientific research and those who are not might still keep a watchful eye on the findings of scientific research and how it affects our treatment of nature to support their arguments about how we treat the natural world and its possible consequences.
- **Environmental activism** Some environmentalist groups engage in specific programmes of action to support the environment. Some of these are *indirect* – educating the public, informing governments, carrying out research, advising and educating. Others are very *direct* – protesting through petitions, public events and even direct interventions to try to stop things which environmentalists think damage the environment (e.g. getting in the way of whaling ships).

- **Cost-benefit analysis** For anyone concerned about the environment, whether individual, group or government, one key issue is balancing up the costs of looking after nature with the benefits. This is extremely complicated. There are wide disagreements about what the costs are, what the benefits might be (and when they might come) and whose responsibility the costs are in the first place. These costs and benefits involve science, beliefs, values, cultures, geography, psychology and many more – and working out the costs and benefits is very difficult: this difficulty can lead to little or nothing being done (or of course the wrong things being done – even if they are for the right reasons!). One other important issue here is about who has the power to do anything about the environment. Some environmentalists claim that most of the problems are caused by the rich industrialised nations while most of the harmful effects are felt by the world's poorest.

There are therefore many different reasons why people understand, value and try to protect nature – and very different ways in which they do this. However, the modern environmental movement is largely agreed that humans have a central role in understanding and addressing environmental issues facing the Earth and that our actions can help or harm the natural world – of which we are a part.

Some religious and philosophical perspectives

Christianity

Within Christianity, the idea of stewardship is central to our relationship with nature. Our planet and all that is on it belongs to God and is valued by God. We should act in ways which preserve and protect it as stewards on his behalf. However, some Christians focus more on the 'dominion' given to humans over the natural world. This can lead them to protecting nature or exploiting it for short-term gain. It is probably fair to say that Christianity has, over time, come to take a much more pro-environment stance which requires Christians to preserve and protect nature and live in harmony with it rather than exploit it – but it has not always been this way within Christianity.

The Church of Scotland

The Church of Scotland's website has a section dedicated to care for the Earth. This gives its views and guidance for Christians on anything from climate change, measuring a church's carbon footprint, to food and sustainable agriculture. In 2009, the Church's General Assembly stated: '*The Church of Scotland is concerned that climate change poses a serious and immediate threat to people everywhere, particularly to the poor of the earth; and that climate change represents a failure in our stewardship of God's creation.*'[49] The Church is also involved in the eco-congregation movement, a group of Christian denominations which works to respond to environmental issues. A document produced by this group, *Theology and the Environment*, considers in some detail the ideas of stewardship and dominion. It states: '*Caring for creation therefore is a way to deepen our Christian spirituality as we reconnect with the living God of creation ... as Christians we are called to avoid and, where possible, to repair the damage humanity inflicts on the natural order.*'[50]

The Roman Catholic Church

In the Catechism of the Catholic Church (2415) it states clearly: '*Man's dominion over inanimate and other living beings granted by the Creator is not absolute; it is limited by concern for the quality of life of his neighbour, including generations to come; it requires a religious respect for the integrity of creation.*' So humans have authority over nature, but this authority should be exercised through care and concern for the natural world now and in the future. In the encyclical letter of May 2015, *Laudato Si'*, Pope Francis outlines in great detail environmental issues and how Catholics should respond. In this he makes an appeal: '*The urgent challenge to protect our common home includes a concern to bring the whole human family together to seek a sustainable and integral development ... I urgently appeal, then, for a new dialogue about how we are shaping the future of our planet ... the environmental challenge we are undergoing, and its human roots, concerns and affects us all.*'[51]

Buddhism

The Dalai Lama stated: '*As a boy studying Buddhism, I was taught the importance of a caring attitude towards the environment. Our practice of non-violence applies not just to human beings but to all sentient beings ... our planet is our house and we must keep it in order and take care of it if we are genuinely concerned about happiness for ourselves, our children, our friends and other sentient beings who share this great house with us ... Until now, you see, Mother Earth has somehow tolerated sloppy house habits. But now human use, population and technology have reached that certain stage "where Mother Earth no longer accepts our presence with silence" ... she is warning us that there are limits to our actions.*'[52] The Dalai Lama points out that the destruction of nature is a result of human ignorance, greed and lack of respect for the Earth. If we do not address it, we will have to suffer the inevitable consequences. Buddhists also consider that animals are fellow-travellers in samsara, which has a major impact on Buddhist treatment of animals.

Humanism

Humanists say that people care for the environment for many reasons. There is a clear reason for caring for the environment: '*We should care about the future of our planet because we care about other human beings, even those not born yet ... human beings must take sole responsibility for sorting out environmental problems. We are the only ones capable of finding the solutions that can lead to a sustainable existence.*'[53] Humanists do not agree that we are 'stewards' of the Earth – we are simply an evolving part of it. They also take the view that science and technology

– as well as changes in behaviour – are necessary to address environmental concerns. Caring for nature is about looking after human welfare and happiness – now and in the future – which of course means that we need to look after the welfare and happiness of all living things – as well as be responsible in our interactions with the natural world. Humanist Society Scotland supports the policy of the International Humanist and Ethical Union on the environment, which stresses that all should have rights, deplores the unequal distribution of wealth and resources and regards it as a human responsibility to pass on to our descendants an Earth which offers the same (or better) benefits as we currently enjoy.

Utilitarianism

Utilitarians would be interested in the cost–benefit analysis of stewardship and protecting the environment. If the costs of any actions outweigh the benefits for the majority, then Utilitarians would be pretty wary of those actions. The trouble with the environment is that costs now may only lead to benefits in the future – so although the majority now *might* not benefit (in fact they *might* have to make sacrifices), their descendants for many years to come *might* get the benefits (and they would therefore make up a majority). Again, for Utilitarians, the difficulty is in working out the consequences of any actions – and in relation to environmental action this is very difficult. In this case too we can't be sure of the benefits (even if there will be any), so this puts Utilitarians in a tricky position. Obviously if treating the environment carelessly leads to environmental damage now, and so harm now, then it would be rejected – but that's often difficult to identify clearly.

Personal Reflection

* *In what ways is your lifestyle 'environmentally friendly' or the opposite?*
* *Do you value nature? Why? Why not?*
* *What one change could you make to your lifestyle to make it more environmentally friendly?*

Active learning

Check your understanding

1. What do you understand by the term 'stewardship'?
2. In what ways might the idea of 'stewardship' be thought of as having religious origins?
3. In what similar and different ways might a non-religious person understand stewardship?
4. How might 'modern environmentalism' have begun?
5. Explain the difference between the intrinsic and extrinsic value of nature.
6. In what practical ways might people act as good stewards of nature?
7. How far do the Roman Catholic Church and the Church of Scotland have similar views about how we should treat nature?
8. In what ways are Humanism and Utilitarianism similar in their views about human responsibility for nature?
9. What are the similarities and differences between religious and non-religious views about how we should behave towards nature?
10. How far do you think responding to environmental issues is the responsibility of everyone or only the responsibility of governments?

Investigate

1. The creation story of Islam, Christianity and Judaism outlines the relationship between humans and God and also between humans and the natural world. Use this story to draw conclusions about how Christians, Muslims and Jewish people should treat nature. For each story you could produce a short report about what it teaches followers of these three religions about the environment.
2. Choose one or more environmental group. Produce a short illustrated presentation on their environmental philosophy and how this translates into action. You can use text, images, film clips, etc.
3. Along with your school history department, produce a timeline showing how humans have interacted differently with nature. For example, hunter-gatherers – agriculture – industry, etc. Along this timeline you could also identify ways in which humans might have helped or harmed the environment at that point in time.
4. Modern environmentalism has a number of key figures/groups and pieces of writing which may be thought of as starting it all off. Choose one of these from the following list (or research your own more local examples). Now produce an illustrated poster showing how this person/group or piece of writing influenced modern environmental thinking.
   - John Muir
   - Georges Monbiot
   - The Sierra Club
   - Rachel Carson
   - Chico Mendes

Analyse and Evaluate

1. How far do the religious and philosophical perspectives you have studied in this section agree that caring for the environment is a human responsibility?
2. For each of the following statements come up with arguments opposing the statements – explaining the reasons behind your statements:
   - Christians should wait for God to put environmental problems right.
   - The Earth was provided for human use alone.
   - Caring too much for nature risks the danger of a Christian worshipping the created not the creator.
   - Everyone should demonstrate environmental responsibility – even the very poor.
   - Individual action can do little to solve environmental issues.
   - The trouble with responding to environmental issues is that no one really knows what to do.
   - The only way to stand up for nature is direct action to stop harm.
3. The Church of Scotland urges churches to 'measure their carbon footprint'. Do you think religious and non-religious people are consistent in what they say about the environment and what they do about it? Discuss in groups and note down any conclusions you reach.
4. To what extent should religious people set an example about how we should treat nature?

Apply

Choose one of the religious or philosophical perspectives you have looked at in this chapter. Prepare a website page for this group explaining its views about the environment and human responsibility for it and suggesting what action this group should be taking to respond to environmental crises.

13 Environmental crises

A large craft approaches a small planet. The craft's occupants have been monitoring this planet for some time in the hope of making 'first contact' and ushering in a new era of intergalactic co-operation. As the craft slows into orbit, its occupants scan the planet for life forms. Life is detected, but the signals are weak. The spacecraft's scanner has difficulty cutting through the thick atmosphere of carbon dioxide and the fierce and unpredictable weather systems which bombard the planet in violent ways. On reaching water – which the planet seems mostly composed of – the scanner detects high levels of radiation; clearly this planet's atmosphere does not have the strength to filter the energy coming from the nearest – quite small – star. The water contains highly elevated levels of toxic chemicals and where it is free from algal bloom – a simple life form but encouraging nevertheless – it seems devoid of any organic life higher than basic microbes. Perhaps the few remaining land masses might hold out hope of communicating with higher life forms. Many of the land masses are pock-marked with huge saline lakes, and there seems to be next to no plant life anywhere, simple mosses at best. At last the scanner homes in on a very weak signal – an organism around three millimetres in length – made up of a simple collection of cells co-operating to form a basic organic life form – feeding on something; it's hard to work it out. There are more of these on this small world, but they number only a few hundred right across this planet. The planet's surface temperature has some strange extremes – extremely hot and extremely cold patches cover the planet with no logical geographical pattern. These extremes would make life almost impossible for anything not having evolved beyond simple multicellular organisms. It looks like the processes of evolution – understood throughout the known galaxy – have not been able to take hold on this small sphere. As the craft scans the planet a smaller sphere appears behind it – held in orbit and now coming into view. Perhaps this smaller world will harbour some higher life: but no, this tiny grey planet has no atmosphere and is covered entirely in large craters – evidence of space debris hitting it with violent force because the planetoid has no atmosphere to slow its path and so ease its impact. On the larger world there is evidence of this too, though less so.

The craft slowly powers up and prepares its systems to leave this world – perhaps never to return. Another world devoid of life in any meaningful sense; another world which the occupants of this craft can add to their list of uninhabited – and uninhabitable – corners of the known universe. The commander of the craft turns to the being responsible for taking the craft out of orbit, and back into deep space saying: 'Karlak! Sta riknor ve 'Earth' triqana shashsput. Sa renawdaro ki tranpat. Nir vek 2098678-18 – serta tranikah 4.54 x 109 ± 1Z Rashta ni krevaxa du-ro: Naq shri."[ii]

[ii] Translated as: "Helm, remove us from orbit of 'the Earth'. Reports of higher life-forms there are mistaken. It is a dead world. Note the date as 2098678-18. The planet registers as 4.54×10^9 billion years old ± 1%. Complex life would have had time to develop there: It has not."

Talk Point

What could cause most of life on Earth to die out?

Environmental issues and crises

Depending on who you ask, there are a range of different environmental issues facing the world today – with some thinking certain issues are more important than others. So when does an environmental issue become a 'crisis'? Perhaps a crisis is when something gets beyond our control to do anything about it. Or perhaps a crisis is better defined as a turning point – where we have to change course or mend our ways before something does get beyond our control. For many environmentalists, humans are now at just such a turning point – and we need to change our behaviours quickly before things get out of control. There are, of course, some who do not think there is any crisis at all – and that environmental change and adaptation is just a normal part of the cycles of life on Earth. Many environmentalists agree that Earth does have cycles and that things change – and sometimes even put themselves right – on a global scale; and have done throughout the 4.54×10^9 billion years ± 1% during which Earth has been in existence. However, they are also likely to argue that it is the *pace of change* which is causing the crisis. Earth can possibly adapt to almost anything given enough time to adapt – but the pace of environmental change is so rapid that Earth is having trouble keeping up. Also, some environmentalists say, it's not just change and pace of change – it's the type and cause of change. Their argument is that environmental crises are – almost entirely – caused by humans. Earth may adapt to this, but it may take a long time and – in the meantime – that adaptation might lead to removing the source of the problem: humans.

What are the crises?

For each of the following environmental crises we'll think about: what the crisis is; what its possible causes and consequences are; different possible solutions. Remember that not everyone will agree that there is any crisis in relation to the issue and that the science behind all this (and all the other factors linked to it) is very complex. It is also important to note that many of the crises below are very closely interlinked.

Talk Point

What do you think are the major environmental crises facing Earth today?

Climate change

The crisis

Climate change is about how the Earth's atmosphere is changing – according to many environmentalists – very rapidly and unpredictably. It is often referred to as global warming, but could equally well mean cooling in some places and warming in others. Life on Earth requires certain atmospheric and environmental conditions in which to survive. Life can adapt to climate change, but only if given enough time to either evolve through adaptation, or make immediate changes to lifestyle to accommodate climate change. The science of climate change is very complex and – at the moment – predicted rather than actual (though some scientists argue that a number of indicators that climate change is here now are present – such as changes to the Antarctic ice sheet and increasingly unpredictable weather patterns).

Causes and consequences

There is disagreement about the possible causes of climate change. Many consider the burning of fossil fuels to be a major cause through their effect on changing the relative proportions of ('greenhouse') gases in our atmosphere, but there are potentially many other causes – such as volcanic emissions, animal emissions and the by-products of many of the normal processes of life on Earth. However, many environmentalists claim that a range of agricultural and industrial processes carried out by humans will lead to quick and dramatic climate change – and that the pace of these processes is faster than nature's ability to respond to them adequately. The consequences of climate change are also unpredictable: climate change could lead to rises in sea levels, droughts, floods, extreme weather, changes to natural habitats and effects on a range of life forms. Of course, all of this could have very serious consequences for all life on Earth – and ultimately many species might not survive climate change (including humans). For humans, these environmental changes might also lead to important social changes, such as movements of population. It could also lead to global tensions as humans battle it out over changing (decreasing) natural resources – such as drinkable water, for example.

Possible solutions

For those who believe that climate change is caused by human activity a range of solutions are suggested: switching from burning fossil fuels and organic matter to renewable energy sources (including nuclear power); changes to agricultural and industrial practices by humans to minimise their effect on atmospheric processes; changes to energy use levels and a 'reduce, reuse, recycle' approach to life; reducing our individual 'carbon footprint' in a wide range of ways.

Energy use

The crisis

All life on Earth and many of our ways of living require energy. The sources of energy on Earth include many different options: oil and gas; organic matter; renewable energy such as wind, wave and solar power; nuclear energy. For many the environmental issue is about the side effects of energy use – the effects of fossil fuels on climate change, or the storage issues for nuclear waste. For many, the crisis is not only the effects of the by-products of our energy sources, but their sustainability over time. Some argue that if we continue to use non-renewable sources of energy we will get to a point where they will run out – and this will mean that they won't be available for our descendants. The crisis will therefore be that if we use non-renewables, then our energy sources will run out. This could have serious implications for much of life on Earth – though by far its greatest effects are likely to be for one species: humans.

Causes and consequences

The causes are simple – in non-renewables, humans use energy sources too much for them to be able to replenish themselves (that would take millions of years for oil and gas and hundreds for some other types of organic fuels). Also, our demand for energy is so high that we might turn to quick sources of energy (such as nuclear) which are limitless sources – but which can come with a heavy environmental cost in their waste and in the dangers associated with them. The consequences of overuse of non-renewable energy sources are equally simple – they might run out. There are also other consequences, for example, getting access to many sources of energy (even renewable ones such as wind power) might cause environmental damage in some way – and the by-products of any source of energy might be environmentally questionable.

Possible solutions

Most environmentalists would probably agree that humans should reduce their energy demands. However, other than that there would be disagreement: most environmentalists reject the environmental costs of sourcing and burning fossil fuels, preferring renewable sources such as solar energy. However, some propose greater use of nuclear energy, which others disagree with strongly. Most people would probably prefer to source energy using something which was a limitless source of energy and which had no negative environmental impact – unfortunately, it probably hasn't been discovered yet. So, the key for environmentalists is to support sourcing and using energy which has the least negative impact on the environment – but there's not any agreement about what that is yet.

Depletion of resources

The crisis

As well as energy creation, human life requires a huge number of natural resources in order to survive. This can be anything from building materials, to food sources, to chemical substances and so on. In relation to resources humans have to use these sustainably – in ways now which safeguard their existence for future generations. Some resources are unlikely to be easily replaced, for example many chemical substances and products of nature take millions of years to form; other resources – such as food products – can be replenished but this also takes time (though some food sources could also run out, for example overfishing could lead to an end to fish as a food source). Again, the potential crisis is that we are taking far more than the Earth can sustain. Like energy creation, the crisis is not just about the possibility that these resources might run out soon, but that 'winning' them from the Earth can have many negative consequences in itself.

Causes and consequences

Many human activities involve taking resources from the Earth – and the balance between need and greed is not, sadly, always clear in our actions. Taking resources in unsustainable ways may not only lead to them becoming exhausted – and no longer available to us or future generations – but also to negative by-products and effects on the natural world. For example, overfishing not only removes a source of food for humans, it would upset the whole ecosystem of the world's oceans – with potentially very unpredictable consequences – not only for humans, but for the planet as a whole.

Possible solutions

Obviously the simplest solution is to reduce our use of resources and to reuse and recycle more. However, we could look for other alternatives to the resources we use. Some might argue that clever humans will always find a new way to do things when a particular resource runs out so we needn't worry – others would think this is a short-sighted and wrong approach.

Pollution and waste

The crisis

The by-products of many human activities are waste products. These waste products can present us with problems in their storage or disposal. Some waste products are potentially harmful to the environment and may lead to climate change and destruction of habitats, life and ecosystems. Pollution can harm nature in a large variety of ways – some of which are hard to put right. This harm can widen to all life on Earth in some cases.

Causes and consequences

Much pollution is 'unintentional' – for example oil spillages, chemical run-off from agriculture and so on. Some is the result of accidents and some is simply the end result of some process or other (breathing, for example!). The causes are many and varied as are the effects. Ultimately, however, the consequences – like many environmental crises – are unpredictable.

Possible solutions

Reducing the processes which produce waste and/or lead to pollution is an obvious solution – as is finding more creative ways of dealing with (and recycling) waste. Avoiding accidental pollution and reducing other forms of pollution would be required – although again there will be disagreement about how best to do this. Some argue that scientific solutions are best – while some argue that we need more than this: we need changes in everyone's lifestyle.

Destruction of natural habitat

The crisis

Many aspects of life on Earth can lead to environmental change. Ecosystems are usually very finely balanced and one small change could put everything else out of sync. This would lead to changes in natural habitats – and so the life processes they sustain.

Causes and consequences

From destruction of rainforest to desertification to changes in land use and the use of our oceans, the causes are complex. Much of the cause is changes in how we use the Earth and the consequences again are highly unpredictable. For example, losing one species might harm another species and so on ... until the situation gets out of control and – perhaps – affects all species. Again, the pace of change is important if it is faster than a habitat's (and its inhabitants') ability to recover.

Possible solutions

Preserving the natural world is key here – so reducing human impact on habitats is part of the answer. Some argue that this change is natural and that we can't control it – others say that we have to think carefully about the consequences of our actions in this respect.

Reductions in biodiversity

The crisis

This is linked to many of the other environmental crises. It means where the number and diversity of life forms is reduced. This generally happens through extinction processes, which can be brought about by many things including climate change and other natural processes as well as very unnatural human processes.

Causes and consequences

Again, a great many causes are possible – from pollution to climate change and so on. Nature is always in a state of change and adaptation – but it needs time to adapt or species can die out. Obviously one consequence is that we have less diversity of life forms on Earth and the problem with that is that as ecosystems are very complex, the loss of one life form can have very serious consequences for another or several others, and so on.

Possible solutions

Again, these are protecting habitats and minimising the negative impact of our actions on everything else. Once more, some might argue for a scientific solution, while others argue that behavioural and attitudinal change is also required.

Talk Point

How important is it that your grandchildren grow up in a world where there are elephants?

Global population increases

The crisis

Human population is on the rise and has been so quite dramatically for some time now. As the population increases, so too do demands on the Earth's systems and resources. It may well be that at some point in the future there is just not enough to go around – whether that's land to live on, food to eat, and so on. If humans affect nature in negative ways, then the larger the population the greater the problems caused by this effect.

Causes and consequences

People are living longer because of improved health care, nutrition and better living standards. Fewer people die prematurely because of advances in medicine and other factors. The consequences are many and complex – from changes to climate and pressure on natural resources to interpersonal tensions caused by increasing numbers of people living in decreasing amounts of space.

Possible solutions

An obvious solution, of course, is population reduction through people having fewer children. However, this is difficult to regulate and may affect the poor more than those who are wealthy. Some argue that we simply need to reduce the resources we take from the Earth – by living simpler lives. Some suggest that we may need to look for more creative ways to cope with increasing population – for example, living in places where we haven't until now (undersea cities?) – but any solution like this could also have negative environmental consequences.

Talk Point

Do you think any of these crises is more important than the others?

The 'H' factor

The key issue in all of these is the role played by humans in *causing* the crisis and what role might be played by humans in *solving* the crisis. No matter the issue or perspective, we are mostly agreed that humans have the power to and therefore perhaps the responsibility of looking after nature. This may involve scientific and technological changes, but also behavioural and attitudinal changes in our lifestyle. It will require co-operation between individuals and countries – and governments which put into action meaningful policies to protect nature now and for future generations. The key issue is how best we can live a sustainable life – and unfortunately, as a species, we have not agreed over this so far.

Some religious and philosophical perspectives

Christianity

The common thread in all of these environmental crises is the relationship between humans and the environment. Christians believe that the Earth is God's and that we are its stewards. This means that for each of these crises we have the responsibility of addressing it properly on God's behalf.

The Church of Scotland

The Church of Scotland has taken very specific views on environmental topics such as climate change. In June 2015, the Church's 'Eco-congregation' responded to Pope Francis' call that action needs to be taken to address climate change now. It said: *'[Climate change] is a unifying subject and the [Pope's] encyclical shows how close the Catholic Church is to other Churches.'* The Church also added: *'Commercial organisations and governments tend to think short term and so they are planning five years ahead. But religions and faith groups are looking at the bigger picture. They are thinking for longer periods of time and acting over longer periods without being restricted in that way.'* [54] The Church considers its role in relation to environmental crises as a positive one in guiding others: *'At a time of widespread environmental crisis, it is important for churches to engage with one of the most serious problems of this time and to offer hope rather than apathy and despair.'*[55]

The Roman Catholic Church

The Papal Encyclical *Laudato Si'* covers a range of specific environmental issues facing us today. In relation to the climate it says: *'The climate is a common good, belonging to all and meant for all ... Humanity is called to recognise the need for changes of lifestyle, production and consumption, in order to combat this warming or at least the human causes which produce or aggravate it ... Climate change is a global problem with grave implications: environmental, social, economic, political and for the distribution of goods. It represents one of the principal challenges facing humanity in our day.'*[56]
The encyclical goes on to state that it is those with the greatest economic or political power who have a particular responsibility to respond to environmental crises – but, of course, that action is a responsibility of all. This encyclical covers in quite some detail a range of environmental crises and outlines the actions the Church thinks we should take in response to these.

Buddhism

In an article entitled 'Buddhism and the Ecocrisis' it is stated: *'Buddhism provides all the essential elements for a relationship to the natural world characterised by respect, humility, care and compassion.'* It goes on to argue that although technological developments have improved life for many, they come with a balancing price linked to their negative effects on the environment. It states that: *'Though change is inherent in nature, Buddhism believes that natural processes are affected by human morals.'*[57] It argues that our greed results in harm to nature and that living a simple life is highly valued in Buddhism. Living such a simple life would have a very low environmental impact, it is argued. It says that Buddhists should not seek to dominate nature, nor to be submissive to it, but to live in harmony with it. Such a harmonious relationship would be more likely to avoid environmental damage.

Humanism

'Humanists for a better world' (H4BW) states that it is: *'Putting humanist values into action – because the whole world is in our hands'.* On its website it includes an article which states: *'I believe that committed humanists are more willing than most to match words with actions, and that together we can help to bring about much needed change and counter the perception that humanists believe the Earth exists just for us to exploit.'*[58] H4BW engages in education and specific campaigns about the environment because it believes that only humans can solve environmental crises. It quotes the famous Humanist Carl Sagan: *'Our posturings, our imagined self-importance, the delusion that we have a privileged position in the universe, are challenged by this point of pale light. Our planet is a lonely speck in the great enveloping cosmic dark. In our obscurity, in all this vastness, there is no hint that help will come from elsewhere to save us from ourselves.'*[59] Humanists regard many environmental issues therefore as at least partly caused by humans, but also only able to be solved by humans.

What benefits does modern technology bring and at what cost?

Utilitarianism

Utilitarians weigh up costs and benefits when making moral choices – and this is equally true in relation to the environment. A lot of damaging environmental processes do produce benefits for many and so each benefit has to be weighed against the costs. Of course, with the environment, the costs are sometimes difficult to measure – because they can be very long term (and unpredictable). The Utilitarian Peter Singer is in no doubt about the problem: *'Now we face a new threat to our survival. The proliferation of human beings, coupled with the by-products of economic growth, is just as capable as the old threats of wiping out our society – and every other society as well.'*[60] Singer argues that the solution to this is an environmental ethic which avoids extravagance, does not measure success in relation to how much we have, and emphasises *'frugality and a simple life'*.[61]

Personal Reflection

- *What part do you think you play in causing and responding to environmental crises?*
- *How would 'the crises' explored in this chapter affect your life?*
- *What might a group of aliens think about our planet's environmental state?*

Active learning

Check your understanding

1. Do you think there is an 'environmental crisis'? What is your evidence for your view?
2. Describe the possible causes and effects of two 'environmental crises'.
3. For one of these 'crises', explain at least two possible solutions to this.
4. Do you think some of the 'crises', you have studied in this chapter are more serious than others? Explain.
5. For three of the crises you have studied describe one possible human cause and one possible natural cause of each.
6. What evidence is there that the Church of Scotland shares the same view about environmental crises as the Roman Catholic Church?
7. What does Pope Francis say in the encyclical *Laudato Si'* about environmental crises?
8. Describe a Humanist response to environmental crises.
9. What do Buddhists see as the link between the environment and human behaviour?
10. In what ways is the Utilitarian view of the environment linked to costs and benefits?

Investigate

1. Choose one of the environmental crises you have looked at in this chapter. Choose a suitable soundtrack and create your own picture montage about this environmental crisis.
2. Choose a different environmental crisis to the one you chose for task one. For this one, you should create a display board which separates the crisis into 'possible human causes' and 'possible non-human causes'. Your display should aim to be as balanced as possible.
3. Imagine instead that the alien spacecraft at the start of this chapter decided to stay and help sort out one of the environmental crises in this chapter. What might they have to do? You should examine carefully a range of suggested solutions to this crisis and prepare a guide for the aliens about how to solve it. (Of course, they may already know!)
4. Many religious and other important figures are held up as models of how we should treat nature (e.g. Francis of Assisi, John Muir). Find out about one of these figures and write a magazine article about this person showing what we can learn from them.

Analyse and Evaluate

1. Choose one of the crises in this chapter and explain the similarities and differences between the religious and philosophical responses in relation to this crisis.
2. For each of the following statements produce a paragraph in support of it and one rejecting it:
   - The rich countries of the world have the greatest responsibility for putting environmental damage right.
   - When it's humans against the environment we should always put humans first.
   - Nature is full of cycles – today's environmental crises are just natural cycles, not caused by humans.
   - Individual action is more important than government action.
   - Governments have a responsibility to people now, not in the future.
   - Families should be limited to one child only to stop global population increases.
3. Choose one famous environmentalist. How did this person's environmentalism come from their beliefs? What sources and teaching did they draw upon when thinking about the environment?

Apply

Choose one of the environmental crises in this chapter. Now design and/or produce a piece of artwork for the entrance to your school which makes people think about this environmental crisis and its possible causes and effects. If you do create and display it you could ask people who pass it to write their feelings about it on a sticky note.

14 Free trade and fair trade

Terry walks into his favourite coffee shop – it's now a fashion accessory to have your own steaming cup of latte in your hand (mobile in the other while checking social media ...). Had he looked up from his phone just for a minute he'd have noticed that his favourite coffee shop – previously known as the Hip Buzz – was under new management and now named A Cup of Kindness. He approaches the barista and quickly rattles off:

Terry: Large skinny latte with a double shot, no syrup – keep the froth away – to go please.

Barista: *Coming right up. That'll be £10.40 ... just when you're ready.*

Terry: (fumbling in his man bag) Yeah man, I'll ... Eh ... Sorry ... I thought you said £10.40! (laughs)

Barista: *Yes sir, I did.*

Terry: £10.40? Seriously?

Barista: *Yes sir, (points to board) I could do you a smaller size for £9.35.*

Terry: For one latte? Are you kidding me? Does it come with gold flecks or something?

Barista: *No gold flecks, sir, just normal coffee and milk.*

Terry: Is this, like, a very expensive cow, or some coffee you can only get once every 50 years or something from some tiny Pacific island which rises out of the sea and then disappears?

Barista: *No, just ordinary coffee – and very nice too.*

Terry: Sorry, I'm missing something here. My usual coffee here at the Hip Buzz is £2.50. →

Barista: *We're not the Hip Buzz now, we're A Cup of Kindness, and yes, our coffee is probably a little more expensive than you've been used to 'til now.*

Terry: You're not wrong. Any specific reason why I'll need to get a bank loan to have a coffee all of a sudden?

Barista: *We use only Fairtrade coffee, sir.*

Terry: Fair to who? Definitely not me I think.

Barista: *Well, that's for you to judge, sir. You see, we pay a fair price to the people who produce the coffee and so our coffee costs a bit more.*

Terry: What's any fairer about what you do than what the Hip Buzz did?

Barista: *No disrespect sir, but the Hip Buzz didn't worry too much about how much the producers of the coffee get for their work – and we do.*

Terry: But all the producers do is plant a coffee tree and then let nature do the rest.

Barista: *It's a coffee plant, sir, and they have to tend it, water it (and water doesn't always come easy where coffee's grown), feed it, protect it from being too cold, too hot, attacked by bugs, fungus and sometimes silly weather. They have to harvest it, transport it carefully and then sell it – and you see, sir, there's the tricky part. It doesn't matter how hard that year's crop was to grow – the price they get will be the cheapest price the buyer can get away with. Sometimes, too, the buyer knows the producers will have to take whatever price he offers – because otherwise they won't sell anything at all.*

Terry: Well, couldn't they just drink it themselves?

Barista: *They could, but there's a limit to how many coffees you can have a day and you can't survive on coffee alone.*

Terry: Well why don't they grow other food to eat?

Barista: *They do, but they use most of their land for coffee because that's what makes them money.*

Terry: So they're just money-grabbing and greedy then?

Barista: *Eh ... no, sir. They need the money to pay for their education and their health care.*

Terry: Doesn't their government provide that?

Barista: *Ah ... it would be nice if things were that simple where they live.*

Terry: Still, I'm not paying £10.40 for a coffee – I'm off to the Caffeine Cabin up the road.

Barista: *Your choice, sir, it's always your choice ...*

Talk Point

What's the maximum amount you'd be prepared to pay for a coffee?

Free trade

In our global economy a whole load of products are traded internationally. These 'commodities', as they're often known, can be anything from coffee to cocoa beans, bananas, sugar cane – and many other things. International markets set the prices for these products and in a free trade system, buyers can seek out the best value products around the world. The aim for the buyer is to make as much profit as possible. This can be achieved by paying as little for each stage of the process involved in producing anything as possible – so that the profit margins are maximised. In a free trade system, there are often very few rules about this – buyers can choose to buy or not – and their purchasing power means that they can often pay far less than the true cost of producing a particular product. The price for a product in this system is decided by 'supply and demand'. If there is a plentiful supply of a product then buyers have lots of choice about where they get it – and so are more likely to source the product as cheaply as they can. If there is high demand for a product they also know that they can sell it at a high price – and the bigger the gap between the purchase price and the selling price, the more profit is in it for the buyer.

These buyers are also often very big, powerful, international companies. As well as holding real power over the producers of any product, they can also hold great influence around the world – especially in countries which are relatively poor and so need these big internationals to support their production.

The prices paid for products in a free trade system are usually decided on the hectic floors of stock exchanges in the world's industrialised countries – and these process often have very little to do with the actual cost of producing the product. In any system too, a number of 'parties' have to take their 'cut' of the price paid for any product: for example, working backwards, the profit made by selling, say bananas, has to be shared between:

- the supermarkets which sell it
- the warehouses involved in the final ripening of the fruits
- those who transport it from warehouse to supermarket
- those who transport it from airport/port to warehouse
- those who transport it by air, sea or land
- those who transport it from producer to airport/port
- the original producers.

That's not forgetting:

- accountants
- insurers
- the many people who support all the processes above – like fuel companies, mechanics, admin staff ...

In fact, the list is very long indeed and it can often mean that the original producers get only a very tiny fraction of the final cost of the product. Most systems of international trade are subject to some kind of regulation by governments and so on but in a completely free trade system this would not happen – it would be everyone for themselves and winner takes all. Of course, the product might never reach the consumer if it wasn't for the various people and industries involved – and of course this would mean that producers would get nothing in the first place. It would, perhaps, be too easy to see large multinational companies as exploitative and unfair – but maybe without these companies and the economic growth they can support, many people's lives would be harder and far less comfortable. However, the issue here is about how much each stage of the process gets – and how fairly the cost of any product is distributed among those involved in getting it from producer to consumer.

Of course, although trade is free around the world and mostly ruled by market forces, there are agreements between world governments about trade. The World Trade Organization (WTO) was set up in 1995. Its role is to regulate trade around the world to ensure that while it is free, it is also fair. It states that there are ten good reasons for ensuring that trade is free but regulated around the world and this is signed up to by member countries:

1. **It promotes peace** Conflicts can begin when one country assumes it is being unfairly treated by another – for example, if a country puts up barriers to importing products from another country.
2. **It handles disputes constructively** Different views about trading practices can lead to very heated arguments as each country tries to stand up for its own interests. The WTO can act as a referee in these cases.
3. **Its rules can be followed by all** Rules about trade which all countries can agree about perhaps make things much more stable.
4. **Trade cuts the cost of living** Free trade rewards producers by improving their living standards – in theory.
5. **Trade leads to better choice and better quality** Where producers have to compete, this encourages them to produce the best good or service.
6. **Trade improves incomes**.
7. **Trade stimulates economic growth** Business and industry are the areas which make profit. Without this profit, social infrastructure like education and health care cannot be effectively built.
8. **This leads to improved lives**.
9. **Governments are protected** Many large multinational companies arguably have greater power than some small governments. WTO agreements prevent these companies from taking advantage of such governments.
10. **This encourages good government** Where governments are under the 'control' of large companies, this could lead to abuses of power and corruption – for example, lowering safety and environmental standards to encourage a large company into your country.

Although member countries sign up to this agreement, many countries have not signed up and it is argued that even those who have might choose to quietly ignore one or more rules if they think it is to their country's advantage.

Talk Point

What kind of 'advantage' might a country feel was important enough to break WTO rules it had agreed to?

Problems for producers

Every business and industry has its own difficulties to face, but the issues faced by primary producers are often particularly tough. The first problem is that many products traded internationally come from relatively poor countries. These countries are often in debt to the wealthier countries and so have to make money to pay this debt rather than provide for their own people. This, in turn, means that in such countries, education, health and social care are not usually free (or are in very short supply). This means that the inhabitants of those countries need to make money to provide for basic things for their families – and this means producing goods for sale. So, those involved in agriculture grow 'cash crops' rather than food crops. They can sell these cash crops and so help their country's economy – although this can also mean that their country then has to buy in food from other countries, even though they have plenty of fertile land and could perfectly well feed themselves. Also, the more a country focuses on producing a limited range of produce, the more it runs the risk of being hit hard if demand for that product falls quickly – or another producer is able to offer the produce at a lower price.

Another problem is the power of the big international companies: these companies can often choose to buy or not to buy in one country or another. This can mean that they seek the cheapest option and may not buy a country's cash crops at all – or may do so for a ridiculously low price. This power can also sometimes lead to these companies having great influence over the governments of poorer countries – which may have had to agree to all sorts of conditions to make sure that they can sell their produce: these conditions may favour the powerful international company but do little for the people of the country producing the goods. In extreme cases, this can lead to corruption in governments as individuals and groups seek to benefit from the power which the international company wields.

An additional difficulty is that as producers strive to produce more and more they run the risk of exhausting the land on which they grow their crops. This may mean that they have to apply expensive fertilisers. Also, crops can be harmed by pests and a whole range of environmental threats, requiring the application of expensive pesticides and herbicides, for example. Often these expensive products come from ... large powerful international companies which can charge producers a great deal for these products.

Another difficulty – particularly in agriculture – is the unpredictability of growing crops year on year. Some years are good years and others are not – and producers generally have little control over that (possible changes to global climate may be a part of the problem). This means that producers may have good years and bad years – unpredictably – and this can make life very difficult.

The final issue ties all of these together. Producers depend on a whole range of things over which they have no control – from global markets, to weather, to international debt. This can mean that producers are at the mercy of so many factors – and no matter how hard they work to produce their goods what they get for their labours is controlled by many others – often unfairly.

Talk Point

Why might producers find it difficult to make sure that their work was paid for appropriately?

The fair-trade solution

To put it most simply, fair trade involves making sure that those who produce the goods in the first place get a fair level of pay for the work that they do. It is about balance – making sure that everyone involved in getting a product from producer to consumer benefits, but that some don't automatically benefit more than others. To this end, the international Fairtrade system was created, represented in the UK by the Fairtrade Foundation. This might occasionally make Fairtrade goods more expensive for the consumers – but this price then reflects the real cost of the production process, not an artificially reduced one based on exploitation of the producers.

As well as ensuring that the end cost reflects the work involved in the product, fair trade can involve a lot more to ensure that producers get a fair deal. Fair trade, for example, might involve organisations supporting the infrastructure in a country (or a part of a country) so that it works more effectively for those who live there. This could be through education, health care or other activities which improve the lifestyle for the people who live there. Once lifestyles are improved, then this can mean that producers have less need to turn to cash crops to provide for their basic needs. Fair-trade programmes might also, for example, support producers to form co-operatives and to work together in selling their produce. Rich buyers might find it more difficult to exploit collectives of producers than they would individual producers. The Fairtrade Mark on a product ensures that it conforms to certain standards linked to the conditions of those who produced the goods. It should demonstrate that the product has been produced in ways which are fair to the producers at all stages of their involvement.

In Scotland, Fairtrade goods used to be found only in fairly specialised shops, but now it would be unusual to find a high-street supermarket which does not sell Fairtrade products and many large chains of supermarkets now use Fairtrade products in their own-brand products. However, no matter how fairly traded a product is, it is only helpful if, at the end of the line, consumers know about it and buy it.

Talk Point

Why might people buy/not buy Fairtrade goods?

Some religious and philosophical perspectives

Christianity

Within Christianity there have traditionally been two approaches to trade and business. The first is the view that having a strong 'work ethic' is something Christians should aspire to – and if this makes them successful in business and in life then that is a good thing. However, alongside this work ethic principle there has always been a very strong trend in Christianity towards care and support for those most vulnerable in society – especially, perhaps, those most economically vulnerable. This means that, in reality, most Christians will support the principles of fair trade – that someone should be fairly rewarded for their efforts.

The Church of Scotland

In 2012, the Church of Scotland produced a report[62] about Christians' 'right relationship with money'. It begins by asking 'What is the economy for?' and answers: '*The economy is for God which means it is also for my neighbour ... all economies are embedded in social relationships. Refusal to name this has created a situation in which society seems too often to exist for the benefit of the markets.*' The Church does not reject economic growth, but it is clear that such growth should be more equal, sustainable, balanced and should ensure that no one is left in poverty. It essentially says that the economy is there to benefit and serve all, not just some and not just itself. The Church has also produced a leaflet: 'Fair Trade: Getting Started' which encourages Churches to support fair trade. In this leaflet it cites three Bible texts which support fair trade: 2 Corinthians 9:6–15; Amos 8:4–6 and Matthew 7:7–12.

Talk Point

In what ways do these Bible texts support fair trade?

The Roman Catholic Church

In the Catechism the importance of the fair distribution of wealth is clear: '*The equal dignity of human persons requires the effort to reduce excessive social and economic inequalities. It gives urgency to the elimination of sinful inequalities.*' (1947) This suggests that the Church recognises that the economy may result in economic differences, but when these become 'excessive' that becomes sinful. The Catechism also states: '*The development of economic activity and growth in production are meant to provide for human beings. Economic life is not meant solely to multiply goods produced and increase profit or power; it is ordered first of all to the service of persons ... of the entire human community.*' (2426) It is quite clear therefore that trade is there to benefit all, not just some. The Catholic Church, like many Christian traditions, was at the forefront of bringing fair trade to people's attention. The Church's official aid agency in Scotland, SCIAF, was set up in 1965 by the Catholic Bishops of Scotland to give practical aid to those in need and to make others aware of that need. SCIAF has supported Fairtrade principles and practice since it began.

Buddhism

The Buddha had lived a life of luxury – with every material need fulfilled. His enlightenment brought immediate renunciation of such wealth and he taught simplicity – separating yourself from the trappings of wealth. However, Buddha also recognised that you cannot attend properly to your spiritual life if your physical needs are not being met. While monks and nuns have few possessions, lay Buddhists live normal lives as part of the economy. Some Buddhists argue that you can be a Buddhist and wealthy – provided your wealth was not gained through the exploitation of others and that you can use wealth to help others. However, other Buddhists suggest that being wealthy is incompatible with Buddhism, because it is too easy to become attached to wealth and let it blind you to other things. Buddhists would support fair trade since fair trade involves compassion towards producers and compassion is a central principle in Buddhism.

Humanism

In an article on the British Humanist Association website it states: '*Development organisations have increasingly come to recognise that trade is the route out of poverty. But this requires more than the free marketers' mantra of 'free trade'. It needs trade justice.*'[63] The article goes on to say that Humanists should be supporting fair trade in practical ways in their daily lives, but also in campaigning to bring Fairtrade to everyone's attention. This article also quotes the UN's Universal Declaration of Human Rights – especially article 25 which says that everyone has a right to an adequate standard of living. Humanists do not oppose people becoming wealthy through their hard work, but they would be likely to oppose wealth which was gained through unfairly exploiting others. Among other things, '*Humanists oppose ... vast inequalities in wealth ... which stand in the way of overall human welfare and progress.*'[64] Humanists believe that everyone should be able to enjoy life and that economic security is part of that. Wealth creation is important, but so too is wealth distribution.

Utilitarianism

In *Principles of Political Economy* published in 1848, J. S. Mill argued that economic forces determine how wealth is *created*, but that human decisions determine how wealth is *distributed*. Mill does not reject free competition as part of creating wealth, but is clear that, once created, wealth should be for the benefit of the many, not just the few. Utilitarians would support economic activity which benefited the majority and if free trade does this then they would support free trade. The issue is how far completely free trade does benefit the majority. Trade is essentially a competition – and in competitions there are winners and losers. Some argue that free trade is more likely to lead to wealth creation for a privileged few – although others disagree, saying that it leads to wealth creation for many. The key issues for a Utilitarian would be: how far does wealth creation bring happiness for the majority and how fairly is wealth distributed? Utilitarians could support or reject fair trade depending on their way of measuring its outcome. If fair trade leads to a fairer, more equal world then clearly that is best for the majority – but if it artificially restricts free trade and so leads to reductions in trade and wealth creation then that might not be good for the majority (although it may be good for the minority!).

Talk Point

In being good for producers, does fair trade benefit the majority?

Personal Reflection

* *Do you buy Fairtrade goods – should you?*
* *What good and bad choices do you make with your money?*
* *Do we each have a responsibility to the poor?*

Active learning

Check your understanding

1 What is meant by a 'commodity' and how are these traded internationally?
2 In what ways might the cost of a product involve a range of people/groups?
3 Describe two of the ten reasons given by the WTO about the importance of regulated trade.
4 Explain two of the key difficulties faced by producers.
5 What is meant by fair trade?
6 In your opinion, is free trade or fair trade the better option? Explain.
7 What is the Church of Scotland's view on economic growth?
8 What does the Roman Catholic Church mean when it talks about economic differences becoming 'excessive'?
9 How far do religious and non-religious views agree about wealth and economic growth?
10 How might a Utilitarian support fair trade?

Investigate

1 Take a trip to your local supermarket. Choose a typical week's shopping and see how much of it you can source from Fairtrade products. Alternatively, you could do an analysis of all products in the supermarket and analyse what proportion of products the store sells are Fairtrade. Perhaps you could then arrange to discuss this with the supermarket concerned and find out what their policies are on fair trade. You could present your findings in graphs, etc. – perhaps to the supermarket. You could also contact a local religious group and analyse how far they use Fairtrade products routinely.
2 Carry out an online search to see which organisations and groups sell Fairtrade products. What kinds of products are most likely to be fairly traded? How are these marketed? What do they cost compared to non-Fairtrade products? You could, of course, run a Fairtrade information event in your school – or offer Fairtrade products at a school event once you have gathered your information.

➜

3 Visit the website of the World Trade Organization (**www.wto.org**) and produce your own report on its philosophy and activities. How far does it promote free trade? What restrictions on free trade do its signatories agree to and what are the benefits for them and others of this? Which countries are 'in' the WTO and which are not?
4 Choose a typical product you buy. Now try to find out how the cost of this product is distributed across all of the people involved in getting it to you. You can display your findings and think about how easy or difficult it is to get hold of this information.

Analyse and Evaluate

1 Run a class debate based on the following statement: 'This house believes that completely free trade is the best option for everyone.'
2 Discuss the following in groups and note your conclusions. What are the possible ways these groups could use Fairtrade products and what are the possible advantages and disadvantages of them using Fairtrade products?
   - Religious and belief organisations
   - Schools
   - Government organisations
   - Businesses (choose a selection)
   - Sports clubs and societies
3 As in other topics in this course, it looks as if the religious and non-religious groups agree about many aspects of the topic (and maybe disagree about some). From what you have learned about the religious and philosophical perspectives in this chapter, how similar are they in their views about wealth, trade and fair trade? You could set this information out in the form of an academic poster.

Apply

Your task is to turn your school into a fair-trade school within one week. What will you have to do and how will you persuade your school to switch to fair trade? If you think your school is already a fair-trade school choose a different local group/place/organisation/business, etc., and consider how you might persuade this to become fully committed to fair trade.

15 Causes and effects of poverty

You don't choose when you are born
You don't choose where you are born
You don't choose to be born a boy or a girl
You don't choose the skills and abilities you are born with
You don't choose your parents
You don't choose how many brothers and sisters you have
You don't choose where you are brought up
You don't choose the quality of education you receive
You don't choose your nation's debt
You don't choose not to pay for your nation's debt
You don't choose how your parents make a living
You don't choose the weather
You don't choose if your country is at peace or at war
You don't choose how successful your crop is
You don't choose the price the buyer pays for your product
You don't choose the job opportunities available to you
You don't choose your health care provision
You don't choose how healthy you are
You don't choose how rich nations behave towards your nation
You don't choose international trade policies
You don't choose whether you get aid or not
You don't choose poverty
Who would?

Choosing to be poor

Would anyone, anywhere, choose to be poor? Certainly some people choose to live life with less than others – but would anyone really choose to be poor, with all the problems being poor can bring? You would have thought not – and yet, isn't it possible that sometimes the poor are treated as if somehow it is their fault they are poor? Think about the things you are in control of in your life now and the things you will be in control of when you are an adult – if you could have control over whether you were poor or not, what would you choose? It is probably fair to say that the world's poor have not chosen to be that way and if they could change it they would – so how is poverty caused in the first place?

The causes of poverty

Like all of the issues in this book, the causes of poverty are many and complex. Poverty has many causal factors – the vast majority of which are likely not to be within the control of the poor themselves. The fact of poverty worldwide is unavoidable. According to the United Nations' millennium project[65]:

- Every year 6 million children die from malnutrition before their fifth birthday.
- Every 3.6 seconds another person on Earth dies from starvation.
- Around 40 per cent of the world's population do not have access to basic sanitation and more than 1 billion people still use unsafe sources of drinking water.

Poverty is also closer to home. Oxfam claims that: '*The UK is the world's sixth largest economy, yet 1 in 5 of the UK population live below our official poverty line, meaning that they experience life as a daily struggle.*'[66] A very quick internet search will reveal the extent of poverty in the world today and it is not comfortable reading. Although the causes of poverty are complex, they can be grouped under a range of headings. Which of these affect individuals will vary, but each – and combinations of each – are likely to lead to poverty.

Economic factors

Poverty leads to poverty

When people have unequal access to the ability to create wealth, they are more likely to end up in poverty. This might mean, for example, starting life off in an economically poor family which means that opportunities to access such things as good health care and education may not be equally available to you compared with someone from a wealthier background. So if your family is already poor, then it is more difficult for you right from the start to 'lift yourself' out of poverty, because your poverty effectively keeps you poor.

Talk Point

Poverty is often referred to as a 'vicious circle'. What do you think this means?

Living in a 'poor' country

Individual economic factors, however, are not the only possible cause of poverty. If you live in a poor country, this can also make it more difficult to escape poverty. This is where it gets complicated because what causes a country to be poor is very complex too: some countries have very few natural resources and so have little to sell on the international markets to support their growth and development. Other countries are rich in natural resources, but don't have the technology, the skilled workforce or the capital to make use of these resources. When this is the case, it can either mean that they get no benefit from their resources because they can't access them – or it can mean that countries which do have the means to access these resources get most of the economic benefits of them. This can lead to poor countries being 'controlled' by richer nations or rich and powerful multinational companies. This can also be made worse by the presence of corruption in a country. The causes of such corruption are themselves very complex, but making economic progress in a country where corruption leads to money and power being held by a few is likely to be harder than where society is stable and well governed. On the other hand some could be attracted to a corrupt government, because they might want to take the chance of reduced health and safety controls, for example, which might increase the profit margin – even if it is at the expense of the workers.

International trade

As you learned in the previous chapter, international trade is a complex idea. It can lead to already powerful countries and companies controlling international trade, which can lead to producers not being properly rewarded for their efforts. If you are under the control of 'market forces' then this can work against you if you are relatively low in economic power. This is another example of how being poor and relatively powerless can lead to further powerlessness and increased poverty.

International debt

Countries might borrow money to support their economy or economic development. Like any debt, this has to be paid back. The sums of money and the timescales involved can mean that a country can be paying back debt for many years. This means that you could potentially be born in a country which has a very large debt. To pay this the country in debt may have to direct money away from other things, such as education and health care for example. It may have to produce goods for export rather than internal use in order to raise capital, and it may have to agree to other countries and companies being able to preferentially access its natural resources. As well as paying back the debt, the countries which owe may also have to agree to certain conditions when repaying the debt – this could be anything from changes to their infrastructure to wider social, political and economic changes. In short, debts often come with 'strings attached', and it is these 'strings' which might lead to or keep a country – and therefore its people – in poverty.

Social and structural factors

Lack of infrastructure

In some countries, poor basic social conditions might mean it is harder to get out of poverty than in others. For example, if health care is poor in a country, then health issues might make it harder to find and hold on to work. Also, for example, where a country has no welfare system it will mean that when you are not working you are not supported – a further potential contributor to poverty. Also, if education provision is poor then it may be difficult to achieve the qualifications necessary to access work. In addition, lack of infrastructure in one country can lead to people seeking work elsewhere. This then means that they migrate away from the country and their work produces no wealth for their country and so things overall get worse. As well as these key social services, other infrastructure issues may lead to difficulties in making economic gains: for example, if there is an inefficient public transport system, then this will limit how far away from your home you can look for work, and if there is little or no child care again this might limit your choice of work.

Social instability

Many countries which are 'poor' are also sometimes relatively socially unstable. Again, there can be many reasons for this which are way beyond the scope of this book, but this instability can make it difficult for economic progress and development to take place. As an illustration, some point to countries which are independent today but which were once controlled by colonial powers: when these colonial powers moved out (for a variety of reasons) they left behind a difficult range of circumstances which have caused problems ever since. In fact, some countries in the world today had their maps 'redrawn' by colonial powers and it is argued that this led to internal issues within the country – for example, ongoing ethnic tensions – which in turn led to difficulties for these countries in making economic progress.

Conflict and war

Sadly, some poor countries experience conflict and war – this might be internal civil/ethnic conflicts or conflict with other countries. The effects of conflict and war can directly harm a country's ability to make economic progress – for example, through the destruction of land for growing food or industrial locations – but there can also be less direct effects – for example, when a country is involved in conflict it is likely to use its economic resources to fund its response to the conflict. This may mean redirecting funds from other areas such as health and education – leading to a further negative spiral of disadvantage and poverty. Also, if the workforce is tied up in conflict then this could further harm the economy and the stress of living in conflict will also harm the economy. Finally, international companies may avoid investing in a country where there is conflict because it will not be able to carry out normal economic activity to support growth – again leading to a negative spiral downwards.

Environmental issues

As if all this were not bad enough, poor countries are often located in places where the climate is very unpredictable and/or extreme. Poorer countries cannot respond to the effects of such natural events as well as richer ones and so this compounds the country's problems because environmental issues can affect the country's infrastructure, reduce its food (or cash crop) yield and so on. Additionally, international investors might be less attracted to invest in countries where climate instability is common – because this could have all sorts of effects on their investment. Some argue that changes to the global climate caused by human activity are disproportionately problematic for poor countries – and so the vicious circle goes on.

In what ways might global climate change affect poor countries 'disproportionately'?

Sadly, it is true to say that poverty affects countries and the individuals in them in many different ways – and that the causes are many and complex. It is also important to remember that poverty is not limited to any particular country or group of people and is present worldwide.

The effects of poverty

So far it should be clear to you that the causes and effects of poverty are sometimes very hard to separate and that one can easily lead to the other in a particularly vicious cycle. There are many effects of poverty, but to simplify the issue we will consider direct and indirect effects.

Direct effects of poverty

At its most extreme, poverty can lead to death. This can be through malnutrition, or through illness and disease brought on by malnutrition, or through increased social unrest or a range of other complex factors. Poverty can also lead to reduced life expectancy, increased child mortality and increases in health-related illness and disease. Also, when a country or individual is poor, the means of responding to poverty-related illness and disease are themselves reduced. All of this can lead to difficult life circumstances for those experiencing poverty, their children and others around them. This in turn can lead to further economic and social consequences – all leading to keeping the cycle of poverty turning.

Indirect effects of poverty

The effects of poverty can be wide-ranging, severe and unpredictable. One possible outcome of poverty is a wider global destabilisation. In 2015, Europe was faced with a refugee crisis which was the most severe it has seen since the Second

World War. Many refugees making their way to Europe were fleeing conflict and persecution – especially in troubled Syria. However, it is also arguable that some were economic refugees – looking to escape poverty and improve their life chances by moving themselves and their families to more affluent countries. As well as these mass migrations which make the headlines, there are more steady refugee movements taking place around the world most of the time. For example, ill-equipped boats filled with refugees from Africa regularly get into difficulties in the Mediterranean – often with tragic consequences. Such situations fuel very deep disagreements. Some argue that these situations are about people taking advantage of more affluent countries and so should be resisted, while others argue that these are desperate people just trying to improve their lives and they should be welcomed and supported: the countries on the 'front line' in these situations – those likely to be the first landfall – argue that the responsibility for the refugees belongs to all of Europe, not just the 'front line' countries themselves.

Talk Point

Do we have a moral responsibility to welcome anyone in need?

Moral choices and poverty

So, poverty involves many factors: the key issue for individuals is how far our own behaviours can contribute to or alleviate poverty; what should we do and what could we do? The next chapter will explore ways in which aid can help alleviate the causes and effects of poverty, but perhaps it is important to consider a more fundamental question about our own individual role in responding to poverty.

Talk Point

What does world poverty have to do with you?

Some religious and philosophical perspectives

Christianity

The vast majority of Christians and Christian groups would argue that one of the key messages in Christianity is love, care and support for those most vulnerable in society. In the Bible, there are numerous statements by Jesus about the rich and the poor – and the responsibility we all have towards the poor. Most Christians would agree that Jesus identifies with the poor and that he teaches that however we behave towards the poor we also behave towards him:

'I say to you, as you did it to the least of these my brothers, you did it to me.' (Matthew 25:40) Christians have always been prominent in movements and organisations which support the poor and many well-known charities have Christian origins. In some cases, Jesus suggests that the way to heaven is to sell everything you have, give away what you receive and make yourself poor. Christians will interpret this in different ways, but are likely to agree with the central idea, that being a Christian involves working to alleviate poverty.

The Church of Scotland

'The Church of Scotland has for many years identified a Gospel bias to the poor and has directed work and resources to be focused on working alongside the most deprived parishes in Scotland.'[67] In 2012, a report to the General Assembly stated: *'A "poverty free" economy is both a hope and an imperative. Realism about achieving it should make us more determined rather than more cynical. It is an economy which ensures that all members of society have a minimum income which allows them to live dignified and healthy lives ... This we owe to God who measures our moral and spiritual wealth on how we treat all members of society.'*[68] So it is clear that for the Church of Scotland, eradicating poverty is the responsibility of all – it is a duty. The Church argues that we will be judged by God on how we treat the poor and on how far we work to alleviate poverty – whatever its causes and wherever it is found. The Church is engaged in a wide range of projects which address poverty – which can be anything from producing reports and lobbying the Scottish Government to working directly with the poor in projects at home and abroad.

The Roman Catholic Church

The Catechism of the Catholic Church is very clear: *'God blesses those who come to the aid of the poor and rebukes those who turn away from them ... it is by what they have done for the poor that Jesus Christ will recognise his chosen ones.'* (2443) It does not come much clearer than this – Catholic teaching requires that Christians support the poor in all that they do – and on this you will be judged. The Catechism goes on to point out that Jesus identified with the poor and calls Christians to do the same: *'The Church's love for the poor ... is a part of her constant tradition'* (2444) and: *'... those who are oppressed by poverty are the object of a preferential love on the part of the Church which, since her origin, and in spite of the failings of many of her members, has not ceased to work for their relief, their defence and liberation through numerous works of charity which remain indispensable always and everywhere.'* (2449) When Jorge Bergoglio was elected as Pope in 2013, he took the name 'Francis' after Saint Francis of Assisi – a saint strongly associated with identification with the poor. Pope Francis has since regularly called on the Church to work for the poor and in one of his first speeches as Pope he declared: *'How I long for a poor Church for the poor.'*

Buddhism

'Our world is increasingly interdependent, but I wonder if we truly understand that our interdependent human community has to be compassionate ... the awesome power that economic institutions have acquired in our society, and the distressing effects the poverty continues to wreak, should make all of us look for means of transforming our economy into one based on compassion ... it is not enough to say that all human beings must enjoy equal dignity. This must be translated into action.' [69] So says the Dalai Lama. In Buddhism, one of the key teachings relates to detachment from material wealth – so for Buddhists, being materially wealthy can be a source of suffering. However, although Buddhism stresses simplicity in life and non-attachment to wealth, it also recognises that poverty causes suffering too. In fact, one of the 'four sights' which led to Buddha's enlightenment was of a man suffering the effects of poverty.

Buddhism therefore teaches that while we should not strive for material wealth, we should also support those who are poor. Buddhist teaching also recognises that poverty can lead to many other problems for individuals and for society and so increases in suffering for all. Alleviating poverty is therefore an act of compassion and has benefits for all involved. For Buddhists the causes and effects of poverty are likely to be linked to the causes of all suffering in life: greed, ignorance and delusion.

Talk Point

Buddhists believe that both great wealth and great poverty can bring suffering. What do you understand by this (and what do you think of it)?

Humanism

The British Humanist Society states that: *'Humanists oppose the vast inequalities and injustices which cause so much poverty and misery. They know that if we are to improve matters it is up to us ... we should care about poverty, however remote it is from us, not because a god or a holy text tells us to, but because we are all members of the same species, co-existing on our small planet and treating others fairly is the right thing to do ... humanists continue to seek rational and scientific solutions for problems of poverty and ignorance around the world.'*[70] Humanists recognise that the causes of poverty are complex, but that we should address these using reason and evidence towards a fairer world. Since Humanists believe that 'this is the only life we have' it clearly makes sense for Humanists to work towards ensuring that this life is fair and just for all – and that means not living in poverty.

Utilitarianism

Modern Utilitarian Peter Singer argues: *'We cannot avoid concluding that by not giving more than we do, people in rich countries are allowing those in poor countries to suffer from absolute poverty, with consequent malnutrition, illness and death. This is not a conclusion that applies only to governments. It applies to each absolutely affluent individual, for each of us has the opportunity to do something about the situation ... if, then, allowing someone to die is not intrinsically different from killing someone, it would seem that we are all murderers.'*[71] Strong stuff! Singer's view is that by not doing enough we allow poverty to take hold and cause misery – but we can do something to put an end to this so we should. Since Utilitarians are all about maximising happiness for the majority and since poverty affects so many, clearly getting rid of poverty would lead to an increase in global happiness. Also, if poverty does have implications for global stability, then getting rid of it will help to stabilise world geopolitics and this too must be good for all. Utilitarian J. S. Mill was equally clear about poverty – referring to it as a 'social evil'. Mill and others recognised that even in his day the causes of poverty were complex, but that, in order to maximise happiness, we each have a duty to address poverty.

Personal Reflection

* *What could you do to help the poor?*
* *How important is it to care for the poor in your own country compared to caring for the poor in other countries?*
* *How far is caring for the poor everyone's responsibility and how far is it the responsibility of world governments?*

Active learning

Check your understanding

1. What evidence is there that poverty is still present in the twenty-first century?
2. Describe two economic factors which cause poverty.
3. Why might a business/industry want to avoid or be attracted to a country where there is corruption in government?
4. What is the relationship between infrastructure and poverty?
5. In what ways can war/conflict contribute to poverty and make it worse?
6. Describe one direct and one indirect effect of poverty.
7. Explain the similarities and differences between religious teachings about poverty.
8. How far do religions and non-religious groups agree that there is a duty to help the poor?
9. What does it mean to 'identify with the poor' and how might this affect action in relation to poverty?
10. Is ignoring the plight of the poor the moral equivalent of murder?

Investigate

1. Create your own presentation on world poverty. This should describe the facts and figures in relation to poverty and prompt people to consider their own responses to poverty. You should aim to cover poverty causes and effects in the UK and around the world.
2. Using scripture sources from the world's religions create a display to get people thinking about the link between religion and poverty. How should religious people respond to poverty and on which scriptural sources should their responses be based?
3. Many charities responding to poverty have very close links with religious and non-religious groups – some in fact have their origins in these. Select a range of charities working in the UK and abroad in response to poverty. Write a report about the extent to which these charities are based upon/linked to religious and/or non-religious groups and organisations.
4. It is easy to think of poverty as something in faraway places. However, poverty is often much closer than you think. Explore the extent of poverty close to you. What evidence is there of poverty? What are its causes? How does it affect people? What responses have local groups and organisations been engaged in? Once you have done this, you could complete an extended piece of writing explaining what you have found and your thoughts and reflections on this. You should, of course, be sensitive to the possible impact this research might have on people in your class when doing this.

Analyse and Evaluate

1 Discuss and reach a conclusion on each of the following statements:
   - Poverty in Scotland is bad, but not as bad as some places in the world.
   - Governments should do more to address poverty.
   - Poor countries have to sort out their own problems.
   - Poverty leads to poverty.
   - The vicious circle of poverty can be broken.
   - Religious and non-religious groups say a lot about poverty, but do not do enough.

2 'Religious people should not be wealthy.' How far do you agree with this statement?

3 Evaluate the claim that there are more similarities than differences between the views of religious and non-religious groups about the causes, effects and ways of responding to poverty.

Apply

Emergency response activity: As a class you should consider and draw up plans to deal with the following emergency situation.

The world's poor have had enough. En masse they begin a march to – what they see as – affluent Europe. The countries they arrive in first have had enough of being 'on the front line' and so they put millions of people on aircraft and send them to Scotland. The authorities in Scotland are overwhelmed and make an appeal for every person in Scotland to play their part in welcoming and supporting these people. Your job is to work out how your town/city/community will respond positively and help those arriving in the true spirit of Scottish hospitality.

16 International aid and charitable work

Agape[iii] means love in action – giving what you can
Your time, your efforts, talents, skills and not just to your clan
It might mean giving money too, once you have paid your rent
And other bills, food, clothes and things – then Tithing ten per cent
And also you can give away your sheeny shiny brass[iv]
In love and friendship helping all – for sure, that's Caritas
There's faith, there's hope, good things it's true, but these are just the rest
For of these three it's Charity which is the very best
While Zakat too means giving for the benefit of those
Who have no shoes, no food, no home or maybe even clothes
You work it out, you give it out, though you don't get a prize
Although it's true through this kind act, you'll find it purifies
If you are kind and show this through the mercy of your heart
You'll give away a set amount, perhaps a whole tenth part
Of your time, your money, all that's yours, this idea will demand
By giving of yourself for others – through practising Dasvandh
For Hindus, Buddhists, Jains too Daana is charity
Detach yourself from wealth's embrace and you'll find clarity
If you're a Jew there's Tzedakah where giving can begin
With little coins dropped often in a simple pushke tin
It's fair to say that all the faiths and those nice Humanists too
Care for all and share with all, for that is all our due
To give, to serve, without the need to ask, or beg or plea
Helping those who share our world – in shared humanity
Give when you can and what you can to anyone in need
No need for a rhyme: Just do it.

[iii] Pronounced 'aga*pay*'
[iv] Another word for money

Charity: giving and doing

It would be hard to find any religious or cultural group which did not have very clear teachings on helping others. Altruism is recognised by psychologists as when we do something for others with no obvious benefit to ourselves – even if there is some cost to ourselves. It seems to be a very human quality. Of course, psychologists also suggest that we are more likely to help those closest to us and with whom we identify, but they also point out that although we are less likely to help strangers, we are still a pretty charitable species. The Talmud of Judaism[72] suggests that some forms of charity are more 'worthy' than others: all are good – but the least worthy is 'giving grudgingly' and the most worthy is 'giving in a way which enables the person to take control of his/her own situation'.

Charity can take a variety of shapes and forms: in relation to individuals it can either be giving or doing (or both, of course!). This might mean giving money, or donating something directly to those in need. It might also be giving to others indirectly, through donating to a charitable organisation or group which then uses what you have given to support others in some way. Charity can also be giving your time and your talents – again this might be very direct, in supporting people in need (doing someone's shopping or some other very practical service) or indirect – in giving your time and skills to some organisation or group which works for those in need. In fact, you can even give to charity without doing anything much at all (!), for example, having a charity credit card means that every time you spend on the card, money is donated to charity – even some websites donate money to charity every time you visit them. There are many ways to give to charity, some of which cost nothing in terms of money and even if they cost your time, perhaps you get more back out of it than you give. Certainly, many people who donate their time to charity work find the personal rewards far greater than the personal costs.

Why give to charity?

Whether it's money, time or something else entirely there are many reasons why people give to charity:

- **Religious obligation** Many religions require that followers give to charity. Sometimes this is a very formal arrangement and at other times it is very private and personal. Some religions consider that giving to charity earns you some kind of 'merit' – like good kamma or favour in the eyes of God. Others simply suggest that it is the right thing to do to show your gratitude for all that you have (which they may consider to have been granted by a divine being, for example).
- **Moral obligation** Many non-religious groups and philosophical perspectives suggest that giving to charity is a sensible human action which is just a natural part of being human, while others might also or alternatively take the view that it benefits us all in the end through creating a fairer, more caring society.

- **Identification with a cause** Some give to charity because they identify with a particular cause – for example, someone who has had a member of the family suffer from cancer might be more likely to donate to a cancer charity. Others may donate to a charity which 'strikes a chord' with them – for example, if they love animals they might donate to an animal charity.
- **To achieve a sense of satisfaction** Some might donate to or work for a charity because it makes them feel good about themselves – it makes them feel they are doing something worthwhile and is personally very rewarding.

There are probably many more reasons why people donate to or give their time and energy to charity – and it probably doesn't really matter why people give to charity as long as they do.

Charity: some moral issues

Some argue that while giving to charity in time or money seems like a good thing to do always and everywhere, it is not without its moral concerns.

- **'Learned helplessness'** Some argue that if charity is too easily available then people might come to depend on it too much – this might make them less likely to find their own way out of poverty, for example, and end up causing problems rather than creating solutions.
- **Which charities?** Some argue that there is a 'hierarchy' of charities which we should support – for example, some say that it is more important to support charities which alleviate human suffering rather than animal suffering. Others say we should support 'home' charities before charities where the benefits are gained abroad. Also, some believe that we should support our own cultures and groups before those of others.
- **How much goes to charity?** There can also be issues here about how much a charitable organisation should spend on its own administration and business and what percentage of the money donated to it should go to those who need it. Some argue that not all charities are equal in this respect and that some spend too much on their own organisation and not enough goes to those the charities are run for. Some charities respond by saying that without investing money they cannot continue to attract giving – so it is necessary. Besides, charities generally publish all their accounts so you can find out how the money you donate is used.
- **How much to give?** Some argue that giving a little is enough (and better than nothing, of course) while others argue that we should give away most of what we have to those in need. There is sometimes disagreement within religions about this too – with some groups arguing that we should all live simple lives and give most of what we have away, while others say that there is nothing wrong with being wealthy and giving only part of our wealth away.
- **'Charity pressure'** Recently there have been some high-profile news reports about people being upset or harmed in some way by charities using overly aggressive tactics in order to get people to donate. While most charities do have to advertise and seek support, perhaps there should be some rules about how aggressively they do this.
- **Letting authorities 'off the hook'** One concern some have about charity is the possibility that it might lead to authorities not carrying out their duties, but leaving it to charities instead. Whether it is buying materials for schools, hospital equipment or foreign aid, some worry that if charity provision is too good, then authorities might ease back on their responsibilities and wait for charities to fill the gap. Of course, some argue that charity work is necessary to fill gaps which would be there anyway – though others worry that charity might be part of the problem and not the solution in this case.

Talk Point

Do you think charities let authorities 'off the hook'?

International aid

It is important to remember that charity organisations and world governments give aid and support where needed. There are very different types of aid given and some of this aid will come from charities while some of it might come directly from governments – particularly those of wealthier countries.

Types of international aid

Again, aid can be direct or indirect – targeting specific needs, or supporting countries towards dealing with their own need.

Direct aid

Emergency relief

Organisations and world governments often give out direct aid in response to emergency situations. This could be natural disasters or in response to conflict and unrest. Aid such as this is often very specific and very short-term. It is designed to address a specific difficulty and may end when the emergency has passed. Aid in this form could be food, shelter, clothing, medicines or even expertise such as doctors and nurses, or emergency crews such as rescue services. Organisations such as *Medecins sans Frontieres*, the International Red Cross and Red Crescent and others may give this type of aid – as might organisations such as Oxfam. In some instances, governments have given armaments to countries (or groups within countries) to support them in fighting in conflicts/wars.

Non-emergency interventions

Similar types of aid might be given by organisations and world governments as a matter of course rather than in response to any emergency situation. The purpose of this aid is also to target direct need, but it has a longer-term quality. This kind of aid deals with ongoing need and often has the aim of supporting countries and communities to be able to be self-reliant at some point after the initial support. Again, this can be in the form of food, resources, expertise, medicines and so on. In this kind of aid, world governments may also give armaments to countries or groups within countries to support them in ongoing conflict.

Some issues with direct aid

Some of the issues here are the same as the issues about giving to charity – though on a bigger scale.

- Perhaps giving aid in any form reduces a country's determination and/or ability to solve its own problems – and simply makes it dependent on other countries (which perhaps those countries don't mind for some reason). Perhaps authorities in some countries might feel they are 'off the hook' if aid is coming from wealthier nations.
- How should world governments decide which countries/emergencies/groups get aid and which do not? Also, how much should be given and in what form?

- Should world governments look after people in their own country first? Every country in the world has poverty – and the majority have very serious poverty within their own borders. Should they sort that out before giving money, resources, expertise and so on to other nations?
- Is it possible that some aid is a case of 'give with one hand and take away with the other'? Some argue that rich nations should not be giving aid, they should be supporting countries to remove their burdens so they don't need aid at all – perhaps rich countries should forget all about the debt of poorer countries as this would be more effective in helping them deal with their own problems than any amount of aid.
- Should armaments ever be given as aid? Some world governments support this because they argue that instability in one area of the world might lead to instability spreading elsewhere – also, they might argue that there's no point in giving other kinds of aid if there is so much conflict that the aid never gets to those it is intended for.

Talk Point

Should world governments look after their own population before helping other countries?

With all of these issues, some argue that while there are concerns with giving aid and especially perhaps some kinds of aid, it is still preferable to not giving aid at all. For others giving direct aid like this has its place, but is of less value than longer-term indirect aid.

Indirect aid

Indirect aid is designed to support a country towards becoming more self-reliant in the long term. Aid like this might be in the form of:

- **Financial incentives** for industries to locate in poorer countries – such as tax benefits, guaranteed markets, etc.
- **Support for a country's infrastructure** – through programmes supporting, for example, capital investment, building programmes, the training of key workers, etc.
- **Support for a country in developing its own infrastructure** – such as education, health care and welfare programmes.
- **'Debt-waiver' schemes** – such as extending periods of debt repayment, reducing debt burdens and perhaps even cancelling debt entirely.

Tied aid

One major concern that some have with these kinds of aid is that they are often considered to be *'tied aid'*. This means that the aid comes at a price to the country receiving the aid. Some have described this as aid with 'strings attached' – this means the country receiving the aid has to agree to a range of conditions. In particular, some aid is linked to *structural adjustment programmes*. These are sets of regulations which countries receiving aid must agree to as a condition of receiving the aid. The stated purpose of these is to *'achieve long-term or accelerated growth in poorer countries by restructuring the economy and reducing government intervention'*[73]. This could involve anything from currency devaluation, reduction of public spending and reduced government intervention through privatisation.

Those who support tied aid might argue that any aid should come with conditions – countries receiving aid have a responsibility to put the aid to good use and conditions attached to aid makes this more likely. However, opponents of tied aid argue that it simply keeps poor countries dependent upon wealthy ones, and that structural adjustment policies cause particular harm to receiving countries' social and welfare programmes. In turn, this can continue to harm economic growth because a country where there is poor health or poor education is going to have difficulty in taking control over its own circumstances and lifting itself out of poverty.

Some religious and philosophical perspectives

Christianity

For Christians, support for those in need is a key aspect of their faith. The Bible is filled with teachings about caring for others, both in practical ways and in financial matters. There are suggestions in the Old Testament about giving to charity according to certain rules and formulae. However, Jesus is clear that his followers should not be tied to such rules, but give freely and cheerfully. Charity is a duty, but not a duty which should be considered a burden. If aid is considered an act of charity then obviously Christians would support it, but charity should allow the receiver to retain their dignity and avoid making the receiver dependent on charity – therefore any aid should reflect this.

The Church of Scotland

The Church of Scotland takes the view that Christian life should be one of selflessness and sacrifice – two qualities modelled by Jesus throughout his life. When we give to charity, or support aid, we act in a selfless way and we also make sacrifices because giving our time and money obviously means we are not using those for ourselves. Jesus continually stresses the importance of caring for the poor – and in doing so with no thought of reward for yourself. The Church of Scotland would support a range of aid programmes, but would be unlikely to support armaments as aid. The Church would want to ensure that those receiving aid did not lose any dignity through doing so and that the aid ultimately helped them to become self-reliant.

The Roman Catholic Church

'The works of mercy are charitable actions by which we come to the aid of our neighbour in his spiritual and bodily necessities. Instructing, advising, consoling, comforting are spiritual works of mercy, as are forgiving and bearing wrongs patiently. The corporal works of mercy consist especially in feeding the hungry, sheltering the homeless, clothing the naked, visiting the sick and imprisoned, and burying the dead. Among all these, giving alms to the poor is one of the chief witnesses to fraternal charity: it is also a work of justice pleasing to God.' (2443) Here the Catechism makes clear that a Catholic's responsibility is to support both the spiritual and physical welfare of others and it stresses the importance of charity. This would apply to individual acts of charity as well as to international aid. Like the Church of Scotland, the Roman Catholic Church would want to preserve the dignity of those receiving aid and help them towards self-reliance. The Church would be unlikely to support aid in the form of armaments.

Are physical and spiritual support equally important?

Buddhism

The organisation Buddhist Global Relief states: *'Bearing in mind the Buddha's statements that "hunger is the worst kind of illness" and "the gift of food is the gift of life", we sponsor projects that promote hunger relief for poor communities around the world. We pursue our mission by:*

- *providing direct food aid to people afflicted by hunger and malnutrition*
- *helping develop better long-term methods of sustainable food production and management appropriate to the cultures and traditions of the beneficiaries*
- *promoting the education of girls and women, so essential in the struggle against poverty and malnutrition*
- *giving women an opportunity to start right livelihood projects to support their families.*

We also seek to raise awareness of global hunger and advocate for an international food system that exemplifies social justice and conduces to ecological sustainability.' [74] Buddhist teaching would support charity and aid for those in need. Buddhists too would be unlikely to support armaments as aid, since Buddhists are generally committed to non-violence.

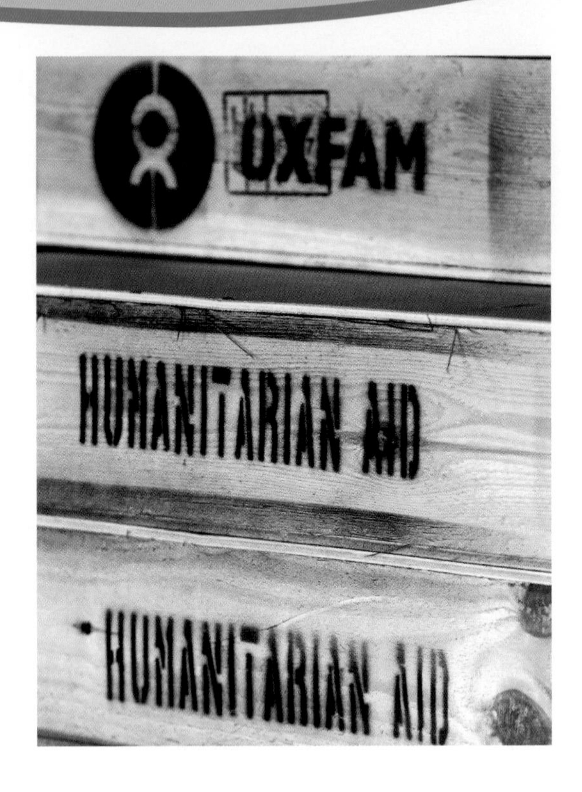

Humanism

The British Humanist Association website responds to questions about 'why there are no humanist charities' by saying: *'when there are so many excellent, non-religious, inclusive charities we generally see no need to set up our own. Most humanists prefer to work for good causes with others (of all faiths and none) and to donate time or money to charities that do not discriminate on grounds of religion (or non-religion) or promote one particular worldview.'* [75] So for Humanists, charity is obviously the right thing to do and again, if this comes in the form of international aid of some type or another, then that is equally acceptable. As for charity in the form of armaments there could potentially be different views across Humanists about this because of different views about how well or poorly this might help those in need to address their situation. Humanist Society Scotland takes a different view. It regards itself as a charity which has a responsibility to protect the rights and interests of Humanists in Scotland and abroad – it will work with other organisations and individuals to achieve this. It also supports a range of international campaigns and fundraising appeals.

Utilitarianism

For a Utilitarian, charity is a balance between sacrifice and benefit. Clearly a world where the majority were in need while the minority were affluent would not be right and so some redistribution of wealth to address this would make sense. As you read in the last chapter, Peter Singer commented that letting the poor suffer is, in his view, the moral equivalent of murder. So obviously any way you can reduce such suffering makes sense – whether that is through charitable action or through international aid. Utilitarians might also have different views about armaments as aid. Armaments could lead to those in need defending themselves and so lead to their country's economic growth but they could of course simply make a situation worse – working out the costs and benefits in this case would be important for a Utilitarian.

Personal Reflection

* *Do you think charity is a duty or a choice?*
* *How much should individuals and governments give to charity?*
* *How should a government decide what aid to give and to which countries?*

Active learning

Check your understanding

1 What is altruism and how does this link to charity and aid?
2 Describe two reasons why people might give to charity.
3 Explain two possible moral issues linked to giving to charity and explain your views on both.
4 Explain the difference between direct and indirect aid.
5 Describe one possible issue with direct aid.
6 What is meant by tied aid and why would some argue that aid should/should not be 'tied'?
7 In what ways are the ideas of selflessness and sacrifice linked to charity/aid?
8 How might Christians respond to the idea of giving armaments as aid?
9 What are the aims of Buddhist Global Relief and how do they link to Buddhist teachings?
10 How do Humanists answer the question about why there are no 'Humanist charities' (and is this true)?

Investigate

1 Choose one charity which is linked to a religion and one which is not. Visit both their websites and note similarities and differences linked to their purpose, their principles and their actions. You could create a table showing similarities and differences.
2 At any one time there are likely to be, sadly, emergency relief aid activities going on. Find out which emergencies are currently being responded to, by whom and in what way. Perhaps you could use what you learn to carry out an activity in support of this in your school.
3 Some of the ways of giving aid to countries through financial schemes can be quite complex. Carry out some research into this (perhaps in collaboration with your business education department) and prepare a simplified summary leaflet about the different ways in which this takes place.
4 Read Matthew 25:34–46 in the Christian Bible. For each of the categories there find out which charities support this aspect of need and also how world governments support this. This could be done in the form of a series of posters: 'I was ...'

Analyse and Evaluate

1 Have a debate in class: 'This house believes that giving armaments as aid is a sensible solution to real problems.'
2 How far are religious groups agreed with non-religious perspectives on the importance of charity and aid?
3 Explain your own views on the idea that 'charity begins at home'.

Apply

There are many examples of ways in which individuals and groups in Scotland can contribute to international aid projects. As a class/school, choose one and run a series of information events/activities to support this aspect of aid. This might involve information evenings, resources and planning and running specific events.

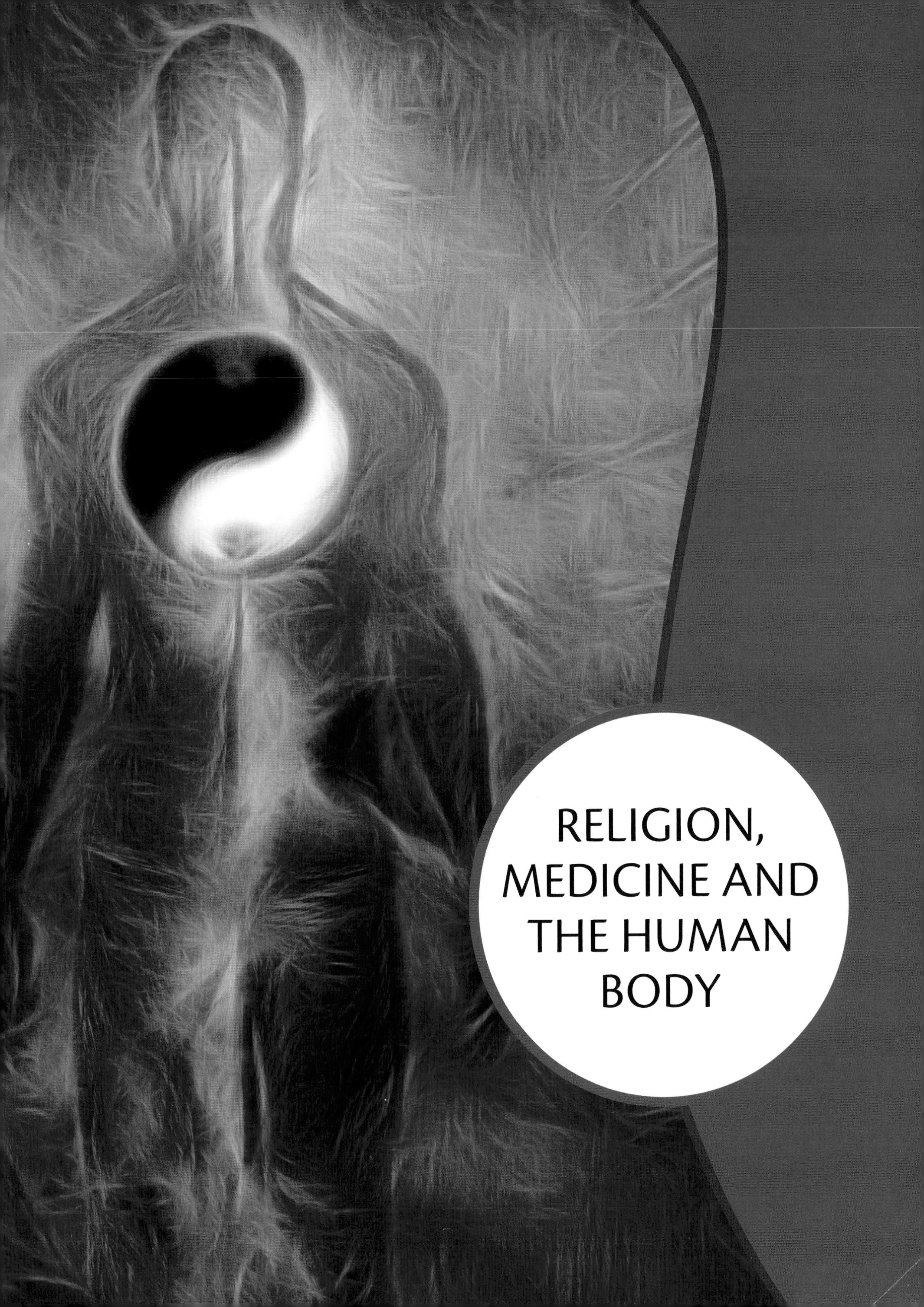
RELIGION, MEDICINE AND THE HUMAN BODY

17 Perspectives on life and death: sanctity of life; right to die

My name is Stephen. I am 62 and I have Alzheimer's. This is an illness of the brain which will gradually see me turn into a very different person. At the moment, I just forget things now and again – though my partner tells me that I am doing this more and more. Sometimes I notice and other times I don't – maybe I forget that I have forgotten! You have to laugh – and life has to go on. But there will come a point – and no one knows how soon this might happen – when my forgetting will become more serious – I may forget important things, like my son's name, or my own name. I may forget faces and look at those I have known all my life as if they are strangers. In fact, one day I may not even know who I am and may wander off and get myself very lost. I could become a danger to myself. Then I may start to lose control of even the simple things in life – dressing myself, tying my laces, feeding myself. However, I won't let it get too far because my partner and I have a clear agreement. There will come a day when I will ask her to help me die – and she will do so. There will be risks for her, of course, but that's what you do for the person you love. I'd do the same for her. I've never really believed in any kind of God and now I'm not likely to start believing. This life is mine. It belongs to no one but me. I have decided how it should be lived for these past 62 years and I will decide how, when and where it ends.

My name is Jen. I am 62 and I have cancer. It will take my life sometime soon. It is often uncomfortable and the medical treatments they give me are not pleasant at all. I've lost my hair and I'm often very sick. I'm in and out of hospital all the time. I know all of my doctors quite well now – we'd probably be best friends if the circumstances were different – but it's not exactly the kind of relationship where you laugh all the time with each other. It's a bit too serious for that. Mind you, it would be hard to believe, but you can see the sunny side of things sometimes, and yes, you can have a joke now and again. But I will fight and fight and do my best to defeat this – but there may come a point when I will know that it has won and I have lost. What will I do then? Nothing. I'll let nature take its course. Life is precious – yes even this quality of life is precious. If I can live five minutes more I will and I will not cut it short for anything. Yes, I do believe in God and I have had my moments when I have been angry with him about this. But he knows what he's doing. For me, life is a gift – and you don't give a gift back to the giver. You treasure it, you cherish it and you enjoy it as long as you can. It's my life, yes, but it comes from God and it will be returned to him – when he chooses it and not before.

Talk Point

Who does human life 'belong' to?

What is 'life' and what is 'death'?

Now this may seem very obvious, but is it? Definitions of death have changed over time – for example, the introduction of ways to measure brain activity changed death from being lack of a heartbeat to lack of brain activity. However, even when people have brain activity, they can still be considered to be 'brain stem dead' – although their heart might still beat, they may breathe independently and so on. Also, medical science now has ways to keep our vital physical functions going which it did not in the past – so someone who would have been considered dead in the past can now be kept 'artificially alive'. Some people also argue that death is not just a physical state – it's a psychological one too. There can be certain conditions where a person might be considered 'dead' even though all their physical life functions are intact. For example, some people with very advanced dementia might be considered by others as no longer the person they were – is this the same as saying the person they once were is now dead? It's not as straightforward as it seems, perhaps. It is also important to remember that for many religious and philosophical viewpoints, the possibilities for prolonging life today have not been around for most of these viewpoints' history – and so they may not have explicit views on many of these issues.

Talk Point

If you lost all of your memories and could form no new ones, would you still be you?

The 'right to die' argument

Throughout your life you make a whole range of choices. You choose what to wear, how to look, what to eat, who your friends are, where you live – and so on: life is full of choices. Some people believe that in the same way that we each have the right to make choices about how we live our lives, we should also have the right to make choices about how, when and where we die. Those who support the right to die argue that each person's life is theirs to do with as they please. It is therefore their choice how, when and where they want to die. In many cases, those supporting the right to die link their arguments to quality of life arguments. These are arguments which state that when a person's life is judged (by them) to no longer be of the quality they want it to be, then they should have the right to end it without any negative consequences for anyone supporting them in this in any way. Right to die arguments are most often associated with terminal illness and changes in quality of life associated with terminal illness. However, they do not need to be linked in this way – some supporters of the right to die argue that people should have the choice about the time, place and method of their death according to their own judgements about the quality of their life. In addition to this, supporters of the right to die argue that people should be assisted in the process so as to make it as painless as possible. This would involve medical staff, perhaps, or others with the necessary expertise – or even others who can simply support the process. At the moment in the UK this is not legal and anyone assisting someone to bring their life to an end could face prosecution – even if their motivation for helping them to die was a compassionate one and something the person they assist to die clearly wanted.

There have been a number of attempts to get the law changed in Scotland so that people can choose when, where and how they want to die. However, the Scottish Parliament has consistently voted against changing the law.

So, why would someone argue that we should have the right to die?

- **Life is only life when it is of sufficient quality** The 'quality of life' argument suggests that when someone judges their life no longer has the quality they want it to have, they should have the right to die.
- **To escape physical pain and suffering associated with illness** Some argue that there sometimes comes a point where medical science can no longer protect us from the physical pain and suffering associated with illness. Pain-killing medication is effective, but some argue that it has its limits – and so to deal with this people should have the right to end their life.
- **To escape psychological pain and suffering associated with illness** Some argue that while the physical pain can be managed, the psychological trauma associated with severe illness is harder to treat – and so the right to die should be an option.
- **To respond to a reduction in quality of life** This can mean many different things to different people – but it really boils down to the point when a person no longer feels their life is worth living.
- **To deal with a physical or mental 'decline' before it's 'too late'** Some argue that the progressive nature of some illnesses is so serious that there may come a point when an individual can no longer make their own choices. Being able to clearly state that you wish to end your life then would have to be made while you were able to rationally make that choice. In some countries this can be in the form of a 'living will' where a person requests to be helped to die (or allowed to die) at some point in the future.
- **To have control over this aspect of your life for yourself** Some simply argue that the right to die should be yours, and that you don't really need a reason other than that it is your choice. They might say that it does not need to be linked to illness or decline – instead it is just about a point in your life where you no longer want to live – and that should be your choice. For example, imagine you are an artist – your whole life has been about art. Suddenly, you begin to lose your sight – everything that you live for might now be difficult or impossible for you. Supporters of the right to die could argue that such a person should have the right to choose to end their life in such circumstances. In fact, some might go further and simply argue that there doesn't need to be any external cause for your choice – it should just be your choice – and you don't need to give anyone any reason for it.
- **The 'dignity in death' argument** Some argue that the right to die provides for greater 'dignity in death' for individuals because they can control when, where and how their life ends.

The right to die argument is often associated most closely with non-religious viewpoints. However, it is important to remember that many religious people would also support a right to die approach – most often only in specific circumstances, but not automatically.

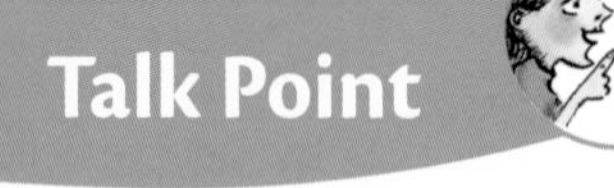

Talk Point

What criticisms of the right to die argument might there be?

Criticisms of the 'right to die' argument

You will think about criticisms of the right to die argument in more detail throughout this chapter, but for the moment, here are some general criticisms:

- **Judging 'quality of life'** Some argue that because 'quality of life' is difficult to judge, we cannot use it as a justification for the right to die. Quality means different things to different people, so making one law that fits all is not possible in relation to this because there are many different definitions of 'quality'.
- **The 'right to die' is different** Although we have rights over most aspects of our lives, we don't have rights over everything. Laws exist to protect us from others and sometimes perhaps from ourselves. Having firm laws about the right to die provides a range of protections for everyone involved.

- **We do not 'own' our lives** This argument generally comes from religious people and groups. Their view is that life is a gift from a divine being, or is so precious that it should never be brought to an end before it comes to its natural end.
- **Accepting the 'right to die' is the start of a 'slippery slope'** This argument suggests that if we accept the right to die in certain conditions, then it might lead to it being put into practice (or suggested) in other conditions. This would be dangerous because it might lead to bringing lives to an end when in fact no one really wanted them to be brought to an end. In fact, it could be abused by those who want to gain out of it in some way.
- **The 'right to die' puts pressure on suffering individuals** This argument suggests that if the right to die is accepted, then individuals might feel pressurised to end their lives (for example, so they are not 'a burden' to others). Also, perhaps, people could be pressurised by others who hope to gain from their death. As well as this, people who are experiencing extreme pain and suffering may not be in the right frame of mind to make a sensible decision about their right to die – or even able to make such a decision.
- **The 'right to die' puts pressure on those around the suffering person** Medical staff, relatives, friends, all sorts of people might feel under pressure to bring someone's life to an end if it is a legal option.
- **The 'right to die' is an easy way out of our responsibility to care for others** This argument takes the view that there are good alternatives to bringing life to an end. Perhaps having the 'easy option' of the right to die might make society less interested in finding ways to alleviate pain and suffering.
- **'Dignity' has many meanings** To argue that the right to die provides greater 'dignity in death' is wrong – because 'dignity' has a range of meanings and to say that dignity only comes with having the right to die is wrong.

Talk Point

Is having the 'right to die' an 'easy way out' of pain and suffering?

The 'sanctity of life' argument

This is arguably the opposite of the right to die argument, because it takes the view that life is so sacred and special that we should hold on to it for as long as we can – no matter what. Most often, the sanctity of life argument is supported by people because of their religious belief. In the monotheistic religions such as Christianity, Judaism and Islam, the view is often taken that because life is a gift from God, only he has the right to take it – and will do so when he chooses to. In religions such as Buddhism and Hinduism, some argue that ending life before it naturally ends is an act which is likely to produce negative kamma and so should be avoided. It is important to remember, however, that within and between religions there are many different views about how strictly the sanctity of life argument is observed – with some arguing that it is never right to end life before it naturally ends and others arguing that it needs to be decided on a more individual basis. So some regard the sanctity of life argument as absolute – never able to be challenged – and others are more flexible about it. It is also important to point out that it's not only religious people who might support the sanctity of life argument; non-religious people too might argue that life is so precious (though not 'sacred') that we should never bring it to an end artificially.

Criticisms of the 'sanctity of life' argument

- **Life belongs to the person who lives it** This generally comes from those who are not religious. Their argument is simple – no divine being 'owns' our lives – we do. This is often based on the view that there is no such thing as divine being anyway – or if there is, what kind of being would permit such pain and suffering, provide a safe medical 'way out' of it and then not permit us to use this? However, some religious people might support this view too – arguing that while God gives life, we are free to choose how to live it and therefore, when it should come to an end.
- **There's no 'slippery slope'** This argument suggests that allowing the right to die in some circumstances will not automatically lead to it in all circumstances.
- **No quality of life** No matter what, life should have a certain quality. Once that quality is gone, people should have the right to no longer live.
- **The 'right to die' removes 'pressure'** Rather than be a burden to the suffering and those around them, the right to die is in fact the opposite. It removes pressure from individuals in living lives they no longer want to live and/or supporting those who no longer have any quality of life. For medical staff, too, it allows for the option of bringing pain and suffering to a controlled and quick end. Rather than this being medical staff 'giving up' it is, in fact, a final act of compassion.

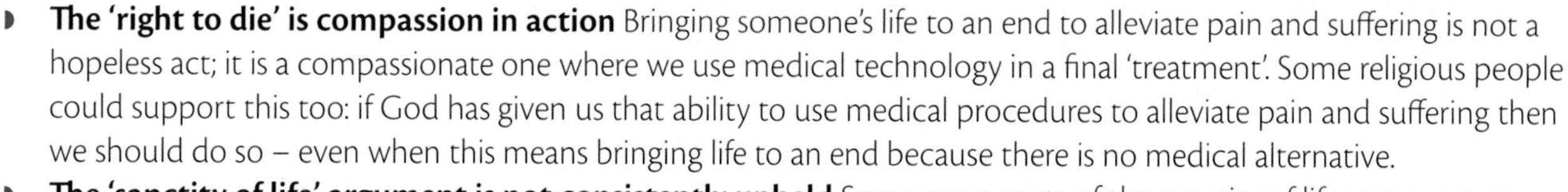

- **The 'right to die' is compassion in action** Bringing someone's life to an end to alleviate pain and suffering is not a hopeless act; it is a compassionate one where we use medical technology in a final 'treatment'. Some religious people could support this too: if God has given us that ability to use medical procedures to alleviate pain and suffering then we should do so – even when this means bringing life to an end because there is no medical alternative.
- **The 'sanctity of life' argument is not consistently upheld** Some opponents of the sanctity of life argument say that although some religious people talk about life being sacred, they might also allow life to be taken in certain circumstances. For example, some religious people support capital punishment and some support the taking of life during war. Therefore, religious people cannot argue that life is sacred because they allow it to be taken in certain circumstances – and so perhaps in circumstances where people want to die they should be permitted to do so.

Some religious and philosophical perspectives

Christianity

Within Christianity, the picture in relation to sanctity of life/right to die is very complex. Some Christians support the right to die argument completely and others oppose it completely – and there are a range of positions in between. In general, the argument links to how far a Christian accepts that life is so sacred that it must never be ended artificially. Some think that only God should choose when it should end, and others think that humans have been given both free will by God and the ability to alleviate pain and suffering – so if this is only possible to do through bringing life to an end, then it should be an available option. Some argue that because many Christians accept the idea of God 'working through' human agents, we should accept that human agents could act on God's behalf to end pain and suffering where possible.

The Church of Scotland

'We are made in God's image; therefore all human life, irrespective of an individual's ability or gifts is precious and holy.'[76] The Church of Scotland supports the sanctity of life argument because it sees all humans as made in the image of God. It has also stated: *'The Church of Scotland has consistently opposed any legislation which would allow the*

deliberate ending of a human life.' In this report from 2010[77] which responded to the proposed End of Life Assistance (Scotland) Bill (which the Scottish Parliament rejected), the Church added that: dignity means different things to different people; no one is truly 'autonomous'; the bill provided no clear indications of who might bring life to an end; there were insufficient protections in the bill to prohibit abuse and so on. It is important to point out that the Church's argument in this case relates to the deliberate ending of life – we will explore the Church's view on 'allowing death rather than causing death' in the next chapter.

The Roman Catholic Church

The Catechism states: *'Every human life, from the moment of conception until death, is sacred because the human person has been willed for its own sake in the image and likeness of the living and holy God.'* (2319) It adds: *'Intentional euthanasia, whatever its forms or motives, is murder. It is gravely contradictory to the dignity of the human person and to the respect due to the living God, his creator.'* (2324) The Church therefore rejects the right to die argument in pretty clear terms. Life is a gift from God and is his to do with as he sees fit. Catholic teaching on 'letting die' is a little different and we will explore this more fully in the next chapter. However, causing death or having any right to die is rejected by the Church.

Buddhism

As in most religions, there are a variety of views about sanctity of life/right to die in Buddhism. On the one hand, some traditions within Buddhism believe that everyone has a 'Buddha nature' – the potential to become a Buddha – and so for some, this potential should be preserved where possible – so not bringing anything's life to an end before it happens naturally. This is similar to, but not exactly the same as, thinking that life has a 'sacred' quality. On the other hand, Buddhists also believe that everyone is free to choose their own path in life, so perhaps that means choosing their death too. However, this is complicated by the fact that Buddhism rejects killing – which could include killing yourself or allowing yourself to be killed. Buddhism also stresses the importance of compassion in life – and so some Buddhists might support the right to die if they considered it to be the most compassionate response to pain and suffering. In an analysis of Buddhist views on suicide, Buddhist scholar Damien Keown concludes: *'A person who opts for death believing it to be a solution to suffering has fundamentally misunderstood the First Noble Truth. The First Noble Truth teaches that death is the problem not the solution.'*[78] Keown goes on to say that by embracing death a person has embraced Maara (the demon who tempted Buddha). This is, of course, only one interpretation of Buddhist teaching on the right to die.

Humanism

Humanists do believe that life is very precious – because it is the only life we have. However, they would reject completely any 'sacredness' associated with life since they do not believe in a God. Humanists have been at the forefront of supporting the right to die argument because they see the right to die as a fundamental human right which allows us to take control of this aspect of our lives and ensure a dignified end to our lives – especially in situations where a person is terminally ill or experiencing a life-shortening condition. Humanists do, however, argue that there need to be sufficient safeguards in place to ensure that no one is under any pressure to take up the option of the right to die and that it cannot be abused in any way. Humanist Society Scotland supported the End of Life Assistance (Scotland) Bill with a dedicated website named 'My life, my death, my choice'. This website makes it clear that the right to die should have sufficient safeguards in place but that while medical care for the terminally ill has improved greatly: *'Most health professionals recognise that a very small number of patients do not get satisfactory relief of their distress, be that physical, psychological or spiritual and these are the people for whom assisted suicide is being proposed.'* [79] Humanists argue that the right to die is a right we should all have.

Utilitarianism

'[The sanctity of life argument] is still defended by bishops and conservative bioethicists who speak in reverent tones about the intrinsic value of all human life, irrespective of its nature or quality. But, like the new clothes worn by the emperor, these solemn phrases seem true and substantial only while we are intimidated into uncritically thinking that all human life has some special dignity or worth. Once challenged the traditional ethic crumbles'[80]. This comes from Utilitarian Peter Singer, who argues against the sanctity of life argument and proposes a quality of life argument. His view is that life must mean something to the person who lives it. Where this is no longer the case then bringing about the end of life is morally acceptable. Everyone has the right to die at a time, place and in a manner of their choosing. J. S. Mill also argued consistently that individuals (generally speaking) were best placed to look after their own interests and this should be respected. It seems therefore that Utilitarians would support a right to die argument. However, it is important to note that Utilitarians would also want there to be safeguards in place so that the right to die was not abused in any way since such abuses could lead to unhappiness.

Personal Reflection

- *What do you think about 'sanctity of life' and 'right to die' arguments?*
- *How far does anyone have the right to make decisions about this for themselves and others?*
- *What makes life worth living/not worth living?*

Active learning

Check your understanding

1. In what ways have definitions of death changed over time?
2. What difference do definitions of death make to the arguments in this chapter?
3. How is 'quality of life' linked to the 'right to die' argument?
4. Describe two reasons which a supporter of the 'right to die' might give in support of their view.
5. For one of these reasons, describe a criticism of this and explain your own view of the criticism.
6. Explain what is meant by the 'sanctity of life' argument.

7 Describe two criticisms of this argument.
8 How far are religious views agreed about the importance of the sanctity of life?
9 Do non-religious views support the 'right to die' argument without exception?
10 How far could a religious person support 'right to die' arguments?

Investigate

1 The 'right to die' varies around the world with some countries supporting this choice and others completely rejecting it. Carry out an online search and annotate a world map showing where in the world the 'right to die' seems to be morally acceptable.
2 Within Christianity, a number of biblical texts have been used to support the 'sanctity of life' argument. Find out which texts are used and how they are used to support the idea that life is sacred. You could display the texts you discover and write explanatory notes about how they support the view that life is sacred.
3 The 'right to die' (End of Life Assistance (Scotland) Bill) was pursued in the Scottish Parliament by the former MSP Margo MacDonald. Carry out your own research into the history of this and how the Scottish Parliament eventually rejected the proposed bill. You could create a short magazine/newspaper item about this.
4 In many religions, helping a person to physically and spiritually cope in the last few days and hours of life is considered very important. How do different religions approach this difficult time and what does this tell us about their beliefs about death?

Analyse and Evaluate

1 For each of the following statements, outline your own views and consider one possible criticism of your view:
   - Life is only worth living if it is of sufficient quality.
   - Giving people the right to die is a slippery slope to treating it all very casually.
   - Pain and suffering are part of being human.
   - We do not 'own' our lives.
   - It is important that people can 'die with dignity'.
   - There is a difference between killing and allowing to die.
2 Explain how a religious person might support 'right to die' arguments and how a non-religious person might support a form of the 'sanctity of life' argument.
3 'No one has the right to tell anyone how, when and where they die.' How far do you agree?

Apply

You are a religious person who believes that in certain circumstances – even though life is sacred – people should have the right to die. You have been invited by your religious group to give a talk outlining your views. Carry out your research and write a short speech. As a class, you could listen to one or more of these speeches and ask some questions of the speaker at the end.

18 Euthanasia and palliative care

What really surprised me about it was just how cheerful everyone was – and it wasn't a forced cheerfulness – it was genuine. People laughed and joked and some of the people in there have a really wicked sense of humour – well beyond their years! Yes, some were in a bit of pain and discomfort, but this was managed so well that it rarely got in the way of doing pretty normal things in life – suppose within reason, of course. There were no people wandering around looking glum – and no doctors and nurses wandering about in cold stiff uniforms – just a group of contented people doing their job with obvious love and care. Everyone knew what the place was for and why people were there – no one hid from that or tried to pretend it was something it wasn't. I dare say people had their more difficult moments, but there was always someone there for them – to support them whatever need came their way. The place was beautifully decorated and – again – felt like a home, not some kind of medical institution. There were items on the walls produced by those who were staying there themselves; there was colour, brightness. One wall had pictures of those who had passed through here – and passed on: you would have thought that this would be depressing, but it wasn't – it was life-affirming and positive and showed the value given to each and every person who has ever made use of the place. Even in their final days and moments, everything that can be done to celebrate life is done – and everyone is supported in every possible way right to the end – including their families and friends. What makes it even more special, I think, is that this is a hospice for children – children with life-shortening conditions. The children here will not recover physically, but their last months and days will be as positive as they can possibly be. These children are cared for and supported through what must be very difficult times – and their parents and brothers and sisters are too. There is no sense of misery about this place – in fact, though it might sound strange – it is a place of hope. What I saw there reminded me of the challenges that life can often present to some, but also how the human spirit – whatever you think that means – can rise above it all and clearly show what humans can do rather than what they can't. It sounds really daft, I know, but when you think about all the terrible things that go on in the world, a visit to this hospice for children can remind you of the good that people can do. From the moment of their arrival to their final departure, someone walks with each child in here each precious moment …

Palliative care

Palliative care means the care given to people who are experiencing life-shortening conditions. This term covers what is also sometimes referred to as terminal illness – that is, any condition from which a person is not expected to recover – and is the care given to the person as they approach the end of life. The aim of palliative care is not to prolong life, but to support a dying person in the final stages of life.

Palliative care can take place in a number of different places. Sometimes it is in hospitals – especially if the person requires very specialised medical support or medical equipment. It can also be in care homes and hospices, which are special places designed to offer palliative care. Hospices may be linked to a range of different organisations – some are secular – and may be linked to charity groups, such as the Children's Hospice Association of Scotland (CHAS) in Kinross – and some are linked to specific religious belief groups such as St Margaret of Scotland's Hospice in Clydebank. According to the situation, palliative care may also take place in the person's home, with visiting specialists providing different kinds of support. Palliative care can involve a permanent stay in a specialised place, but it can also be in the form of respite care – which means that the person with the life-shortening condition can be looked after for shorter periods of time in order to give their primary caregivers a break from providing this support. Wherever it takes place, palliative care can have a number of components:

- **Pain relief** Often people with life-shortening conditions are in pain. They may be given different kinds of pain medication to enable them to be as physically pain-free as their condition allows. Such pain medication is administered and regulated by trained staff, though in some circumstances it may be administered by family members.
- **Other medical interventions** In life-shortening conditions, other medical interventions may take place. These are generally not treatments towards recovery, since recovery is not expected, but have the purpose of making the person with the condition more comfortable in some way or other, or alleviating aspects of their life-shortening condition even although they cannot reverse it.
- **Emotional and psychological support** Life-shortening conditions can affect people emotionally and psychologically in many different ways and different kinds of palliative care address this in different ways. This may involve counselling or other forms of emotional and psychological support according to the person's need and the kind of care being offered. This may simply be the creation of a positive environment in which the person can live out the final part of their life.
- **Spiritual support** Many places which offer palliative care also offer spiritual support – because they recognise that this set of life events has spiritual significance for some people. This support might be in hospitals with chaplains and others providing spiritual care, or it may be in hospices and involve visiting or permanent staff, depending on the kind of hospice it is.
- **Support for relatives** When a person has a life-shortening condition, this can have important implications for their family members. Sometimes palliative care extends to the family of the person with the life-shortening condition – supporting them in whatever ways might be appropriate.

For many, palliative care is a vital service at a very difficult time. It provides focused and skilled care to deal with specific situations and so is a final act of compassion for those with life-shortening conditions and those close to them.

Talk Point

What 'issues' do you think there might be with palliative care?

Palliative care: some possible issues

Some argue that effective palliative care is a mark of a society's concern for everyone, no matter what their circumstances and is a fundamental right which should come with our National Health Service in Scotland. However, although it is likely that everyone would support the availability of palliative care for those with life-shortening conditions, it is still possible that there can be issues around it:

- **The allocation of scarce health-care resources** Of course, everyone would want anyone who is ill or who has a life-shortening condition to receive the best possible care they can, but perhaps the cold hard facts of economics have to be taken into account too. Health-care resources are often scarce – the reasons for this can be very complex – and so they have to be allocated where they are most useful. Some might argue – as harsh as it may seem – that perhaps health-care resources should be allocated where there is a chance that they could help someone live, rather than support care in a situation where recovery is not possible. This may seem cruel, but some argue that this is the reality – health-care resources are not infinite and have to be allocated wisely – perhaps using them to care for the dying is not the right way to use them. Of course, others would respond that you cannot put a price on care for the dying and that our job as a society is to ensure that health-care resources are available for everyone – no matter what their need or their circumstances.
- **A 'social lottery'?** Some might argue that because palliative care isn't necessarily available to the same extent to everyone everywhere, some people might benefit more than others. Perhaps, too, those who are better off might be able to afford 'superior' private health care whereas those who are poorer may not be able to access it in the same way. Some might counter this by saying that at least in Scotland we have the NHS, which is free for all, and so, in principle, no one should be unable to access good palliative care. However, some argue that palliative care is not high on priority lists for medical resources and so may not attract the funding it requires and deserves.
- **A social duty not a charity** Some take the opposite view, arguing that palliative care is so vital that it should be a social responsibility taken on by authorities and not left to charities. However, again, governments might argue that the money available to them is not unlimited and that it should be allocated where it might do most good. Besides, it is surely better that charities take on this role than it is not provided at all because authorities may not be able to afford it.
- **An 'admission of defeat'?** Some might argue that palliative care is an admission that we have 'given up'. They might argue that treatment should go on for as long as possible with the aim of helping the person to recover and that we should never accept that an illness cannot be reversed. Opponents would counter this by saying that there are simply times when all the treatments have failed and there is no other option but palliative care – to continue to try to reverse an illness is a delusion and might actually make the person suffering the illness (and those close to them) suffer even more physically and/or psychologically.

Euthanasia

Some argue, however, that no matter how good palliative care is, it still cannot alleviate all pain and suffering and it still does not provide a person with sufficient 'dignity in death' (or in the process of dying). Besides, it might be argued that each person has the right to die in the place, time and manner of their choosing. You have already considered the arguments relating to the 'right to die'/'sanctity of life' and this section will delve a little more deeply into those, because although euthanasia would be supported by those who have a right to die stance, it can also be supported by those who support the sanctity of life argument according to the 'type' of euthanasia we are considering.

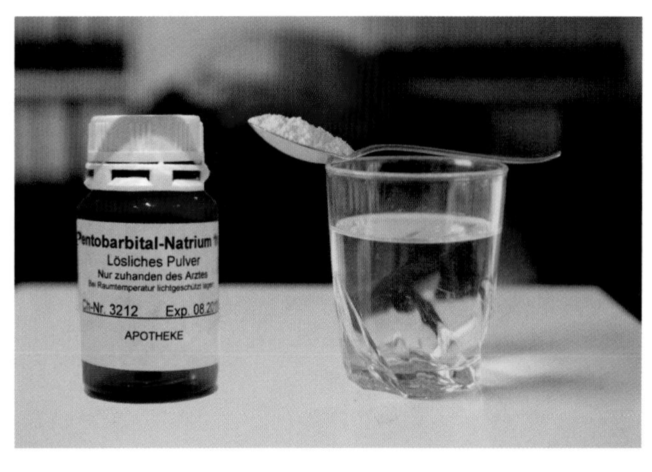

Non-voluntary euthanasia is where a person's life is brought to an end in a situation where they cannot make the final decision for themselves. (NB: Some sources will also refer to this as involuntary euthanasia; however, you need to be aware that some sources include situations where death is brought about *against a person's wishes* under involuntary euthanasia, for example, in cases of capital punishment. Here we will use non-voluntary euthanasia because this indicates that you are not in a position to make a decision, but if you use involuntary euthanasia the SQA will probably not mind.) This inability to make the decision is known as *incapacity*. In Scotland, the Adults with Incapacity (Scotland) Act (2000) covers what happens when someone no longer has the capacity to make decisions about their treatment. No matter what the situation, the courts will try to work out what the person would have wanted done if they had capacity.

Voluntary euthanasia is where a person expresses a conscious decision to have their life ended on their behalf. This may be in the form of an 'advance directive'. It may also be expressed during an illness or long before as an expression of what the person would want to happen in certain circumstances. Voluntary euthanasia might be requested by a person experiencing or anticipating a terminal or life-shortening illness or in any other situation where they are experiencing (or anticipate experiencing) a reduction in what they consider to be quality of life.

Regardless of the form of euthanasia, here are two main methods of carrying out euthanasia:

- **Active euthanasia** This is where active measures are taken to bring someone's life to an end (*causing to die*). This might be through administering lethal medication to end life. Currently in Scotland this intentional bringing of someone's life to an end is illegal – no matter who has requested this (even if the patient did so before they were no longer able to express this desire) or what the situation is – and anyone involved in such an activity could be charged with murder or culpable homicide. Any decision about prosecution in this kind of situation would be taken by the Crown Office and Procurator Fiscal.
- **Passive euthanasia** This is where instead of actively causing death by doing something, death is allowed to take place through not doing something (*allowing to die*). It could mean, for example, the withdrawal of life-sustaining medication or the 'switching off' of life support technology. Some make the distinction between 'ordinary measures' to preserve life and 'extraordinary measures', arguing that not carrying out extraordinary measures which result in death is not the same as killing. It is also important to point out that definitions of 'treatment' can vary. Some may argue that treatment does not include basic life-sustaining processes such as hydration and nutrition while others argue that these could be considered as treatments. The principle of 'double effect' is also important here. This is where an action is taken which has one intention but can lead to two consequences. For example, withdrawing certain medications might not have the intention of bringing about death, but may do so. How far that was the intention will have a role in considering whether it was a moral act or not.

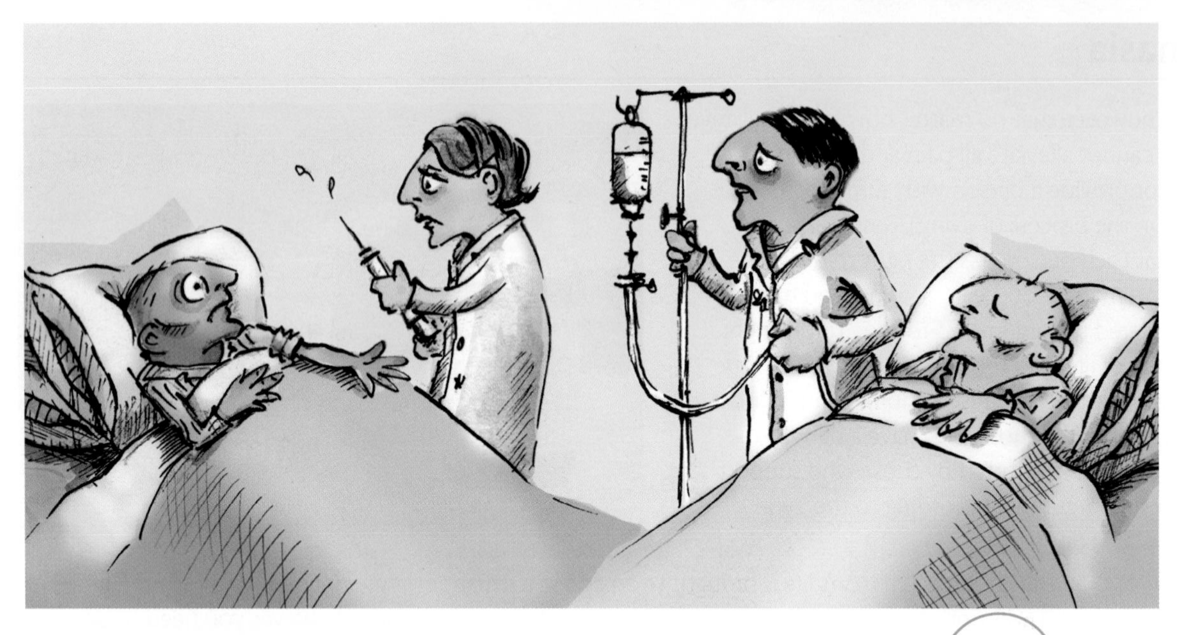

Talk Point

Do you think there is a difference between 'causing to die' and 'allowing to die'?

When might euthanasia be considered?

- **In a situation where it is agreed that the person has no hope of recovery and is judged to have no quality of life – or perhaps is not considered living in any meaningful sense**
  In Scotland, if medical staff consider that there is nothing to be gained for the patient in receiving any medical treatment, then they may withhold that treatment. If this is challenged in court, the court has to make a decision about what the person would have wanted in this situation – which is often difficult. The courts can also go against the wishes of the relatives if the court thinks that the patient would not have agreed with their choice about treatments. The law in Scotland, however, does not guarantee that withholding treatment will not result in prosecution.
- **When requested by the patient at a point before they were unable to make the request**
  In Scotland, adults have the right to refuse treatment of any kind – as long as they have the capacity to do so (such treatment could include anything from CPR through to basic needs such as food and water). In Scotland this is referred to as an 'advance directive' and in other countries as a 'living will'. This is when the patient states clearly that if they are in a state where they can no longer make decisions for themselves, medical staff can make the decision to withhold treatment on their behalf – even if that would lead to their death. However, in Scotland, advance directives are not legally binding – though it is claimed by some that in practice they would be taken into account by the courts in any legal proceedings.

Euthanasia: the moral issues

Euthanasia is a serious matter with many conflicting viewpoints held. Different countries around the world have very different laws about euthanasia. In some countries it is legal, in others not – although there are always very carefully worked out guidelines about it in places where it is available. (Although some would argue that these can never be careful enough.) What are the key arguments?

Arguments in support of euthanasia

- **It is a final act of kindness on behalf of someone unable to make their own decision** Whether active or passive, it is an act of kindness in bringing suffering or a life considered no longer worth living to a merciful end. For this reason it is sometimes referred to by supporters as 'mercy killing'. It is important to note that some supporters of euthanasia might support passive, but not active, euthanasia.
- **It is a final form of treatment** Some argue that it is the job of medical staff not to preserve life at all costs, but to manage pain and suffering. If all else has failed then perhaps euthanasia is a final way to ensure that pain and suffering comes to an end through medically controlled measures, whether active or passive. Organisations such as the British Medical Association provide very detailed guidance for medical staff about the circumstances around euthanasia.
- **It is a human right** Some argue that regardless of the situation, everyone has the right to choose how, when and where they die. In the case of euthanasia, this would be in the form of a legally binding 'advance directive' which could result in being allowed to die through withholding treatments. It could also be a request for an intervention to cause death.
- **It provides 'dignity in death'** Although an adult with capacity can refuse any treatment in Scotland, the situation is more complex where there is no capacity. Supporters of euthanasia might argue that having this as an option allows each individual to have a dignified end to their life.
- **If we accept 'allowing to die' why not accept 'causing to die'?** Supporters might argue that the laws and rules around euthanasia are currently too confusing: why is causing to die any more morally unacceptable than allowing to die? Both have the same intention and the same outcome, so both should be equally acceptable.
- **It means that scarce health-care resources can be directed where they are needed** Supporters argue that there can be situations where prolonging life is not a good use of scarce health-care resources. Perhaps the resources used to prolong life or maintain it where it is of little quality should be directed to situations where patients have a chance of recovery.

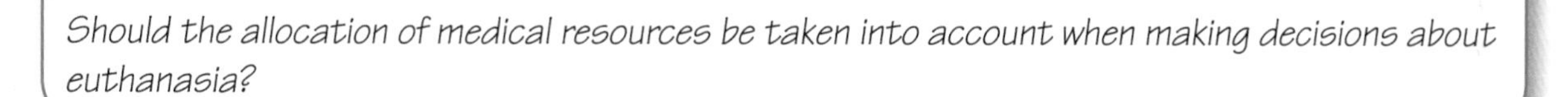

Talk Point

Should the allocation of medical resources be taken into account when making decisions about euthanasia?

Arguments opposing euthanasia

- **It is a final act of hopelessness, not kindness** Some argue that we should preserve life at all costs and that anything else is wrong. We have duty of care towards patients – no matter what their condition – and this duty involves preserving life: it is not anyone's job to judge what is and is not quality of life. Medical staff should preserve life, not end it through any means – no matter what the circumstances are.
- **It places unacceptable pressures on medical staff, the courts and those close to the patient** Making the final decision about ending a life (or allowing to die) is a serious matter which no one should have to be burdened with.
- **It could harm the relationship between patients and medical staff** Patients should be confident that medical staff are there to support them – not end their life.
- **It is not a human right** While people have rights over many things in life, they do not have the right over their own death – nor does anyone else.
- **The 'slippery slope' argument** If we accept non-voluntary euthanasia in some circumstances, what is to stop it being used in any circumstance? Perhaps especially where health-care resources are limited this could lead to euthanasia being carried out in 'borderline' cases – or simply where it is not justified in order to make medical resources available elsewhere. Also, it could lead to some very dubious decisions being reached about what is and is not 'quality of life'.

- **Euthanasia of any kind could be abused** There could be all sorts of reasons why treatments may be withheld or active measures taken to bring life to an end. This could be subject to all kinds of abuses – and if it were legal, then these abuses might be more likely to go unnoticed and unchallenged. What also might it do to patient/doctor relationships – could its availability lead to a possible lack of trust between the two?
- **Mistakes cannot be put right** The diagnosis that there can be 'nothing more done to preserve life' or that life is of 'no quality' might be wrong. There have been cases where people in persistent vegetative states have been written off as having no hope of recovery – and have then recovered (which obviously would not have happened if euthanasia had been an option). Also, how do we judge the quality of life of someone who is unable to communicate what quality of life they are currently experiencing?
- **The 'dignity in death' argument is wrong** Some argue that suggesting that a life brought to an end or allowing someone to die is somehow more dignified is simply wrong. They would propose that it can be equally 'dignified' to aim to preserve life where possible. They might also argue that a life brought to an end through euthanasia may not be any more dignified than any other death.
- **Is it really their choice?** When a person 'voluntarily chooses euthanasia' how do we really know how voluntary this is? Maybe they are under pressure in some way – perhaps they are not in their right mind (which might possibly be more likely if they are in the advanced stages of illness).

The debate about euthanasia may well continue for a long time to come – and no one can predict what changes might result. It is a complex moral issue because it is linked both to arguments about the 'sanctity of/quality of life', as well as how far we (or anyone else) have 'rights' over life and death. The most recent attempts to change the law in Scotland have been rejected by the Scottish Parliament (though none so far have called for active euthanasia to be legalised), and responses to euthanasia across the world's governments and legal systems can be very different.

Some religious and philosophical perspectives

Christianity

There are likely to be a wide range of views about euthanasia within Christianity and some important differences in thinking according to whether active or passive euthanasia is being considered. In general, Christians would wish to preserve life where possible since they believe it is a gift from God. However, many Christians would argue that this does not mean preserving life at all costs – and that there can be situations where allowing people to die is the compassionate and right thing to do. In general, Christians would oppose any intentional action which *brought about a person's death*, though many would accept withholding of treatment where this would *allow death to occur*. It is also important to note that Christians would reject euthanasia by any means which was only motivated by the need to reallocate medical resources.

The Church of Scotland

'The Church of Scotland has an obligation before God to assert God's interest in life, rather than death; to exercise Christian compassion towards the sufferer, the disabled and the dying, and to encourage the relief of symptoms and improvement in quality of life for such people. The Church cannot support euthanasia as a means to anything of these ends, and rejects the introduction of death as a treatment option in any clinical situation'. The Church of Scotland therefore rejects anything which would be considered intentional killing because it also considers that: *'the Christian recognises no right to dispose of his own life.'*[81] The Church does not support any intentional action which is designed to cause death since life is sacred – even if a patient requests it. In 2009 it reaffirmed this position[82].

The Roman Catholic Church

The Catechism states: *'Whatever its motives and means, direct euthanasia consists in putting an end to the lives of the handicapped, sick or dying persons. It is morally unacceptable.'* (2277) The Church rejects any intentional killing, including anything which may have been requested by anyone in any kind of advance directive. However, the Church also adds:

'Discontinuing medical procedures that are burdensome, dangerous, extraordinary or disproportionate to the expected outcome can be legitimate; it is the refusal of "over-zealous" treatment. Here, one does not will to cause death; one's inability to impede it is merely accepted.' (2278) It also accepts that competent individuals can request no extraordinary measures, as can others on their behalf if they lack capacity. So, the Catholic Church does accept that it is morally permissible to withdraw certain types of 'extraordinary' treatments even if that is likely to cause death – as long as that is not the intention. In *Caritas in Veritate*, Pope Benedict summarised the Church's teaching about life being from conception to natural death.

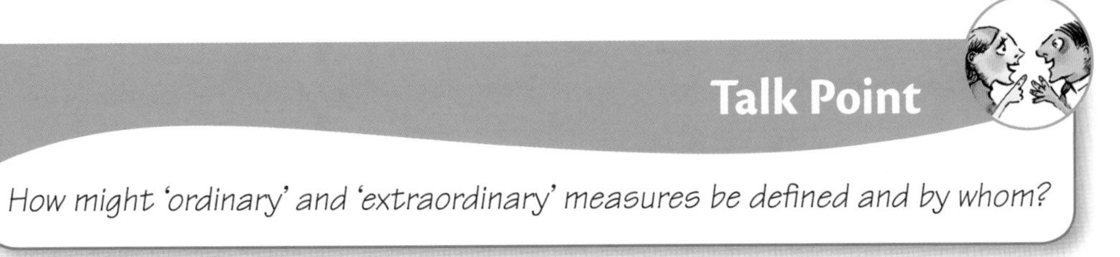

Buddhism

For Buddhists, three principles apply in relation to euthanasia: firstly, the precept which prohibits killing; secondly, teachings about the importance of compassion; and thirdly, the expectation that Buddhists will use 'skilful means' wisely in all situations. So, while this means that Buddhists would be likely to reject any intentional killing this is not impossible if it seems to be the 'skilful' thing to do in order to alleviate suffering and so act with compassion. The best that can be said is that in Buddhism, each situation should be considered on its own merits rather than there being any one rule which applies always and everywhere – both motive and consequence are important. This means in practice that a Buddhist could support both active and passive euthanasia according to the circumstances.

Humanism

For Humanists, quality of life arguments are central. If a person is judged to have no quality of life, then euthanasia in any form would be considered an option. There would be no real difference between causing death and allowing to die – provided of course that this was managed compassionately and with appropriate medical and other safeguards in place. For Humanists, advance directives would be accepted since we all have the right to die according to our own views. *'Humanists ... see a special value in human life, but think that if an individual has decided on rational grounds that his life has lost its meaning and value, that evaluation should be respected.'* It adds: *'There is no rational moral distinction between allowing someone to die and actively assisting them to die in these circumstances: the intention and the outcome are the same in both cases, but the more active means is probably the more compassionate one.'*[83] A section on the 'Right to Die in Dignity' from the European Humanist Federation gives a full explanation of Humanist views on the right to die and would be supported by Humanist Society Scotland. The key issue for Humanists is personal autonomy and choice: Humanists would oppose death without consent.

Utilitarianism

Utilitarian philosophy would generally be in support of euthanasia. One of J. S. Mill's key principles was the principle of autonomy. In *On Liberty* in 1859, Mill stated: *'Over himself, over his own body and mind, the individual is sovereign.'* This would mean that any individual was free to make an advance directive requesting euthanasia (active or passive) and that this should therefore be granted. In relation to non-voluntary euthanasia, modern Utilitarian Peter Singer argues that the concept of personhood is important. His view is that there are certain situations in which it is no longer meaningful to refer to someone as a person – because they lack self-awareness, consciousness or the ability to think in any rational way. In this instance it is permissible to treat such an individual in a morally different way. Singer also suggests, perhaps more controversially, that the use of scarce medical resources in keeping 'alive' someone who is no longer 'a person' has to be taken into consideration.

Personal Reflection

* *How far do you think any form of euthanasia is morally acceptable?*
* *Should the law in Scotland be changed to make euthanasia 'easier'?*
* *For you, what does 'quality of life' mean?*

Active learning

Check your understanding

1. What are the main components of palliative care?
2. Should all palliative care be provided by the authorities?
3. Why might some argue that palliative care does not receive the funding it should?
4. Describe one possible situation where euthanasia might be considered.
5. Explain the difference between active and passive euthanasia and non-voluntary and voluntary euthanasia.
6. What issues are there around the principle of 'advance directives'?
7. Describe two arguments in favour of euthanasia.
8. For one of the arguments above, describe a counter-argument and your own view on this and the counter-argument.
9. How far are Christians agreed about euthanasia?
10. Is euthanasia an issue which religious people and non-religious people completely disagree about? Explain your answer.

Investigate

1. A number of charity organisations run hospices. Choose one and find out about how it raises its money and the palliative care it provides. You could use the information to produce an information pack about the hospice and perhaps run a fund-raising activity to support its work.
2. One of the key issues here is 'when does life end?' This is perhaps both a medical question and a philosophical one too. Produce a short report on the medical, philosophical and other definitions of 'life' and 'death'. You could cover how this has changed through history and how modern technology has affected the definitions.
3. A number of high-profile individuals and situations have been used in various ways during the debate about euthanasia – for example, Diane Pretty, Tony Bland and Margo MacDonald. Find out about one of these situations and the part this played in the debate about euthanasia.
4. As well as the religious and philosophical perspectives you have covered in this chapter, there are many other religious and philosophical views about non-voluntary euthanasia. Find out about these and produce your own summary of their views.

Analyse and Evaluate

1 For each of the following statements, explain your own view and consider ways in which someone might oppose your view:
   - Palliative care should be available for all, no matter what the cost.
   - Hospices encourage us to 'give in' to death.
   - There is more than one definition of 'alive'.
   - Euthanasia provides an opportunity for 'dignity in death'.
   - Active and passive euthanasia amount to the same thing.
   - You need to be 'in your right mind' to request any form of euthanasia.
   - Although many believe that life is sacred, very few put this into practice.

2 The major issue for religious people is that legalising euthanasia would lead to a moral 'slippery slope'. Evaluate this statement.

3 'No one should have to choose when someone lives or dies.' How far do you agree?

Apply

What should a hospice be like? Your task is to prepare some guidelines for a new hospice. Perhaps this hospice could cater for specific people (such as children, or teenagers, for example). Draw up ten principles this hospice should observe so as to make its work as effective as possible. In addition to this you could think about the physical design of the hospice, decoration, etc.

19 Assisted suicide

'Helping another person to die would be terrifying and upsetting ... but it would be the right thing to do. How can you love and care for a person all your life and then abandon them when they most need you? How can you watch them slowly deteriorate before your eyes, suffering physically, mentally, spiritually? How can you do nothing to help them bring this all to a controlled and gentle – and dignified – end? How? And why can't you ask for help if you have no medical qualifications? Why can't you ask for someone who knows what they're doing to help you support your loved one on the final stage of life's journey? Why does society support us with all our minor ailments and illnesses throughout our lives and then turn a blind an uncaring eye when our need is greatest? And why should it affect anyone else? It's an individual choice – one person's choice, one person's life, one person's end – what has that got to do with anyone else? Why can't someone ask for help? Why can't we give it? I support assisted suicide.'

'There's no simple answer to any of this. But no one need be abandoned in their time of greatest need. They can be cared for and made comfortable – physically, emotionally, spiritually, right up to the end. Where is the dignity in turning away from the dying by bringing it all to an abrupt and unnatural end? And why should any such death be gentler than any other? Why should anyone be burdened with supporting the taking of a life – what would they think each morning on waking up? And why should someone who doesn't even know the person be called upon to help – just because they have qualifications? Care for the dying is the opposite of abandoning them – it is walking with them through all that the end of life may bring – why might someone think of this as the opposite of caring? The choice of an individual has consequences for all of us – why should anyone feel pressurised into taking their own life just because someone else has taken that step? How will we ever know that it's what the person really wanted – not what they think they should have wanted? I reject assisted suicide.'

Talk Point

Which of these two views is closest to your own?

Suicide

Suicide – or attempted suicide – is not illegal in Scotland and never has been. In England it was illegal until 1961. Before this if you attempted suicide and failed you could be fined or imprisoned; if you succeeded then you would not be allowed to be buried in consecrated ground (like a church graveyard) and you might even have a wooden stake driven through your body after death. As if this wasn't enough, the family of someone who had committed suicide might have their possessions taken from them as punishment. Nowadays, anyone attempting suicide or expressing the wish to do so ('suicide ideation') is offered treatment and support rather than punishment – and so too is the family of anyone who has threatened to take or taken their own life.

Assisted suicide

Assisted suicide is when a person requests someone to aid them in committing suicide themselves. It is different to euthanasia because it is not requesting anyone else to end your life – you end it for yourself, but you are assisted to end it by someone else. What is meant by 'assistance' can vary according to individuals and circumstances. In places where assisted suicide is legal, such as in the 'Dignitas' system in Switzerland, *'for legal reasons, the patient must be able to undertake the last act'* (which may be ingestion of a drug – generally Sodium Pentobarbital – or pressing a button to administer the drug intravenously). *'If this is not possible, Dignitas is unfortunately unable to help.'*[84]

Talk Point

Why might someone feel they might need to be 'assisted' to take their own life – and what might such assistance mean?

There are few places in the world where assisted suicide is legal. In those places where it is, it is claimed that there are enough protections involved in it to ensure that the person does not suffer and that those assisting are protected from possible prosecution. For example, in Switzerland a person can be imprisoned for supporting anyone in suicide if the person assisting has 'selfish motives'. This means that in practice assisting suicide is not illegal if it is carried out for selfless reasons.

In Scotland, aiding anyone to commit suicide could result in the person being prosecuted for murder or culpable homicide: a decision about this would be taken according to the circumstances by the Crown Office and Procurator Fiscal. Margo MacDonald MSP tried to persuade the Scottish Parliament to legalise assisted suicide in the Assisted Suicide (Scotland) Bill which she introduced to parliament. Margo herself had Parkinson's disease and died in April 2014. Often politicians are guided by (or told by) their party about how to vote in parliament. However, in this case a free vote was given – which means that MSPs could vote according to their own views on the matter. This gives some idea of the complexity and depth of feeling around this issue. In the end, the Bill was rejected by 82 to 36.

The Bill had proposed that assisting the suicide of another person should result in: *'No criminal liability for assisting suicide: no civil liability for assisting suicide.'* It also proposed a number of safeguards which the proposers of the Bill argued would prevent any abuses of the change in the law:

- The person requesting assistance with suicide (must be over 16) would make a preliminary declaration in the presence of a witness (someone independent) and this would be supported by a medical practitioner's note.
- This would be recorded and noted in the person's medical records.
- This first request would be supported by a medical practitioner.
- There would be a need for a second request similarly supported by a medical practitioner.
- The person making the request would need to have full capacity (be able to make, remember, understand and communicate the request).
- The person making the request would have to have an illness that is terminal or life-shortening, or a condition that is, for the person, progressive and either terminal or life-shortening and the person's conclusion … that the person's quality of life is unacceptable is not inconsistent with the facts then known to the [medical] practitioner.

- The proposed Act includes this statement: 'Nothing in this Act authorises anyone to do anything that itself causes another person's death.'
- The suicide would be assisted by a 'Licensed Facilitator' governed by a group set up by Scottish Ministers[85].

Arguments supporting assisted suicide

Many of the arguments related to euthanasia are also used in support of assisted suicide, though there are some which are specifically related to this practice. In Scotland, any form of assistance in suicide is illegal, though in some countries it is legal. What arguments might there be in support of assisted suicide?

- **It is a human right** Supporters argue that each person's life is theirs to do with as they see fit – as you choose how to live your life so you should choose how to end it. Supporters argue that a person with capacity should be permitted to make this decision either before they are in a life-shortening situation or during it. Most supporters argue that there should be some safeguards about this – such as an age limit – though some argue that because it is a right, it should apply to everyone, no matter what their age or personal circumstances.
- **It is a final act of loving kindness** Some argue that there are individuals who die in pain and alone, when they could be supported through both by their loved ones. This is currently not possible because being in the presence of someone committing suicide could be interpreted as supporting them in doing so and therefore will be considered a criminal act. Some who would want assisted suicide argue that it is wrong that they have to worry that their loved ones might face prosecution after their death.
- **It should be an option when quality of life has deteriorated** In Scotland, supporters of assisted suicide have so far mostly argued that it should be reserved for extreme cases where a person is terminally ill or has a life-shortening condition and where the associated reduction in quality of life makes life no longer worth living. However, others who support assisted suicide have argued that it should be available no matter what the circumstances because judgements about quality of life are very individual: why should someone need to be terminally ill, experiencing a life-shortening condition or in pain before assisted suicide is acceptable? Perhaps it is up to each individual to decide what is and is not quality of life. They might argue that quality of life is not just a physical idea, it is a social, psychological and emotional one too – and so it is up to each individual to decide what is and is not quality of life.
- **It provides a safe and dignified way to end life** One of the key arguments around assisted suicide is that as suicide is not illegal for anyone attempting it, why should it be illegal for anyone to assist someone attempting it? Suicide can be very difficult and it can go badly wrong – meaning the person dies in great pain or fails in their attempt with terrible consequences. Skilled support in committing suicide can stop this happening – making sure that the suicide is completed and is done so in a way which minimises pain and suffering. For this reason, many supporters of assisted suicide argue that trained medical staff should be allowed to provide this support – because they have the medical expertise. This has led to assisted suicide often being described as 'physician-assisted suicide'. However, some argue that anyone should be able to provide the support. In addition to this, some argue that being able to take your own life with assistance is more dignified than your life being 'taken out of your control'.

Talk Point

Should only medically trained people be allowed to assist with suicide?

- **It does not lead to a 'slippery slope'** Many supporters of assisted suicide argue that if proper safeguards are in place then it will not lead to abuses or to euthanasia being carried out on people who do not want it (or cannot express their view on it). In fact, they might say, why should making assisted suicide legal have any effect on the circumstances in which it is carried out or how often it is? Suicide is not illegal in Scotland and it would be hard to say how this affects suicide rates compared to countries where it is illegal. So, if assisted suicide was legal, how does anyone know what effect this might have?

Arguments opposing assisted suicide

Again, many of the arguments linked to euthanasia apply here, though there are some which are unique to this situation:

- **Life is sacred and no one has the right to take it** This is generally a religious view based on the belief that life belongs to a divine being, not the person living it.
- **It is a hopeless act and not one of kindness** Some argue that assisted suicide does not need to be an option because pain relief is so good nowadays and because a person suffering should be supported by those around them. Making assisted suicide legal would be an admission that we had failed as a society in our duty of care to those who carry out any form of suicide.
- **It places unacceptable pressure on a range of people** Although no one is being asked to take anyone's life, they are being asked to be present while someone else does so and not intervene. This is a very difficult thing to ask anyone to do – whether medical staff or loved ones. No one should be put in this position. It is also possible that the person committing suicide is under pressure too – this could be in numerous ways, but it would be difficult to work out just how 'freely' the person had chosen to end their life.
- **It is open to a range of abuses** From medical staff wanting to use medical resources elsewhere, to relatives wanting to gain from a person's death, to individuals worrying that they are 'a burden' to others and so committing suicide when they really don't want to – the options are many. Making this legal opens up many ways for the situation to be abused – no matter what safeguards are put in place.
- **It could lead to a 'slippery slope'** No matter how well intentioned any legalising of assisted suicide might be, it could still lead to a 'devaluing' of human life (or of some 'kinds' of human life). If it is legal in some cases, what is to stop someone pressing for it to be legal in others – where some might think that it is not justified?
- **How does anyone know that it is pain-free** One of the arguments in favour of assisted suicide is that it provides a pain-free way to end suffering: however, although it might look pain-free and medical indicators might suggest this, no one can experience what someone else experiences – and successful suicides cannot return to describe the experience. Perhaps taking your own life is painful and horrible no matter how it is done; perhaps the human body protects itself from pain and suffering during a 'natural death'.
- **Why might suicide be any more 'dignified' than any other kind of death** 'Dignified' means different things to different people, but perhaps it is wrong to suggest that suicide is automatically more dignified than any other kind of death. Some religious people argue that there is dignity in accepting death – however it comes.

Some religious and philosophical perspectives

Christianity

No matter how it is carried out, Christians believe that suicide is morally unacceptable. Christians believe that God has the right to determine when our life comes to an end – not us – and we should not bring it to an unnatural end before he chooses to do so. In the past, Christianity tended to condemn those who attempted or committed suicide because of the sinful nature of suicide. Nowadays Christians are more likely to offer support, love and care rather than condemnation although suicide and assisting suicide would still be viewed as sinful.

The Church of Scotland

'The Church of Scotland has reaffirmed its opposition to the assisted suicide bill ... the overriding opposition is an abiding concern for the most vulnerable in our society and the negative impact right to die legislation may have on their quality of life. In our focus on autonomy and personal choice, there is the danger that we forget that personal choice does not exist in a vacuum and a choice for some may undermine choices for others. Every personal choice has a community impact.'[86] The Church therefore rejects any legalisation of assisted suicide because of the impact this could have on people and society. The Church argues that 'assisted dying' violates the sanctity of life. Its main arguments against the Assisted Suicide (Scotland) Bill were: there is no evidence that assisted dying is any more dignified than any other death; it is not a simple personal choice – all choices affect others; the nature of the assisted dying was not clear enough in the Bill; it does not sufficiently prevent any kind of coercion of the person requesting it; it places medical staff in unacceptable positions; it does not sufficiently protect the person requesting it should they change their mind; the Bill 'misappropriated' scientific evidence in support of its position.

The Roman Catholic Church

In response to the Assisted Suicide (Scotland) Bill (2013) the Bishops Conference of Scotland said: *'We believe human life must be fully protected by law at every stage. It is not appropriate for any person to make judgements about the "quality" of another's life as this bill would require ... [the bill] contradicts claims that there is no danger of a "slippery slope" and the consequent threat to innocent life.'* This response goes on to reject: the proposed age of 16 for assisted suicide to be available; the Bill's lack of clarity about what is and is not a qualifying illness for which assisted suicide might be an option; the pressure it would put on medical staff and others; the lack of clarity about how life would be ended; the removal of important safeguards. It argues that time and money would be far better spent on improving palliative care and concludes: *'The proposal is wrong in principle and would be impossible to implement in practice while ensuring the safety of inhabitants of our country.'*[87]

Buddhism

In Buddhism there is no universally accepted view about assisted suicide. On one hand assisting someone to take their own life might be considered as assisting someone to carry out an act with very serious negative kammic consequences; on the other hand it might be seen as an act of compassion. In Buddhism, all life involves suffering – and therefore perhaps no stage in life is more associated with suffering than any other stage. The process of dying may be long, drawn out and appear to involve more suffering than other stages of life, but life is filled with suffering. On the one hand all Buddhists would like to escape suffering, but in Buddhist thinking, death may not necessarily lead to this, since further lives (also involving suffering) may be to come. In theory and practice, therefore, assisted suicide could be accepted or rejected in Buddhism. Buddhists argue that the Buddha himself suffered a painful and terminal illness in the final stages of his life – he did not choose to end his life before it came to an end naturally. Some Buddhists suggest that this is a model for Buddhists to follow, while others argue that the Buddha asked each of us to make our own decisions – not just follow his model uncritically.

Humanism

'Humanism respects the autonomy of the person, and so we are in favour of the right to choose to end one's own life, subject to

appropriate qualifications and safeguards.'[88] Humanist Society Scotland was central in the 'My Life, My Death, My Choice' campaign in support of the Assisted Suicide Bill and argued that the Bill was the right approach to assisted dying because it: was limited to those with terminal or life-shortening conditions; only applied to those who chose to 'opt-in' to assisted dying; provided proper safeguards for vulnerable groups; required the individual to take final action to end their life; ensured that no one could be involved who might benefit financially. Humanists argue that each individual has the right to end their life as they see fit and that as a society, this should be supported in any way which will benefit the person making this choice.

Utilitarianism

First of all, Utilitarians tend to respect the rights of the individual over their own circumstances – including death. This, of course, would be provided that such control did not lead to effects for society which reduced overall happiness. Opponents of assisted suicide often argue that legalising it could lead to pressure being brought to bear (or felt) by some who would not choose it if it was not available to them. A Utilitarian would reject assisted suicide if it led to a society causing undue pressure on vulnerable people at a difficult time of their life – this would hardly lead to universal happiness. However, the case might have to be made that legalising assisted suicide did lead to this effect on individuals. On the other hand, Utilitarians could argue that legal assisted suicide is a mark of a civilised and caring society – since it provides support for a person in an extreme situation; this could potentially lead to greater happiness for the majority because we would all know that in a similar situation we would be able to make a choice about the end of our life. Therefore there is no one clear position on assisted suicide within Utilitarianism.

Personal Reflection

* *Was the Scottish Parliament's decision to reject the legalisation of assisted suicide right or wrong?*
* *Do you think assisted suicide will ever be legal in Scotland? Could anything lead to it becoming more acceptable?*
* *How far do and should individual choices have implications for wider society?*

Active learning

Check your understanding

1. How have laws and attitudes changed towards suicide over time?
2. What is meant by 'assisted suicide' and why might someone want to take up this option?
3. Give an outline of the history of the Assisted Suicide (Scotland) Bill.
4. Describe the key features of this Bill.
5. Discuss two arguments in support of assisted suicide.
6. Explain two arguments which oppose assisted suicide.
7. Which of the arguments in support of assisted suicide (if any) do you think are the 'strongest' arguments?
8. Which of the arguments opposing assisted suicide (if any) do you think are the 'strongest' arguments?
9. To what extent are Christians agreed in their views on assisted suicide?
10. How is assisted suicide viewed differently by religious and non-religious people?

Investigate

1 The website 'My Life, My Death, My Choice' (www.lifedeathchoice.org.uk) argues in support of assisted suicide and includes a range of resources including video clips. Have a look through this website and: if you support assisted suicide, consider how well this website makes its case and what you would suggest to improve the website; if you oppose assisted suicide, explain your views on the content of this website (or devise your own website which matches it, but rejects its claims).
2 Around the world, attitudes to and laws about assisted suicide vary. Carry out your own research into the differences and display your findings.
3 During the various stages of the Assisted Suicide Bill, numerous views were sought about it and many responses gathered across a whole range of different groups. Devise and carry out your own anonymous questionnaire which gathers views about assisted suicide. What differences are there between groups, ages, different lifestyles and so on? Remember that this is a very sensitive area for some and your questionnaire should be carefully constructed to avoid any distress to anyone (including you). If you have a psychology teacher in your school ask their advice about appropriate ethical safeguards for questionnaires.
4 There are many religious and philosophical perspectives not covered in this book – find out about some of their views on assisted suicide and compare these with the ones you have covered in this book.

Analyse and Evaluate

1 'Assisting a person who wants to take their own life is society's duty.' Evaluate this statement taking into account religious and non-religious views.
2 'Helping another person to take their own life is never morally acceptable.' How far do you agree?
3 'Assisted suicide is one issue about which religious and non-religious people will never agree.' Evaluate this statement.

Apply

If you support assisted suicide Have a careful look through the Assisted Suicide (Scotland) bill and the responses to this Bill. Now rewrite the Bill in a way which might lead to it being more acceptable to those who objected to it.

If you oppose assisted suicide Using the Assisted Suicide (Scotland) Bill as a model draw up your own bill which is designed to ensure that assisted suicide never becomes legal in Scotland.

20 Organ donation

Hardeep was 25 when he died. His death was sudden and unexpected – the result of a road traffic accident. As he lay in the hospital bed, medical staff agreed that Hardeep was brain stem dead with no hope of any kind of recovery. So, gently, they discussed with his distraught parents the option of discontinuing the artificial support for Hardeep's breathing and circulation. His parents agreed that this was the right thing to do – as they accepted that Hardeep was gone. As his parents were coming to terms with their grief at the loss of their son, medical staff approached them to request that organs and tissue be taken from Hardeep so as to be used to save the lives of others. Hardeep's parents had never given this any thought – nor had Hardeep. At 25, he had not considered the possibility of a sudden death – and so had never signed up to be an organ donor. Hardeep's parents, however, knew that their beloved son was the kindest soul you would ever meet – and that if he thought he could help someone else – even after his death – he wouldn't hesitate to do so. So his parents agreed to Hardeep's organs being taken for transplant.

Thomas, a 19-year-old with heart disease, received Hardeep's heart; Calum, a dad of two young children, received his liver; Amir received one of his kidneys, as did Hilary. Corneal tissue was transplanted to Iain. One of Hardeep's lungs went to Arthur, while the other went to Benjamin. Each of these recipients went on to live a normal happy life, as did their loved ones and families – all grateful for the donor of these organs and tissues: the donor who gave life back to their loved ones.

What is organ donation?

Most organs and tissues can be donated after death – it is even possible to have a face transplant using an entire donated face and, in fact, it has been done. The whole face can be removed from a dead person (cadaver) and reconstructed on top of the bone structure of another (living) person. This may be because the living person has lost his or her face to varying degrees because of illness or accident. This is so far extremely rare, while heart, lungs, liver, kidneys and other organs are routinely transplanted from cadavers to living patients. To be able to use organs for donation, certain medical rules apply:

- Organs/tissue cannot be taken where the person has had cancer which has spread in the last 12 months.
- Organs/tissue cannot be taken where the person has/had a severe or untreated infection.
- Organs/tissue cannot be taken where the person has/had Creutzfeldt-Jakob disease.[89]

As well as organ and tissue transplant from cadavers, some organs and tissues can be transplanted from living donors to other living recipients. Generally whole organs can only be transplanted where they come in pairs and so the donor would be left with one – so, for example, you could donate one kidney or one lung, but as you only have one heart you cannot donate that.

In Scotland and the UK there are very strict guidelines about organ and tissue transplant which require that the person donating the organ/tissue must have clearly and freely chosen to do so (before their death in the case of cadavers of course). This is generally recorded through being on the register of organ donors and carrying your organ donation card – which you have to actively sign up for. Organs and tissue are never allowed to be sold and the person donating cannot specify who receives their organs or tissue. Organs or tissue cannot be taken where this would cause the death of the donor. In the situation where organs are taken from a cadaver, the status of the person as dead has to be agreed in the normal way for determining that a person is no longer alive. Importantly, too, there is a distinction made between those who are 'heart-beating dead' and those who are 'not heart-beating dead' because different organs are more likely to be viable from someone whose heart is still beating (although they are 'brain dead') as opposed to someone whose heart has stopped.

Talk Point

Why do you think there are different definitions of death?

Why is there a need for organ donation?

The reasons why living people might need transplants are generally linked to illness/disease and/or accidents leading to the failure of specific body organs or tissues. The failure of these organs and tissues can have different effects, depending upon the organ or tissue – the functions of some tissues/organs can be sustained artificially in some cases, though this is often a short-term solution. When some of the 'vital organs' fail this can mean death, of course, whereas other organs and tissues can fail and not result in death.

There is widely agreed to be a shortage in the availability of donor organs. There are many people in need of transplants, but not enough donors. This is complicated by the fact that donated organs have to be a close match for the recipient. In short, a donated organ may be rejected by the recipient's body (which treats it as an 'invader' or 'infection' and fights it): the greater the difference between the donor organ and the recipient, the more likely the recipient's body will reject it. This possibility can be reduced through the use of particular drugs, however it is not certain that these will stop the recipient body rejecting the organ and so the transplant may fail. To reduce the likelihood of rejection, organs have to be as closely matched between donor and recipient as possible. Close family members are the best match, then more distant relatives and so on: matching donor to recipient can be difficult for a variety of reasons – and because organs can deteriorate quickly after death, the 'window of opportunity' between a suitably matched organ becoming available and the recipient being ready and able to receive it can sometimes be very short and very fragile.

Moral issues linked to living donation

Firstly, we will think about the specific moral issues which are associated with donation of organs by living donors.

The right to donate

Very few people probably disagree with the right of an individual to donate their organs if they choose to do so. The donor will have to accept some risk associated with the process because any medical procedure can involve risk – and, of course, if one of a pair of organs has been donated then the donor has to accept that this puts them at increased risk if their remaining organ fails for some reason. However, even though there are risks, most would probably accept the donor's right to take on these risks as they see fit – as long as they are fully aware of these risks and prepared to accept them freely.

Donor/recipient relationship

Donation of an organ is most likely to take place between close relatives, or people who are in a close relationship of some kind: apart from anything else, the closer the biological relationship the more likely it is that the donation will be successful. Also, since organ donation is a big step for an individual to take, it will probably be more likely to occur where the donor values the recipient highly. However, there have been cases – sometimes referred to as 'extreme altruism' – where donors donate an organ to someone they don't know. There can be many reasons for this, but again, few people would probably object to an individual's right to do this – and in fact may see this as a very significant act of selflessness and courage.

The right to donate where there is unacceptable risk

In Scotland, it would not be possible to donate an organ where this would cause your death – because this would effectively be assisted suicide and so illegal. However, morally, is this always unacceptable? For example, most parents would do anything to care for their children – even give their lives for them. If you could save your child by donating an organ – even if this resulted in your death – should you not have the right to do so?

Should someone be allowed to donate an organ where doing so would cause their death?

The right to choose the recipient of your organ(s)

Again, this is not currently permissible, but morally speaking should it be? Some people of course might choose to donate only to certain 'types' of people – and most people would probably agree that allowing this would be wrong. However, what if the choice was not something widely agreed as unacceptable, but something else? The recipient of a donated organ is based on *objectively measured and unbiased medical need* – but let's say that one possible recipient was an unrepentant serial killer and the other was a young mum with four children. Although the serial killer's medical need was greater ... should it be morally permissible for a donor to have some say about which person receives their organs in this case?

Medical rights v. moral rights

At the moment, recipients of organs are decided based on objective measures of medical need – the person in greatest medical need gets the organ first. Now while this is medically acceptable, is it always morally acceptable? For example, let's say that two people need a liver transplant – one has suffered liver failure because of illness and the other because of a lifetime of alcohol abuse which, in the opinion of doctors, isn't likely to change after the liver transplant (even though the recipient claims it will). Let's say the person suffering liver failure through alcohol abuse has the greatest medical need – should this 'cancel out' any moral concerns about this person receiving the donated liver?

Pressure to donate

One issue which may arise is the possibility that some people may be pressurised into donating when they don't really want to – this might be direct pressure from relatives, for example, or indirect pressure in other ways. For example, imagine you have a close relative in need of an organ transplant and the only match for them is you. You might be scared to donate because of the risks – or not want to for other reasons. Is it morally acceptable that you might have to deal with pressure to donate when you would rather not?

Selling your organs

Of course, this does not really qualify as 'donating' an organ and so is perhaps not what the SQA would like you to think about. Morally, however, it raises important questions: why should someone not be free to sell their body organs or tissue? We sell other things which belong to us, so why not our organs? Some argue that if this is considered an acceptable risk by the person then that is their choice to make – others might even argue that this is in some way morally acceptable even if it results in your death (for example, if someone saw this as the only way to provide for their family and save them from death). Opponents would argue that this is open to so many possible forms of abuse that it should never be permitted, and besides, it would involve exploitation of the poor and vulnerable – because who else would take such a risk just for economic reasons? Selling organs would not be permitted in any form in Scotland.

Moral issues linked to organs taken from donors after death

Some of the moral issues linked to living donation may also apply to donations after death and there are some which are unique to donations after death.

The right to donate

Should relatives have the right to donate the organs of their dead loved ones even if their loved ones had not expressed this wish during their life? Perhaps the person just 'never got round to it' or was too young to even contemplate it (as in the case of babies). Some might argue that since the person is now dead, use should be made of them to help others and that relatives might have some kind of moral responsibility to agree to this. In fact, perhaps – morally speaking – relatives should donate organs even if the possible donor had rejected this option while alive. This would not happen currently, but in relation to the morality of the issue, should it be permitted at some time in the future? This could also extend to the right to sell body organs – again, although this is not legally permissible, would it be morally right to allow relatives to benefit economically from selling the organs of their loved ones or would this possibly result in pressure to let people die (or even end their life prematurely)?

Talk Point

Should relatives of a dead person be permitted to 'override' the person's views about organ donation during life?

The right to choose recipient characteristics

In the same way that living people may want to choose who receives their organs (although they can't), should the relatives of a dead donor be permitted to have any say in who receives the organs of their loved one (they currently don't)?

Medical rights v. moral rights

Similarly, recipients of organs from dead donors will be based on medical need – but should this always be the case? Are some recipients more 'worthy' of receiving a life-saving organ than others?

Pressure to decide that someone is dead

Some argue that one of the issues with organ donation is the possibility that it could lead to people being declared dead too hastily – or allowed to die when they might be kept alive. The NHS in Scotland is very clear that the regulations currently in place would never allow any of this to happen. Decisions about preserving life or deciding that it has ended are based on agreed objective medical criteria and the decision that a person is dead (or that extraordinary measures should not be taken to preserve their life) is officially completely separate from whether the person is a potential donor or not. However, morally speaking, could the fact that you have a potential life-saving donor in front of you who will definitely die soon put pressure on medical staff (or relatives) to allow the person to die sooner than they would naturally – or to be less precise about deciding that the person is dead?

Donor card issues

Currently, you can sign up to be part of the register of donors in the event of your death – you can do this online **www.organdonation.nhs.uk** and you can carry a donor card. By registering as a donor, you can choose to donate selected organs/tissue, or any organs/tissue of use. Once you die, your closest relatives will be asked to confirm that you had not changed your mind about this. If they agree that you haven't, then your organs will be taken for use. Your closest relatives do have to give permission for your organs to be taken and if they reject this option then your organs will not be taken. In most cases this is likely to be very straightforward, but it will be a difficult time for your relatives and they may not find making the decision easy. Also, there have been cases where relatives disagree about taking organs from their loved one – and if the relatives are all at the same degree of kinship to the donor, then this can become very complicated (bearing in mind too that some organs have to be taken very quickly after death so that their viability is maximised).

So, at the moment, being an organ donor is an *opt-in system* – you have to consciously choose to do it. However, some have argued that it should be an *opt-out system*. This would mean that it would be assumed that your organs can be taken after your death unless you had consciously stated otherwise during your life. Some argue that this would reduce the shortage of organs and that many people in life simply don't get round to signing up as an organ donor – because most of us don't think about our own death very much. If we knew how beneficial organ donation would be after our death perhaps we would have signed up. Some reject this option because they argue that being a donor should be a positive choice. There may also be those who believe that organ donation should be *compulsory*: most people would agree that it is 'socially compulsory' to save someone's life if you can – walking on by when someone needs your help would be considered morally unacceptable by most people. So, if you can save someone after your death through organ donation should this not also be a social duty and therefore compulsory? Some would reject this, because they would think it harms our personal freedoms – although our freedoms are limited in many ways during life.

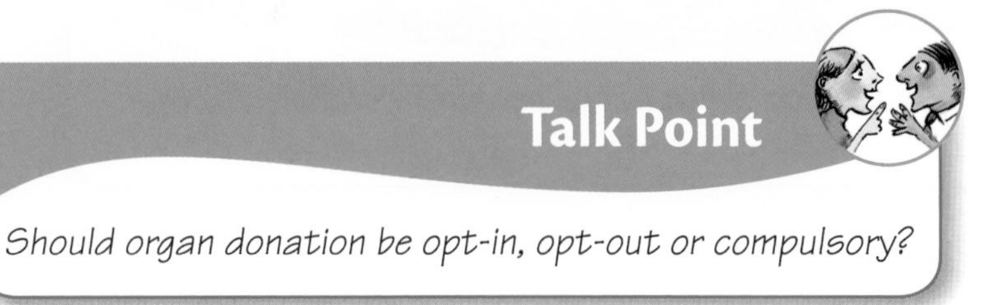

Alternatives to human organ donation

While it is not specifically linked to the issue of organ donation, it is interesting to consider the morality of alternatives to human organ donation.

Artificial organs

The function of certain organs can currently be partly or wholly replaced with technological interventions – for example, artificial heart valves and dialysis machines can fulfil these bodily functions. In the future perhaps this use of technology might become more advanced – and potentially solve shortage issues if they are sufficiently complex to enable them to take over the function of organs/tissues. While it is argued that this is simply an effective use of technology to solve medical issues, others may be concerned at the possibility of humans becoming more 'machine-like' and so this might somehow bring into question what it means to be human.

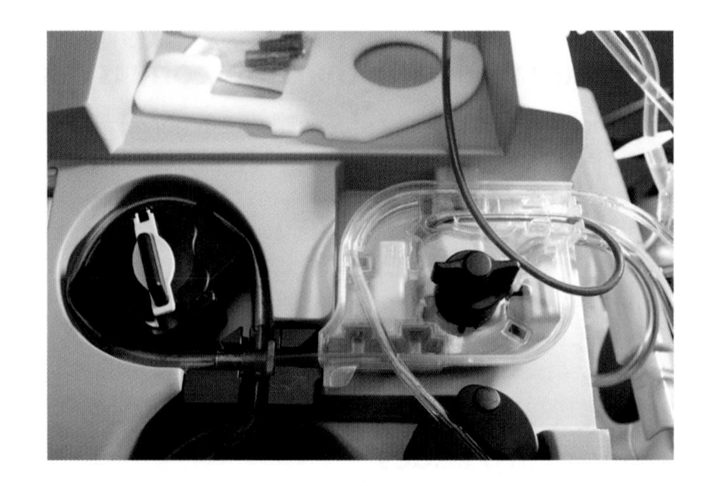

Xenotransplantation

This is the use of organs and tissue from non-human donors (animals) in humans. Some argue that – properly regulated – this would be an effective way to deal with donor shortages, while others argue that no matter how well regulated, the ethical issues here are simply too extreme to ever allow this. There are many concerns about xenotransplantation, which are usually focused on:

- The possibility that this will allow illness/disease to 'cross over' from animals to humans once animal organs/tissues become part of a human body.
- The dangers associated with the genetic modification of animal tissue for use in humans (organs/tissue may have to be genetically modified to make it 'closer' to human tissue to reduce the risk of rejection and this could have unforeseen consequences for the animals and humans).
- A range of ethical issues around the rights of animals (the treatment of animals, killing them to harvest organs, the fact that they cannot consent to any of this, etc.).

Some religious and philosophical perspectives

Christianity

In general, Christians consider organ donation to be an act of selfless kindness – a gift of life to someone after your death. They would reject any pressure being put on anyone to donate organs as well as anything which brought about death before it came naturally. Christians would be highly likely to oppose any kind of selling of organs, as this would be exploiting the most vulnerable in society.

The Church of Scotland

The Church states: '*The Church of Scotland ... supports the practice of organ and tissue donation. We believe that this is part of humanity's commitment to healing and, with the real potential for the death of one person to prolong or greatly improve the quality of life of another, an action with strong symbolic Christian resonance.*'[90] This statement was part of a response to a proposal that organ donation be opt-out rather than opt-in. The Church made it clear that it was not in favour of such an opt-out approach, mainly because it takes the view that donors should clearly express their consent to organ donation during life, so that donation is a gift rather than an expectation. So organ donation is an act of kindness on the part of the donor. In March 2015, the Church spoke out strongly against any trade in selling organs by supporting moves in the Scottish Parliament to include the selling of organs as part of the Human Trafficking and Exploitation (Scotland) Bill. It considers organ trafficking to exploit the poor and vulnerable. In line with its views on assisted suicide and euthanasia, the Church would also oppose any situation where death was hastened unnaturally in order to make use of a person's organs. In relation to who receives organs, the Church would argue that all matter in the sight of God and so medical need should decide who has priority in receiving organs.

The Roman Catholic Church

In the Catechism it is clearly stated: '*Organ transplants are in conformity with the moral law if the physical and psychological dangers and risks to the donor are proportionate to the good sought for the recipient. Organ donation after death is noble and meritorious and is to be encouraged as an expression of generous solidarity. It is not morally acceptable if the donor or his proxy has not given explicit consent. Moreover, it is not morally admissible to bring about the disabling mutilation or death of a human being, even in order to delay the death of other persons.*' (2296) So this is pretty clear and covers most of the options for donation. It is kind, it must be consented to and, in the case of living donors, it should balance the needs of the donor with the benefits to the recipient. It should involve no pressure on anyone and must not bring about death before it naturally occurs. The Church would reject the selling of organs because organ donation should not be commercialised and this would be likely to involve exploitation of those who are poor and vulnerable. The Church would also argue that since all are equally valued by God, medical need should decide who receives organs.

Buddhism

There are no hard and fast rules in Buddhism about organ donation – each Buddhist must make their own decision about this.[91] Buddhists are more concerned about the state of the mind at death than the state of the body: the body is impermanent and we should not become attached to it – so donating our organs after death is perfectly acceptable. However, some Buddhists believe that consciousness remains in the body for a while after death and during this time the body should not be disturbed – which would mean removing organs would not be possible. Most Buddhists would regard organ donation during life or after death as an act of compassion and so something which results in good kamma. Some Buddhists could accept donation of organs where this results in death – in the Jataka tales, one of the previous incarnations of the Buddha saw him sacrifice himself to provide food for a starving tiger and her cubs and one tale tells of a King who gives his eyes to a blind beggar – resulting in donated corneas being very common in Buddhism countries. However, many Buddhists would question the act of donation involving harm to a person since Buddhists reject causing suffering – including to yourself. Buddhists would be likely to argue that organ donation should be your expressed wish – though if an opt-out system helped people then this too would be considered. Buddhists would be likely to reject anything which brought pressure on an individual (or their family) to donate organs since this would not be an act of compassion even if the outcome was good. Buddhists would also be likely to reject the selling of organs since this would have the potential to exploit the poor. Buddhists would be likely to support organs going to those in most medical need.

Humanism

In relation to organ donation, the British Humanist Association states that: *'We support medical advances for the improvement of human health and wellbeing.'*[92] It rejects the trafficking of organs, and completely supports current bans on selling organs. It supports an opt-out system of organ donation after death because it argues that many simply don't get round to thinking about it and an opt-out system could increase the availability of organs for transplant considerably and because *'We have a moral responsibility to allow our organs to be used for transplantation, if that will improve the quality of life for others and contribute to the wellbeing of the human family.'*[93] Humanists would regard altruistic donation of organs by the living as a matter of individual choice, as long as individuals have enough information to allow them to make a rational choice about the risk to them compared to the benefits of the recipient. Humanists would want organs to be received according to medical need and would be likely to reject any pressure on individuals, relatives, or any hastening of death in order to secure organs for transplant. Humanist Society Scotland supports changing the law in Scotland to 'opt-out' as this would increase the number of organs available for transplant.

Utilitarianism

Utilitarians could support a range of positions on organ donation: in general, if organ donation results in increased happiness, then it would be welcomed whether it is during life or after death, whether opt-in or opt-out. However, if it was accompanied by any pressure on individuals or families, or resulted in actions which brought about death prematurely, then Utilitarians would be wary of it: that's not to say they would reject any of this completely, because a balance has to be found between need for organ transplant and supply if happiness is to be maximised. As to individuals donating organs which would result in harm for them, a Utilitarian might accept this as a possibility depending upon the balance of sacrifice to benefit – besides, Utilitarians generally support individual freedoms where these do not conflict with the rights of others, so choosing what to do with your organs might be entirely that – your choice. This could also extend to the selling of organs. While, in practice, Utilitarians would be very cautious about this (and many would reject it completely) because of the potential for abuse of the vulnerable, in theory Utilitarians would have to allow this possibility because it could be seen as a matter of personal choice. In relation to who receives organs, Utilitarians could support decisions based on matters other than medical need since the value of one person receiving an organ compared to another may be much wider than their individual need.

Personal Reflection

- *Do you carry a donor card? Should you?*
- *Should organ donation be opt-in or opt-out?*
- *Should deciding who gets organs be based on medical need alone?*

Active learning

Check your understanding

1. What conditions are currently applied to taking organs after death and during life?
2. How does the definition of death link to organ donation?
3. What possible reasons are there for organ shortages?
4. Describe two moral issues associated with organ donation by the living.
5. Describe two moral issues linked to organ donation after death.
6. Explain the difference between an opt-in and an opt-out system for organ donation.
7. In general, why are most of the perspectives you have studied opposed to the selling of organs?
8. How far do you agree that in relation to organ donation, religious and non-religious perspectives have the same views?
9. What moral issues are linked to alternatives to human organ transplants?
10. How far are religious and non-religious perspectives agreed about organ donation?

Investigate

1. Find out about the range of ways in which you can donate body organs during life and after death. Create your own information leaflet about this. You could explore which organs and tissues can be donated during life/after death as well as other ways in which you can donate your body for use after your death (e.g. for use in the study of anatomy or as practice for surgical procedures).
2. There are a range of online sources which explain organ and tissue donation to a variety of audiences. Choose a potential target audience and create an outline of a website based on the websites you investigate. For example, increasingly children and young people are given a say about matters which affect them. Should children and young people have organ donation explained to them so that they can express their views about it too?
3. Choose one of the religious or philosophical perspectives you have examined in this chapter. Carry out some further research into its views on organ donation of various kinds – including its more detailed views on the selling of organs and the right to donate where this might be harmful to the donor.
4. Carry out some questionnaire research in your school regarding views about organ donation. Remember that this is a sensitive subject and so your questionnaire should be carefully expressed so as to avoid any distress. Report on your findings in a format of your choice.

Analyse and Evaluate

1 One-minute challenge: no matter what your view is, prepare a one-minute talk in favour of or opposing one or more of the statements below. You could do this as a class with half for and half against:
   - Relatives should be able to donate organs of loved ones after their death even if the loved one has said that they would prefer this not to happen.
   - A donor should have some rights in choosing who gets their organs.
   - An individual should have the right to donate their organs no matter what the risks are.
   - Receiving an organ transplant should be based on more than medical need.
   - Doctors should make treatment decisions bearing in mind that the patient is a potential organ donor.
   - Organ donation should be compulsory for all.
   - Children should be able to donate organs.
   - More effort should go into finding alternatives to organ donation such as xenotransplantation.
   - An individual should have the right to sell their organs/tissue.

2 'On organ donation, religious and non-religious views are almost entirely agreed.' To what extent do you agree?

3 'The benefits of making organ donation compulsory far outweigh the possible drawbacks.' To what extent do you agree?

Apply

Imagine that a bill was to be introduced to the Scottish Parliament as follows:

'Bill proposing the right of an individual to donate/sell organs/tissue including in situations where this would result in the donor's death.'

1 This proposed Bill argues that each individual has the right to do with their own body whatever they want, and if this includes donating organs which would result in their death then that person would have the right to do so.

2 This proposed Bill argues that in the same way a person has the right to sell anything which they own for benefit then this right should be extended to bodily organs.

As a class, split into groups and take one of the religious/non-religious perspectives you have studied in this chapter. Write a response to this proposed Bill from your chosen perspective explaining your views about this proposed Bill.

21 Status and treatment of embryos

Jean: Dae ye e'er gie a thocht tae afore ye wur quickenin?

Jane: *Nae, I hivna gien it much thocht masel tae be honest.*

Jean: Bit, aire maun hiv been a time fin ye wisna aboot.

Jane: *Aye, richt eneuch. Sae fin de ye think ye yokit tae be human?*

Jean: Startit? We maun aye be human sin we wis born.

Jane: *Aye, I ken yon, bit whit aboot afore ye wis born, wis ye human then?*

Jean: Aye, whit else cwid ye be – a cuddie?

Jane: *Nae, dinna be daft, bit fin did ye yoke tae be human?*

Jean: Ahm no sure at a' – fur I canna mind a'thin aboot it.

Jane: *Yon's ma aweers ...*

Jean and Jane are discussing when their life began. Jean started with the premise that her life began when she was born, however she quickly reviewed her position by thinking about what she therefore was before she was born. Jane pressed her argument by pointing out that there must have been something which could be identified as Jean before Jean was born to which Jean responded that she couldn't be certain since she had no memory of anything before she was born. Jane concluded that argument by suggesting that this lack of memory was crucial – thereby implying that simply having no memory about your own life before birth didn't give much of a clue as to when life begins ...

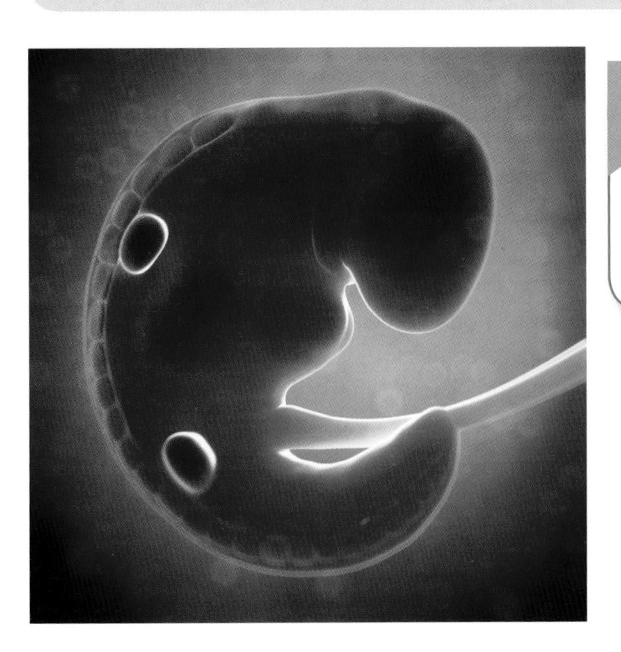

Talk Point

Does the fact that you cannot (consciously) remember anything before your birth mean that before birth you were not you?

The beginning of life

All humans everywhere have certain rights. These rights are summed up in customs, rules and, of course, laws. There are even laws which many countries sign up to, for example, in the United Nations Declaration on Human Rights. These rights which we give to fellow humans are – for the most part – different to the rights we give to animals (though there are some who think they shouldn't be), plants, machines and anything else not human. However, although we mostly agree that humans should have certain rights, how far do we agree about what is and isn't human? What is a human? Is it something biological, psychological, spiritual ... or something else entirely? When a baby is born it is a simple matter to decide that this baby is human (although even that might be disputed by some in certain situations) – but before birth, when did the being that became the baby become a human? There are some very different views about this which are very important for our thinking in this chapter. Before we look at different views about when life begins, let's get some important terminology out of the way: the SQA has chosen to call this section the 'Status and Treatment of Embryos'. For our purposes, therefore, we will consider an embryo to be something which comes into existence at the moment of conception. However, medically, it is important to be aware that there are different names for the various embryonic stages after fertilisation occurs.

So, what different views are there about when life begins?

The moment of fertilisation

Prior to fertilisation there is simply (usually) one oocyte (egg) and many millions of sperm(atozoa). One spermatozoa successfully penetrates the outer wall of the oocyte and this is 'the moment of conception' when sperm and egg join, share DNA, and begin the process of the development of the embryo. From this point onwards, all the required genetic material is present to become the (biological) person the embryo will become. For many, the moment of conception is the beginning of life, because from now on, the embryo is everything biologically that the walking, talking, breathing, heart-beating human the embryo will become. In other words all the potential ingredients for the next stage are present at this stage and if this continues in an unbroken continuum, then human life too progresses in an unbroken continuum. Some argue that at this stage, the embryo is a potential person and that a potential person is due all the rights, privileges and protections which a fully developed person should expect. It is also important to remember here that many people who regard the moment of conception as the beginning of life would also support a special status for both oocyte and sperm – since they too have the potential for life.

On the other hand, some argue that although the moment of conception is a crucial stage in the development of a person, there is an important difference between a potential person and an actual person. Although all the biological material is here, they argue, many of the other components that go to make up a person are not, and so the fertilised embryo remains a collection of cells rather than something they would consider as human (or at least not fully human).

The point of 'ensoulment'

For some religious people, life begins when a divine being has granted the embryo a soul. Most consider this as the moment of conception, but some think it happens at a later stage of the embryo's development. From this point on, having a soul makes the embryo a person and so deserving rights and protections. Some argue, of course, that this point only has meaning if you are a religious person – and doesn't explain complicated religious issues such as spontaneous abortion (why would a god have granted a soul, only to take it away sometimes shortly afterwards?).

Implantation

At around seven days after fertilisation, the embryo attaches itself to the wall of the womb. Some propose that this is the point at which life begins, because now the fertilised embryo can begin to grow and develop towards birth. Others, however, might say that this stage of development only indicates that the embryo is dependent upon the mother (some would argue that at this point it becomes 'part of' the mother) and so is not yet a person.

The 'primal streak'

At about the fourteenth day of development, the embryo cells start clustering together in order to form some of the basic bodily systems (such as the nervous system). At this point, some argue, the embryo can now experience pain and so it has developed something which marks it out as different to a collection of cells. Certainly, they would claim, if something can feel pain, then we have certain responsibilities towards it and it should be protected from the possibility of experiencing pain.

The 'quickening'

This is the point at which the embryo is first felt by the mother to move. For some, this is an indication that the embryo has moved to a different stage of its development. However, the embryo has been moving pretty much continuously since the moment of conception – even though the mother will not have felt this.

The attainment of consciousness

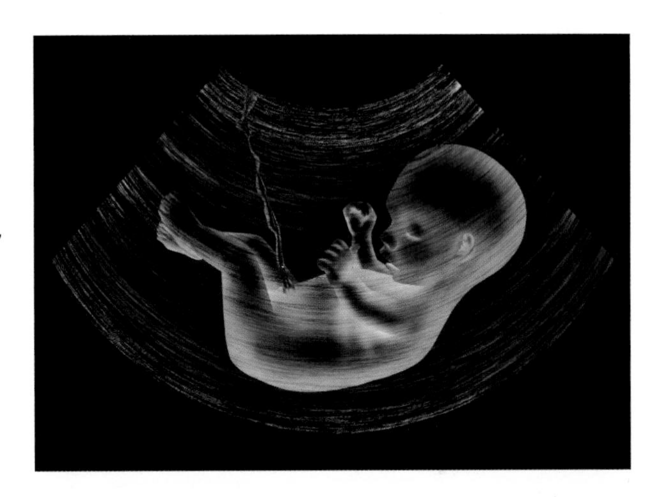

Now this is a really complex one. Some argue that life begins when the embryo starts to experience consciousness. However, there is still scientific debate about what exactly consciousness is. Brain activity is recordable in some cases at around 40 days after conception. However, there is no clear agreement about what this brain activity is or what it means, and whether this means that the embryo can be given the status of being a person. Even if it was agreed that this was consciousness, some might argue that consciousness does not automatically confer human status on a living being. On the other hand, some argue that consciousness is not really relevant because consciousness is not required to be considered human. Throughout life, many people lose consciousness – temporarily or in some cases permanently; does this mean that they are temporarily or permanently no longer a person?

Talk Point

What do you think 'consciousness' means and at what point do you think a human starts and stops being conscious?

Viability

This is the point at which the embryo (now more likely to be referred to as a foetus) could survive outside the uterus. For some, this marks the point at which the foetus can be thought of as a person. However, viability varies according to individual foetuses and also is linked to the availability of suitable medical and other support for the foetus. In fact, when you consider it, no foetus or baby would be likely to survive very long out of the uterus without support (which might be no more than feeding and keeping warm). However, for some, this marks a definitive shift in the status of the embryo from being something completely dependent on the biological processes of the mother to being something which can survive without these direct biological support mechanisms and so it has moved on considerably in its status as a person.

The status of the embryo: general principles

Following on from the previous discussion about when life begins, there are really three positions you can take about the moral status of the embryo.

- **The embryo is fully human from some point during its development** This means that no matter what you think of its consciousness, or how far you think it is a 'person', it deserves all the respect, protections and treatment that any other human being should expect. In fact, some might argue that it demands even more protection because of its inability to express its desires and wishes (and/or because it is not yet at a stage where it can be considered to have desires and wishes). When this fully human status becomes a reality depends on your point of view – with some people thinking it is from the moment of conception and others at some other point in the development of the embryo/foetus. From this point, morally speaking, the embryo should be considered as human and therefore all the moral safeguards available to humans should also be available to the embryo (regulated and protected by others on its behalf of course).
- **The embryo is partly human from some point in its development** Being human is a complex concept – and being a 'person' even more so. However, this position considers that there is something uniquely different about an embryo compared to any other collection of cells (in the same way that any human is a collection of cells). However, this position might recognise that although the embryo is a potential person, it is not yet a person, or at least not a fully human person (until some point, the exact pin-pointing of which will vary according to different people). This means that while the embryo does have some rights, it does not necessarily have all the rights which a fully human person should expect.
- **The embryo is a biological entity – a collection of cells** This position takes the view that the embryo is a collection of cells which are increasing in complexity as they develop towards being human. However, it makes little sense to think of this collection of cells as human and certainly not a person. Again, when this 'collection of cells' becomes human and/or a person will vary according to individuals, but until that happens the embryo has no more moral importance than any other collection of cells. It therefore makes little sense to talk of an embryo having rights.

Talk Point

Which of these three positions most closely matches your viewpoint?

How you treat embryos will therefore vary according to which variety of the three positions above you accept. There can be many reasons why you might adopt one of these three positions (or some mixture of the three): your religious beliefs could shape your thinking, or your philosophical standpoint, or your upbringing – or even just your gut feeling about it. Whichever position you adopt about the moral status of embryos will affect your views about their treatment.

Treatment of embryos: general principles

Again, the broad principles here can be set out in a fairly straightforward way – although, again, combinations of each of these three positions are possible.

- **An embryo is fully human (or fully potentially human)** therefore should be given the same rights and protections as any other human – with special consideration perhaps taken of its vulnerability and inability to act on its own behalf.
- **An embryo is partly human** and so while it does not deserve all the protections of a full human person, it does deserve a degree of special protection and has some rights – though these are less precise and comprehensive than the rights which a fully human person should have.
- **An embryo is not a human person** therefore should not be given any special rights or protections.

In what ways can embryos be treated?

The treatment and use of human embryos is very tightly controlled in the UK by the Human Fertilisation and Embryology Authority (HFEA) which is an *'independent regulator overseeing the use of gametes and embryos in fertility treatment and research.'*[94] The HFEA considers medical and ethical discussion about the status and treatment of embryos and so regulates practice in this area. Just as for the HFEA, the view you have of the moral status of the embryo is very likely to affect your response to the morality of the following possible ways in which embryos can be treated.

IVF

In-vitro fertilisation (IVF)is using technology to support conception. Failure to conceive naturally can be for a variety of medical reasons or a result of social preferences (for example, same-sex couples who wish to have children may use IVF technologies to facilitate conception). One of the complexities with IVF is that the processes can involve 'superovulation' (production of many oocytes) and also the fertilisation of multiple oocytes with the most 'viable' ones being selected for re-implantation back into the uterus and then allowed to proceed to birth. 'Viable' in this case is a medical decision based on which of the fertilised embryos is considered most likely to survive. The less viable ones may be used for research up to a 14-day limit after which they must be discarded (as will any which are not used for research). While some argue that IVF is a helpful medical procedure in the case of couples who cannot conceive naturally, others are less persuaded by it when it relates to the establishment of pregnancy in other situations (for example, in the case of same-sex couples). There have also been recent concerns raised about the possibility that embryos fertilised in-vitro could, potentially, have more than two parents. Some are concerned about the use of the non-viable embryos, and some are concerned at the morality of 'discarding' any fertilised embryo (as well as the issue of deciding that one is 'more viable' than another). For some, this also raises the difficult question of 'designer babies' – which means selecting viable embryos based on more than simple likelihood of survival, instead somehow trying to choose aspects of the embryo which are personal preference rather than medical matters (for example, choosing to re-implant male rather than female embryos).

One other concern linked to IVF which is important in many of the matters you have looked at in this section is the issue of human intervention in natural processes (referred to by some as 'playing God'). This takes the view that humans should not interfere in natural processes such as conception, pregnancy and birth. Of course, there are a range of views about this, but those who object to human 'interference' in relation to embryos might claim that while medical interventions can be perfectly acceptable in many cases, the unique processes of conception, pregnancy and birth should not be interfered with. In their view, there is something particularly special about these processes and medical science should place some limitations on what we do here. They might argue that although we can use medical science to support conception and pregnancy, this does not always mean that we should.

Genetic screening and selection

More 'viable' embryos are re-implanted in the case of IVF – which relates to their likelihood of survival. However, even following natural conception and during the normal course of pregnancy, a number of tests can be carried out on the developing embryo. These tests can uncover a range of things, from the gender of the embryo to the likelihood that it may develop specific (sometimes genetically determined) conditions. In the case of IVF, the option to not re-implant an embryo with a particular condition may be available. In the case of otherwise normal conception and pregnancy, the option to terminate the pregnancy may also be available should some condition be identified in the developing embryo. This raises a range of moral issues:

- For example, is this taking 'playing God' too far? Perhaps it is one thing to discard an embryo which seems to have little chance of successfully developing and another to discard an embryo because it has been identified as having some condition. Are we deciding here that some lives are more worth living than others? Have we the right to make this decision? What might this say about the value that we place on different people?

- Could this lead to a 'designer baby' approach – where we select (or allow to continue to develop) only those embryos we consider to be 'worthy'? Could this lead to a future where we can screen for all sorts of things and then choose whether that is the kind of child we want or not (eye colour, height, intelligence, sporting ability ...?) Could we, through genetic selection of embryos, shape the future make-up of the human species (or speed up the evolution of our species ...)?

- More widely, do we ever have the right to terminate a pregnancy because we judge that it is not going the way we think it should? (And who would be 'we' in this case?) We'll look at this in more detail later when we consider abortion, but for the moment it is worth considering how our view about the moral status of the embryo links to anyone's right to terminate an embryo for whatever reason.

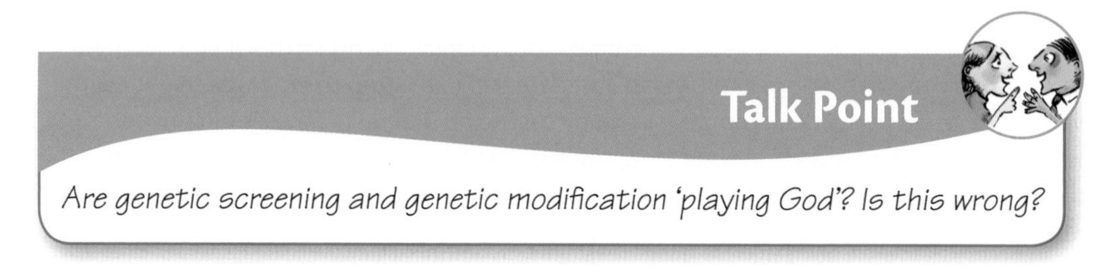

Talk Point

Are genetic screening and genetic modification 'playing God'? Is this wrong?

Genetic modification

As well as choosing to allow to develop or terminating specific types of embryo, what about the genetic modification of embryos? In 2015, scientists in China made the claim that they had genetically modified human embryos[95]. This was followed by a great deal of ethical debate. In September 2015, scientists in a UK research facility were claimed to be seeking permission to genetically modify human embryos[96] (although these embryos would be discarded after this and not re-implanted into the womb). So, what about genetically altering human embryos: what ethical issues might this raise?

- There are issues about what we could and should do to 'improve' an embryo – and, of course, if we should *ever* try to 'improve' an embryo, especially as an embryo cannot express any views about this.
- Is there a moral difference between allowing genetic modification of human embryos which are subsequently discarded and genetically modifying embryos which would then be implanted into a womb and allowed to grow towards birth?
- Should we permit genetic modification in some cases but not others? Some argue that if we have the ability through genetic modification to prevent the development of medical conditions in life (often genetically caused conditions),

should we not do so? In fact, might we have a moral obligation to do so? Opponents say that this could lead to us valuing some people and not others and this would be wrong – besides, again perhaps this would be taking 'playing God' too far.

- Is there a moral difference between cosmetic and medical genetic modification? Some might argue that using genetic modification to prevent medical conditions is one thing, but genetically modifying embryos for 'cosmetic' reasons is another. Cosmetic reasons might include, for example, body shape, hair colour, and so on. The argument here would be that using genetic modification processes for this would be wrong.
- Are the possible costs and possible benefits in genetic modification too difficult to predict and so suggest that genetic modification is a bad idea? Genetic modification may change one 'undesirable' thing, but it *may* also affect something else (unpredictably). Should this level of unpredictability in the outcome of genetic modification mean that we should reject it right at the start? Also, any medical procedure involving an embryo – for whatever reason – involves risks. Are such risks acceptable? Do these risks depend on the reasons for our actions?

Pure research

As well as issues linked to the treatment of embryos which are associated with the intention to continue a pregnancy, there are also issues related to the use of embryos where there is no intention that they are ever permitted to develop towards birth. The use of embryos in this way is regulated very carefully by the HFEA, who sets out clear guidelines about what can and cannot be done and at what stage of embryonic development certain procedures are and are not permitted.

Firstly, the sources of fertilised embryos for research and other processes can involve moral differences: some think that no embryo should ever be 'discarded' while others think that in certain situations, embryos which have been discarded should be allowed to be used – especially if this use brings benefits. This issue is further complicated by the fact that some embryonic tissue used in research and for other purposes may be the result of deliberate terminations of pregnancy (abortion) which raises a whole range of other moral concerns for many. So, for some, how an embryo has been 'obtained' is a moral issue to begin with, no matter how it is used after it has been obtained.

Pure research is research with no specific *therapeutic* aim. Its purpose is to further human understanding and so, of course, could have important implications for therapies as a by-product of the research. Depending on your view of the status of the embryo you will approach this differently: some argue that using an embryo in this way is morally justified as the embryo is 'sacrificed' for the benefit of others. Others would oppose this because the embryo is human, and because the embryo has no ability to consent to its being used in this way. Some might also argue that pure research does not provide enough justification for the use of embryos because it has no clear aim in mind and no direct therapeutic use. Others would disagree, arguing that pure research could lead to unexpected breakthroughs and so does justify the use of embryos.

Stem cell research

Stem cells are cells which are basically able to divide and renew themselves. Stem cells are undifferentiated, which means that they have no specialism of their own, but can divide and develop into highly specialised cells. Stem cells can therefore be used to treat certain diseases like Parkinson's disease and Type I diabetes among others. This means that they are highly valuable as cells which can help treat a range of diseases. One major source of stem cells is human embryos – usually those involved in IVF treatments. The stem cells are removed from the embryo and the embryo is then destroyed – although scientists are working to develop ways to remove stem cells from embryos without subsequently having to destroy the embryo. (Stem cells can also be harvested from adults, obviously without any requirement to destroy the adult in the process.) For many people, stem cell research offers great hope that certain diseases will be able to be more effectively treated, so the benefits outweigh the drawbacks. However, for some, stem cell harvesting and the subsequent destruction of the embryo are morally unacceptable because the process involves the deliberate destruction of an embryo which is a potential human being. Some also argue that the possibility that embryonic tissue might be financially valuable might lead to a market for it and so potentially lead to women agreeing to terminations for this reason alone.

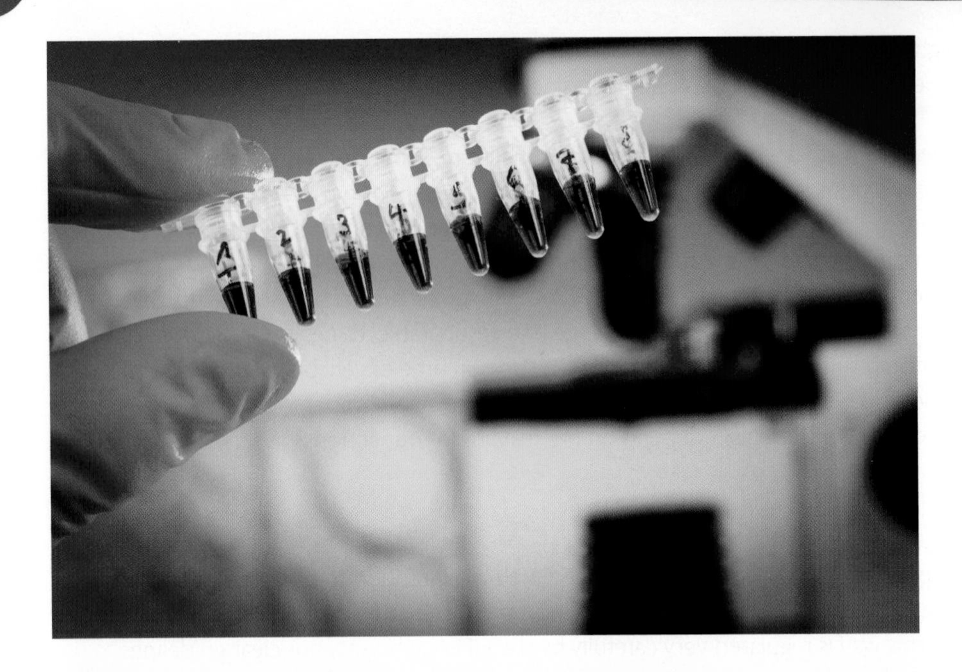

Talk Point

Is it right to use embryonic material for research and/or therapeutic treatments?

Abortion

Many of the medical and scientific issues around the treatment of embryos ultimately boil down to the rights and wrongs of abortion. This is a very complex and emotional topic which involves a range of views linked to opinions about the status of the embryo/foetus/unborn child. Using embryonic material in IVF is considered by some as using embryonic material which would otherwise be discarded anyway and so it is morally right to make use of it for scientific purposes. Others, of course, disagree with the processes involved in IVF and therefore any associated use of embryos and embryonic material, while still others see value in IVF, but do not support deliberately discarding embryos. As well as embryonic material resulting from IVF, there may also be additional moral concerns around using embryonic material which is the result of planned abortions not linked to IVF. To try to simplify this complex issue, a view about abortion is likely to be linked to the status of the embryo you examined above: that is, the embryo as fully human from conception; as potentially human from the moment of conception; as partly human at some point in its development and fully human at another; as only fully human at a specific point.

Your views about the status of the embryo in relation to how much it can be thought of as a human person will, at least partly, decide your views on abortion. However, views about abortion can also involve views about:

- The morality of killing human life – of any kind at any stage
- The view that abortion is a women's right to choose or not
- How far it is believed that the embryo is part of/independent from its mother
- The relative rights of mothers and fathers in relation to abortion.

Abortion is a complex issue, and further complicates the moral debate around the status and treatment of embryos.

Some religious and philosophical perspectives

Christianity

The status of embryos

Within Christianity there is a variety of views about the status of embryos, from those who think that the embryo is fully human from the moment of conception to those who think full humanity begins at a point much later than this. Christians believe that life is sacred and a gift from God and so therefore deserves to be cherished and protected – so how far you consider an embryo to be a fully living being will then affect how much protection and care you think it (s/he) deserves.

The treatment of embryos

In addition to this, Christians believe that the most vulnerable in our society deserve special care and protection – so if you think of an embryo as an especially vulnerable thing/human/person, then you will want to ensure that it has special protections, not just because life is sacred, but because vulnerable life deserves even more dedicated protection. There will be differences of opinion in Christianity about specific ways in which embryos are treated because some will support some 'uses' of embryos, some will argue for only certain uses and some will reject any use of embryos.

The Church of Scotland

The status of embryos

'*The Roman Catholic Church and many individual Christians believe that from conception onwards the embryo should be accorded the fully human status. In principle this allows no embryo research at all. In 2006 the General Assembly of the Church of Scotland took a middle position, which affirmed the special status of the embryo but also recognised potential benefits of embryo research under limited circumstances.*'[97] The Church of Scotland therefore considers the embryo is special (but does not necessarily have 'absolute specialness') but also considers that in some limited circumstances it can be used for research purposes. This therefore implies that the Church of Scotland does not consider life to begin at the moment of conception.

Treatment of embryos

So the Church accepts the use of embryos in some circumstances. The Church's Science, Religion and Technology project produced a report on human stem cell research and embryology in 2006[98]. '*The General Assembly agreed with the report's main conclusions:*

- *That embryo stem cell research might be permitted up to 14 days, using supplies of IVF and PGD embryos, but only for a very good reason*
- *To oppose the creation of IVF or cloned embryos for research, except under exceptional circumstances*
- *To oppose animal-human and parthenogenetic embryos*
- *It also urges the Government not to relax the present regulations governing embryo research in forthcoming legislation.*'[99]

It is important to note that this report was drawn up by twelve experts in fields relevant to the science around embryo research, but that within this group there were also differences of opinion leading to the final report.

The Roman Catholic Church

The status of embryos

'*At the second Vatican Council, the Church for her part presented once again to modern man her constant and certain doctrine according to which "Life once conceived must be protected with the utmost care; abortion and infanticide are abominable crimes." More recently, the Charter of the Rights of the Family ... confirmed that "Human life must be absolutely respected and protected from the moment of conception".*' This clearly restates the Church's long-held position that life begins at the moment of conception and is therefore due all the rights and protections due to a person from that moment on. This has led some to summarise the Church's position by stating that it does not see an embryo as a potential human being, but instead is a human being filled with potential.

Treatment of embryos

The Roman Catholic Church is equally clear about any use of embryos for research purposes: *'The Charter of the Rights of the Family published by the Holy See affirms: "Respect for the dignity of the human being excludes all experimental manipulation or exploitation of the human embryo".'*[100] In summary, the Church rejects any medical interventions, research, use or treatment which does not have the aim of preserving the life of the developing embryo.

Buddhism

The status of embryos

There is no one agreed Buddhist view on the status of the embryo. Some argue that personhood begins at the moment of conception, since this is when the pattern of the previous life merges with the fertilised egg. From this moment on, the embryo is a person in the same way that any other person is.

Treatment of embryos

Like other issues in this chapter the interplay of three important Buddhist principles will affect the treatment of embryos, and how each Buddhist applies these will determine their view of various kinds of treatment.[101] The first is the principle of refraining from taking life. If an embryo is human, then this could mean that nothing should be done which might involve harming it. The second is the principle of compassion – which could mean showing absolute compassion to each embryo. However, individual Buddhists might interpret this as meaning that embryos could be used in some ways, since the beneficial outcomes would be compassionate for many more people in the long run. Finally, the principle of 'skilful means' involves making the right decision based on knowledge and wisdom. This could lead a Buddhist to accepting certain uses of embryos if this seems the wise thing to do for some reason or other.

Humanism

The status of embryos

'In the case of embryo research, Humanists would focus on two issues: whether an embryo is indeed a person, and whether the research on and subsequent use of embryo cells would do more good than harm.' This comes from the British Humanist Association which goes on to argue that at the early stages of embryo development: *'an embryo has few of the characteristics we associate with a person'.* Humanists therefore are likely to argue that the embryo has no special moral status at the early stages of its development.

Treatment of embryos

'If an embryo's cells can be used to alleviate human suffering, the good consequences seem to outweigh the harmful ones as long as the legal cut off point for research is sufficiently early.'[102] Humanists therefore accept properly regulated research using embryos, since they do not accept that early embryos can be considered human in any meaningful sense. In fact, Humanists argue that the argument that people are 'playing God' in using embryos does not make sense because humans 'play God' every time they make any medical intervention. Most Humanists, in fact, are likely to take a modified Utilitarian position on the use of embryos, accepting that embryo use is morally justified if the benefits outweigh the drawbacks.

Utilitarianism

The status of embryos

There is no specific Utilitarian position on the moral status of an embryo, since Utilitarians may have very different views about when life begins, and also, once life is considered to have begun, what actions are morally permissible in relation to that life.

Treatment of embryos

In an article in *The Scotsman* in 2012, Utilitarian Peter Singer argued: *'Why should a being's potential to become rationally self-aware make it wrong to end its life before it has the capacity for rationality or self-awareness? We have no obligation to allow every being with the potential to become a rational being to realise that potential.'* [103] Singer was writing in response to questions about 'risking a woman's life in order to preserve an unborn child'. Singer has often stated that to be deserving of full human rights a being must be a human person in a meaningful sense and he thinks it is far from clear that an embryo can be considered as a full human being. Utilitarians therefore could support – or reject – any treatment or use of an embryo: if this is likely to lead to greater good for the majority then it would be morally acceptable to use an embryo, but if doing so led to a society which was less caring of 'more vulnerable life', then that might not be beneficial for the majority. The decision would have to be made by the Utilitarian around whether the embryo was a person – if the embryo could feel pain, if the embryo has interests and how far we have a responsibility as conscious beings towards a being which is not yet conscious in the way more developed humans are.

Personal Reflection

* *To what extent do you think an embryo is a person?*
* *In your opinion, what ways in which embryos might be treated are morally acceptable/morally unacceptable?*
* *How far do you think the central question in relation to the treatment of embryos is linked to the idea of the 'ends justifying the means'?*

Active learning

Check your understanding

1. What different views are there about when life begins and what are these views based upon?
2. How far is there disagreement about whether an embryo is a person or not? What is your view?
3. What is IVF and what moral issues might it raise?
4. Describe in detail two ways in which an embryo can be used in research.
5. How do the moral arguments about abortion link to the treatment of embryos?
6. What do religious people generally say about the status of embryos?
7. How might a religious person respond to different ways in which embryos can be treated?
8. What two key issues might a Humanist focus on when considering the treatment of embryos?
9. Would a Utilitarian support all forms of research using embryos?
10. Do Buddhists think of an embryo as a person?

Investigate

1. Each part of this chapter could easily be a book in itself. Choose one of the ways in which embryos can be/are treated and carry out further research. Display your findings in an academic poster format where you explain the key facts and opinions and discuss the various responses across beliefs and philosophies.
2. For a different aspect of the status or treatment of embryos, create an 'infographic'. This is a series of drawings accompanied by a script explaining the key issues behind a particular topic.
3. You have covered some religious and philosophical perspectives in this chapter. Select a different religion/viewpoint/philosophy and prepare a presentation on its views about the status and treatment of embryos. You could, again, focus on one issue or idea in this chapter.
4. In this chapter you have not explored human cloning, human/animal hybrids, and parthenogenesis of embryos. Find out what each of these is all about and what moral issues they raise. How might the viewpoints you have studied in this chapter respond to these?

Analyse and Evaluate

1. To what extent do you agree that an embryo is special and deserves special rights and protections?
2. 'In relation to the treatment of embryos, religions are more agreed on this than on almost any other topic.' To what extent do you agree?
3. Is there a 'gap' in thinking about the status and treatment of embryos between religious and non-religious perspectives and do you think this gap could ever be 'closed'?

Apply

It is argued by some that complex issues such as the status and treatment of embryos should not be left in school until you are in your senior years, but should be taught at a much earlier stage. Choose one of the issues you have studied in this chapter. Your task is to create some materials which could be used by S1 pupils to help them explore these complex issues.

RELIGION
AND
CONFLICT

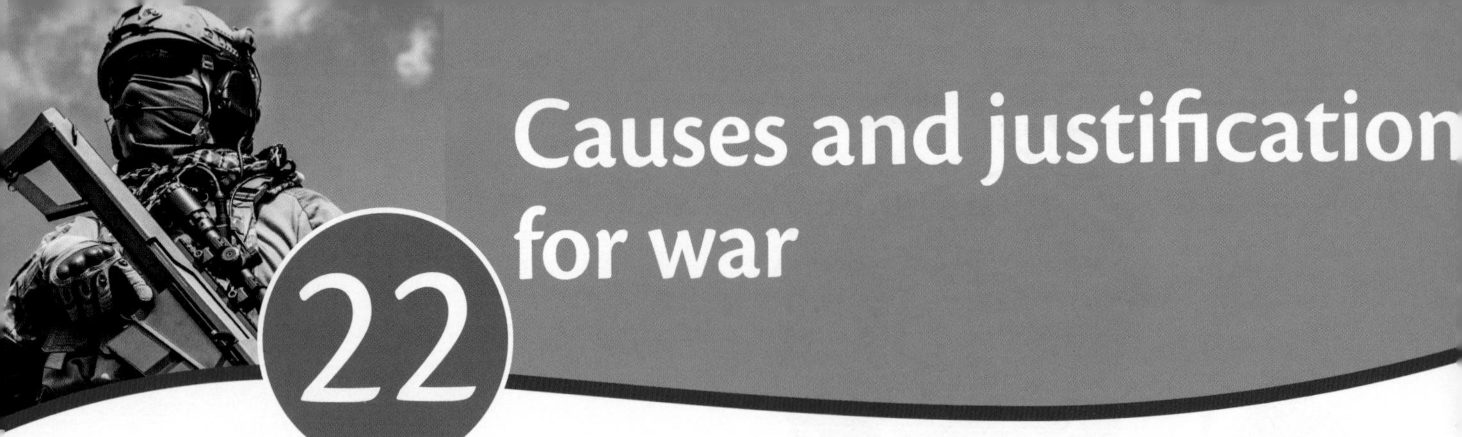

22 Causes and justification for war

Once upon a time the Bilurians lived together in peace with the Trilurians. No one cared that Bilurians liked everything in twos and Trilurians liked everything in threes. For example, Bilurians cycled on bicycles, which Trilurians thought was really funny and quite strange compared to their much more sensible habit of tricycle riding – although the Trilurians' habit of using two forks and one knife or two knives and one fork usually raised a chuckle from any watching Bilurians.

Bilurians and Trilurians lived next door to each other, worked together and went to school together. They ate at the same restaurants, often the same foods (two courses or three as you would expect), went to the same cinemas, night clubs and so on. They even watched the same TV programmes – though Trilurians preferred 3D TV for obvious reasons. In everyday life you would never be able to tell who was a Bilurian and who a Trilurian unless they were cycling, eating or watching TV ... However, and the reasons for it all are lost in the mists of time, there came a point where Bilurians and Trilurians no longer lived so harmoniously together. Before anyone knew it, Bilurians were talking really quite unpleasantly about Trilurians and then things started to take a turn for the worse with more than verbal attacks. Eventually, although they had all shared one beautiful country for as long as anyone could remember, all the Bilurians moved to one end of the country and all the Trilurians to the other and before too long these areas became known as Biluria and Triluria. The tensions remained as each country built up its own two or three-dimensional identity ... and worsened: Bilurian leaders made great speeches against all things Trilurian, as did the Trilurians against their Bilurian neighbours. →

The Lurian war has now been raging for many hundreds of years and it's a wonder that there are any Bilurians or Trilurians still living. Rusted tricycles and bicycles litter the wastelands where violent battles have been fought and no one has the time for TV any more. The numbers killed have been too many to document and most Bilurians and Trilurians have never known anything but their countries at war. No one knows how it started and worse still, no one has any idea how, or if, it might end; what each side does know, however, is that whatever the reason for the war ever starting in the first place, the war is the right thing for their mighty nation to support and that one day their side will be gloriously and finally triumphant ... or perhaps biumphant ...

Talk Point

How similar is the Lurian war to any other war you know about?

What is war?

It is important to define what we mean by war: for the purposes of this chapter we will include all forms of conflict within and between countries as war – or rather conflict which goes beyond individuals and relatively small groups. Technically speaking, wars between countries have to be formally declared in most cases – and generally link to international laws and agreements about the point where it is considered that the only course of action left is war. Civil wars are conflicts between groups and/or factions within countries. Other conflicts have all the properties of war but are not always formally declared as wars. So we will include any relatively large-scale conflict which includes fighting which leads to destruction of property, land and, most importantly, people.

The complex causes of war

Like all the issues in this course, the causes are rarely straightforward. There are usually a very large number of different causes involved in each issue, all of which lead to certain behaviours, beliefs, practices and outcomes. It's the same with war: every war is different, and every war has a different set of circumstances which come together to create the conditions for war – it would be a lot easier if the causes were simple, because then the solutions might be simple too ... perhaps. Wars can be complex mixtures of history, psychology, personalities, social and cultural factors, philosophical and religious positions, politics, ideology, economics ... to name but a few. To simplify the issue as much as possible we will group the causes of war into 'aggressive' and 'defensive' causes.

Talk Point

What do you think are the major causes of war?

Aggressive causes of and justifications for war

What we don't mean here is angry world leaders or people (although that might not help matters). 'Aggressive' in this sense refers to wars which begin in a purposeful way with – most likely – a specific outcome in mind, or a real or perceived cause. Aggressive wars are those where one country (or group within a country) engages in war from the outset – for very specific reasons – or, more likely, as a result of very complex combinations of these reasons.

To increase or secure land or resources

Some wars between countries begin because one country wants what another country has – this might be land to live on, to cultivate, or to make use of in some other way. It might be that one country wants the resources that another country has – to increase or stabilise its own economic power – and decides to take these by force. It could also be that one country thinks that the control another country has over a specific resource might harm their country and so going to war about it is the best approach (for example, to ensure a suitable water supply in one country which is seen as being threatened by another 'upstream' country). In civil wars and conflicts it may be that one group wants to extend its living space or to take from another group what it thinks it should have – for example, power from the government or 'control over its own affairs', or control over a country's resources. Wars such as this may be based on objective assessments of particular situations – or they may be based on assessments of situations which are closely tied to the way one country or group 'sees things'. Wars like this can easily escalate as allies of countries/groups attacked might rush to their defence and allies of the aggressive country/group might support them since they might think that they are acting perfectly reasonably.

To spread or settle ideological differences

Some wars may begin because of ideological differences between countries, or between groups within countries – or even, in some cases, between the ideologies of powerful individual leaders or ruling classes. These ideological differences may be real or perceived. Ideologies are simply different ways of seeing things – though they can easily draw in other real or perceived differences between countries or groups within countries in a complicated mix. Sometimes these ideologies are based on philosophies, political views or religious differences, or support for one group in a society as opposed to another – for example, different ethnic groups or different social/economic classes. Such ideological differences can easily become polarised – which means that there end up being extreme views held on one 'side' and the 'other' side and then people line up with whichever 'side' best matches their view. This polarisation can easily lead to people not being very subtle about differences within countries or groups. For example, once a country goes to war, it is very easy for most people in that country to start identifying themselves with that country's 'national identity' and so, even though they may have as much in common with someone from the country they are at war with than someone in their own country, because the other country is not theirs it can lead to them thinking that going to war with them is morally acceptable regardless of any similarities. Sometimes people refer to this as 'jingoism' which means identifying with everything in your country (or group) and thinking it is best because it belongs to your country/group. Wars like these can easily escalate as allies with similar ideologies might support the aggressive or defending country/group because they share their ideology and/or want to promote it further.

Personalities, policies and posturing

In the past wars could be fought because of differences between leaders – which then drew everyone in the country or group into conflict. This is less likely nowadays since most countries are not ruled by one absolute leader who can make decisions like this. However, some argue that the power and attitude of individual world leaders can still result in war. Political policies can also lead to conflict because if a group or country has committed to a particular position on something, then they might have to pursue that through aggressive conflict. Finally, sometimes aggressive wars are posturing which has got out of control. This might be a leader or group 'taking a stance' about something; such stances are all very well when they are 'just talk'; however, sometimes these can escalate into conflict when the posturing gets to a point where there's 'no turning back'.

Talk Point

Can 'aggressive' causes for war ever be justified?

Defensive causes of and justifications for war

Many wars and conflicts are therefore aggressive acts which do not respond to any external cause in particular. However, many wars and conflicts can be thought of as defensive wars – wars which come about as a response to something. Defensive wars are about protecting yourself (or your way of life) and/or protecting others. Defensive wars can be further categorised into wars which begin because of actual or perceived threat.

Actual threat

Clearly if one country has actually attacked another (or one group has attacked another) then one of the possible responses is to fight back as an act of 'self-defence'. Perhaps the attacked country or group had no intention of engaging in war/conflict, but the attack prompted it. One difficulty with this is the question of when an attack is an attack. Obviously if one country's armies have marched into another country and are engaged in killing people, then that is clearly an attack. Such activity would be relatively straightforward as a justification for war (perhaps): however, what if the attack is more 'subtle'? What if country or group A thinks that country or group B is much more subtly attacking them? This could happen, for example, where insurgents are carrying out specific acts of violence against a particular country or group. In this case, is it justifiable for a country/group to respond by carrying out acts of war? And if so, a full-on war, some bombing, limited attacks on the aggressors? Also, is it right for one country to support another which claims that it is under attack? Let's say country/group C claims it is under attack and asks country/group D for support. Does country/group D have the right to support country/group C? Is there a moral obligation to support a country or group in this situation? Some argue that the 'war on terrorism' was an example of a justifiable response to an actual threat, while others argue that while the threat was real, the response was not justifiable: some, of course, argue that while there were identifiable acts of terrorism, the origins of these actions were not straightforward and so any response against the origins of these actions were dubious.

Perceived threat

You are walking along the street and you see someone coming towards you. You think they are going to attack you, so you hit them first. Is this morally acceptable? Some wars and conflicts begin precisely in this way. A country or group decides that there is a threat against it and it is going to take a 'pre-emptive' strike against the perceived aggressor as an act of defence in advance of a real attack. Now again, there can be differences here too – if a country has lined all of its armies up on your border it might be quite reasonable to assume they are going to attack you – although there's still the question of whether it is right or not for you to attack them first because they 'look as if' they are going to attack you. On the other hand, perhaps things said by the leader of another country or group gives you reasonable cause to think that they are planning an attack – should you strike first to gain the upper hand? There is also the potential issue here of perceived ideological threat – what if you think a country or group has the aim of spreading its ideology into your country or group and so replacing your ideology – do you have the right to defend yourself against an 'ideological threat' even though there may be no actual violence or aggression involved?

Talk Point

Is it right to strike first when you think an aggressor is going to strike you?

Justifications for war: Just War Theory

So, there can be a wide range of causes of war and the justifications for these can be linked to aggressive or defensive positions. However, Just War Theory aims to summarise justifications for war – although many argue that Just War Theory isn't about justifying war, it is about preventing it – because it sets out very clear conditions for acceptable and unacceptable reasons for going to war (*jus ad bellum*) and then what is acceptable when at war in order to bring about a swift return of peace (*jus in bello*). Just War Theory has become predominantly a Christian theory (although it can be found in the teachings of ancient non-Christian philosophers and in viewpoints expressed in other religions) which tries to make sense of three conflicting ideas:

- There is a responsibility on leaders to protect their people and do what is right.
- Sometimes doing this may require being prepared to use violence.
- It is wrong to take human life.

The basic principles of Just War Theory and some moral concerns these raise are:

- **The war must have a reasonable cause** Issues – who decides what is a reasonable or unreasonable cause and based on what evidence? Even if the war has a reasonable cause for one country or group, does this automatically match the understanding of 'reasonable cause' for another country or group?
- **The war must be a last resort** Issues – who decides when everything else has failed, after how long and based on what? What other options are there to avoid war? In waiting for a decision about the view that everything else has failed, might one country or group end up weakened by their inactivity while another country or group has been able to ready themselves for war?
- **Be declared by a proper authority** Issues – who might this be? Clearly in the case of a country it would be their leader/s, but what about in other situations such as civil wars where even who is the 'proper authority' might be one of the sources of conflict? Does this mean that wars not declared are any less problematic – or real – than any other kinds of conflict?
- **The war must be for the right intention** Issues – in an ideal world, any war would have the ultimate aim of leading to peace, but is this always the case? Who decides what a good/justifiable intention is and what is not? One country/group's 'right intention' may not be shared by another.
- **Have a reasonable chance of success** Issues – how can this be decided and by whom? Most countries/groups hope to – or perhaps expect to – win any war they engage in but what makes them think so? How do you measure success in a war – other than perhaps whether it ends or not? Does this mean that small minority groups who feel under threat should never go on the offensive because there is a strong likelihood that they will not be successful?
- **Should ensure that the ends are proportional to the means** Issues – who decides what 'proportional' means? How, in practice, does anyone ensure that anything is 'proportional' in war? If there are differences of opinion between groups/countries about the ends of a conflict, how might there be any agreement about what are and are not acceptable means to these different ends? Is the death of even one person in a conflict 'proportional'? How far should wars involve just the military and how far should civilians be involved?

We will return to some of these points in the following chapters, but for the moment the key question is this: Would accepting Just War Theory be more likely to prevent wars beginning in the first place, lead to earlier resolution of conflict and eventual peace ... or not?

Talk Point

Would Just War Theory be helpful to a group/country/leader considering war?

Some religious and philosophical perspectives

Christianity

In general many Christians are likely to consider war as a 'necessary evil' in some situations – especially when all attempts to avoid war have failed. While Christians generally support the idea that life is sacred and that it should not be taken, they might also accept that there are situations where it is justified in order to lead to a greater good. Many Christians of course oppose war as an idea and reality in all its forms – arguing that the commandment 'You shall not kill' does not allow for any exceptions. However, those Christians who accept that war is sometimes necessary would argue that defensive wars are acceptable, though it is unlikely that Christians would support aggressive acts of war which had no reasonable foundations.

The Church of Scotland

In 2009, the Church's Church and Society Council produced a report examining the ethics of defence. In this it stated: *'In the context of the ethics of defence then, the Church itself is called to live out of the heart of God having put us in the right with himself, and to seek to work out the very difficult issues in defence out of this perspective. This is not to say that we cannot defend ourselves from an attack, but use of defensive weapons must be thought through very carefully. There may well be considerable disagreement among Christians as to what defence means.'* [104] The Church's position is therefore that war is sometimes necessary and morally acceptable. However, careful thought needs to be given to the methods of warfare as well as being clear about whether some forms of defence are more morally acceptable than others. The Church supports Just War Theory, and has argued that all the criteria of Just War Theory should be met if a war is to be considered morally acceptable. In responding to the war in Afghanistan in 2011, the Church appointed an ecumenical group which stated: *'If a specific conflict is no longer considered to be a "just war" then it is clearly very hard for a Christian to support or continue to participate in it.'*[105]

The Roman Catholic Church

The Catechism is clear about the morality of defensive war: *'Legitimate defence can be not only a right but a grave duty for one who is responsible for the lives of others. The defence of the common good requires that an unjust aggressor be rendered unable to cause harm.'* (2265) It also argues, however, that *'All citizens and all governments are obliged to work for the avoidance of war.'* (2308) The Church effectively supports Just War Theory and is keen to stress that all attempts to avoid war should have been exhausted before war is engaged in. It stresses that aggressive acts of war are wrong, but defensive actions are legitimate as long as they conform to Just War Theory principles. The Church therefore takes a common approach within Christianity which is based on the idea that war is occasionally a regrettable, but necessary, evil in order to protect yourself or others.

Buddhism

The first of the five precepts is clear that Buddhists should avoid killing and avoid harm to anything living. As well as a central commitment to peace and non-violence, and an approach to life which stresses the avoidance of aggressive thoughts and actions, it would be expected that Buddhists would universally oppose war. In the Dhammapada it states: *'Hatred is never appeased by hatred, hatred is only appeased by love. This is an eternal law.'* All of this would imply that even a defensive war would not be acceptable to a Buddhist – and for some Buddhists this is the case. However, some Buddhists take the view that engaging in war may be necessary in order to protect those in need – as an act of defence and doing no more than is necessary to resolve the situation. Some also argue that war can be engaged in to protect Buddhism, or to keep the kammic harm of war to a minimum. Then again, some Buddhists would respond that it is more in tune with Buddhism in all situations to prefer to be killed or allow killing rather than kill, whether this is a defensive act or not.

Humanism

The British Humanist Association states: *'Some say that war is "natural" ... Humanists would respond by saying that we should use our intelligence and ability to reason to overcome some natural instincts, and that, in the case of something as terrible as war, we should always seek non-violent solutions first. But to resort to violence in self-defence or for altruistic reasons – to protect the lives and rights of others – can sometimes be justified on a national level, just as it can on an individual level.'*[106] Humanists therefore consider that there are times when war is necessary, though they too would expect that all ways to avoid war would have been attempted. However, it is also important to note that many Humanists also support the view that war is wrong and so have been heavily involved in pacifism and conscientious objection.

Utilitarianism

Utilitarians could support or reject any kind of act of war. The key issue for many would be the possible consequences of going to war or not going to war. Clearly a decision would have to be reached about how far the likely consequences would justify war – or inaction. The difficulty here, as in many instances in Utilitarianism, is the complexity of working out what the possible consequences of war might be and then making a decision based on that. Going to, or avoiding, war might have many consequences, but working out what they are won't be easy. If the war would result in temporary and limited suffering leading to an eventual long-lasting and universal happiness, then war would be morally acceptable, but if not, it would not be.

Personal Reflection

* *Do you think defensive and aggressive reasons for war are morally different?*
* *Should there be a 'clear and present threat' before war is justified?*
* *Would you fight in war?*

Active learning

Check your understanding

1. In what different ways can war be defined?
2. Why might it be true to say that most wars have more than one cause?
3. Describe how increasing your land or resources might lead to war.
4. In what ways can ideology be linked to war?
5. What might be considered reasonable and unreasonable causes of war?
6. Is there a difference between perceived threat and actual threat?
7. What are the main points of Just War Theory?
8. How far do all religions support Just War Theory?
9. Might a Humanist support Just War Theory?
10. How might a Utilitarian make a decision about whether war was justified or not?

Investigate

1. Sadly, humans have been involved in war for a very long time. In groups, choose one war from history. Carry out research into this war; explain how it began and what kept it going (and what caused it to end if it did).
2. How far are the personalities of world leaders important in the causes of war? Choose one war/conflict from the past or present and prepare a short report about your views on the contribution of 'personalities of leaders' to this war/conflict.
3. Similarly, for a different war/conflict, think about how far it matches up to Just War Theory. Prepare a short presentation on your thinking.
4. For a war/conflict which is currently ongoing, find out how much people actually know about its causes and the justifications people have for engaging in this war. Be sensitive in your research and either create a questionnaire or carry out some interviews in your school.

Analyse and Evaluate

1. 'While the Just War Theory provides safeguards during war, the fact that no country observes these means that it might as well not exist.' Discuss.
2. Evaluate the view that followers of religions should always be pacifists.
3. 'War can never be justified.' To what extent do you agree?

Apply

Arguably, world leaders are probably very familiar with Just War Theory – but you never know. Design an information pack on Just War Theory.

Strategies of modern warfare

23

One thousand years from now, this may be possible ... modern warfare 3016!

As humans began to get closer and closer to technology, so personal computers turned into tiny tablets, letters turned into tweets, medicines turned into nanobots ... humans began to be incapable of going for even a millisecond without updating their online status and checking the progress of their online lives. No longer was it considered fast enough to switch on a phone or – imagine – switch on a computer and wait for it to load up! No, humans wanted everything live and in real time, and instantly and constantly. So the solution was simple: microscopic implants controlled by thoughts alone. Want to send a message to a friend? Just think it and it will be sent directly from your implant to their implant. Want to buy something? Just imagine it and a range of implants will be activated in bankers, shop owners, distribution warehouses and so on. No need for keyboards, screens, batteries, WiFi ... but there was one problem. Soon some governments wondered if everyone's implant could be turned against them and so the experiments began. Implants were placed in mice (who surprisingly don't think about cheese) and humans thought harmful thoughts about the mice. The mouse implant received this communication and the mouse simply died. What power! Now, if a world leader was becoming a little too powerful, or a little too vocal in her opposition to another country, then her implant would simply be overwhelmed by commands which would lead to her immediate self-destruction. Of course, as soon as everyone realised this potential for implants, the race was on to protect their own implant from such hostile actions – but every time a solution was found to stop their own implant receiving the deadly instructions, another method to override this protection was discovered and the implants race was on.

Now you would think everyone would simply remove their implants so as to avoid this possible killing strategy, but human beings sadly are endlessly capable of making some bad decisions and, rather oddly, very few removed their implants – for most people there was no real need, because 'nothing bad would ever happen to them', and for world leaders there would always – more or less – be sufficient protections. Besides which, the whole process was much less wasteful and messy than the ways people went to war a thousand years ago where people actually physical engaged in fighting against each other ... imagine that ...

Technology and modern warfare

So what counts as 'modern' warfare? This is not a straightforward question to answer because warfare has changed as time has gone on and in the recent past has become much more technologically advanced. The first human wars would likely have been fought with bare hands and then rudimentary weapons. Before long, specialised weapons such as spears and swords would have been devised, then specialised war machines such as huge catapults able to lob great rocks at the enemy. These low-tech machines would gradually be replaced by higher-tech machines, such as mechanised and armoured vehicles, bombs, guns of increasing complexity and accuracy and intercontinental missiles able to attack

locations many thousands of miles from their point of origin. In addition to this, nuclear technology enabled weapons of mass destruction to be devised in the form of nuclear weapons.

In the recent past, weapons have become ever more complex and, perhaps more importantly, ever more remote. Intercontinental missiles can be launched from a control room with the person launching them never seeing them and/or never seeing their targets. Most recently, drones have been used to deliver attacks on enemies. These remote-controlled aircraft can be used to strike at targets with the human 'pilot' safely out of danger in a control room far away. There has even been talk lately of fully independent airborne attack drones which plan and execute the attack themselves using smart technology. Perhaps this could lead to ground-based attack machines too at some point in the future. This has led some to express concern at the danger of giving 'robots' the ability to plan and attack without human involvement – leading to the possibility of a 'terminator' scenario where these 'robots' might eventually turn against humanity.

Talk Point

Should humans always retain control of warfare?

Advantages of technological approaches to modern warfare

- Some argue that the more advanced your war machinery, the greater its deterrence value. This is based on the idea that your country will be less likely to be attacked by another country (or group) if it has very advanced ways of defending itself, because the attacker will take this into account in their thinking and so may be less likely to attack you in the first place.
- Perhaps technological ways of engaging in war are beneficial precisely because they are remote. The operator never sees the horror which they bring about through pressing a button which controls a missile. This is less traumatic for your people and more efficient. Also, it means that your military is not put into any situation of risk – no one needs to be 'on the ground' or piloting aircraft in order to deliver an attack.
- The power of technology might be so great as to bring a more traditional war to an end more quickly. Wars can drag on for many years, but perhaps a huge display of firepower in the form of a barrage of missiles (or one nuclear missile) might lead to a country or group quickly surrendering and so ending the war quickly. This could, perhaps, save lives in the long run.
- Technology might be relatively cheap – although missiles, for example, are expensive, perhaps they are much cheaper in the long run than supporting physical armies of people.
- Perhaps if we do improve our technology in the future, all wars could be fought by machines on our behalf. The winner of the war would be the group or country whose machines won and, as long as everyone agreed to accept this outcome, then no human need ever die in a war.

Disadvantages of technological approaches to modern warfare

- Technology still currently requires human operatives. Human operatives can make mistakes. This means that although some technologies can be targeted very specifically to avoid civilian casualties, mistakes can be made.
- Technology can malfunction. Technologies can go wrong and lead to terrible accidents. If we ever do enable technology to 'make its own decisions', what would stop technology deciding to turn against us?
- The remoteness of technology distances us from the reality of war. Sitting in a control room not seeing the horror of war might save you from trauma, but it might also prevent you from caring. Perhaps seeing the terrible reality of war first-hand might make people less likely to engage in it in the first place.
- It is morally unacceptable to have vast amounts of war technology just to threaten others. This creates tension and could potentially be more likely to lead to war than to sustain peace.
- The immense power of some technologies – nuclear weapons, for example – is out of proportion and cannot be targeted specifically. Such weapons kill indiscriminately and widely and may have long-lasting effects for many years to come. These are so 'efficient' at killing (although not if you take that to mean discriminate killing) that they would never be morally acceptable to use, and if it is wrong to use them, why have them?
- Some technologies are very expensive – is it morally acceptable for a group or country to use its finances in such a way?

Biological warfare

This is warfare where biological agents are used to target the enemy either directly, through killing people, or indirectly through targeting crops and animals so reducing food supplies and potentially weakening a country's economy or a group's ability to survive. A range of biological agents can be used as weapons and these can be targeted at the enemy in a variety of ways. They can be used to disable rather than kill your enemies, which could make traditional strategies of warfare more straightforward for you to engage in.

Advantages of biological warfare

- There is no need for any military action on your part – so your people are not in danger because they do not need to attack.
- Biological agents can be very effective and very powerful. They can also kill living things while not affecting infrastructure and many natural resources – which means that the infrastructure/resources can be taken by you once the biological agents have been cleared away.
- They can be deployed quite 'stealthily'. This means that all you have to do, for example, is introduce a virus into a population using one carrier. The virus then spreads and the war is won. This might also have good deterrent value for other enemies you may have.
- They are relatively inexpensive. Biological weapons can be terrifyingly cheap to make and virtually free to put into action.

Disadvantages of biological warfare

- There could still be risks to your people in the creation, storage and application of biological weapons. If the biological agent is accidentally released in your country or among your group then that could lead to many deaths among your people.
- Biological agents can mutate. This could lead to them no longer being under your control and turning into even more deadly varieties and heading your way. Perhaps you might kill all your enemies, but wherever they were based might be off-limits to you forever. So although your enemy is now gone, so too is any other benefit you might have

been hoping for from the war. Also, biological agents know no boundaries – so perhaps mutated biological agents could eventually reach your population and kill them all too (for example, if the agent became airborne). In short, there are just too many risks associated with biological agents. Also, perhaps many of your enemies might adapt to the biological agent and come back to get you – and they would probably want retribution.

- The simplicity and accessibility of some biological agents could mean that they might too easily fall into the hands of your enemies – with negative consequences for you.

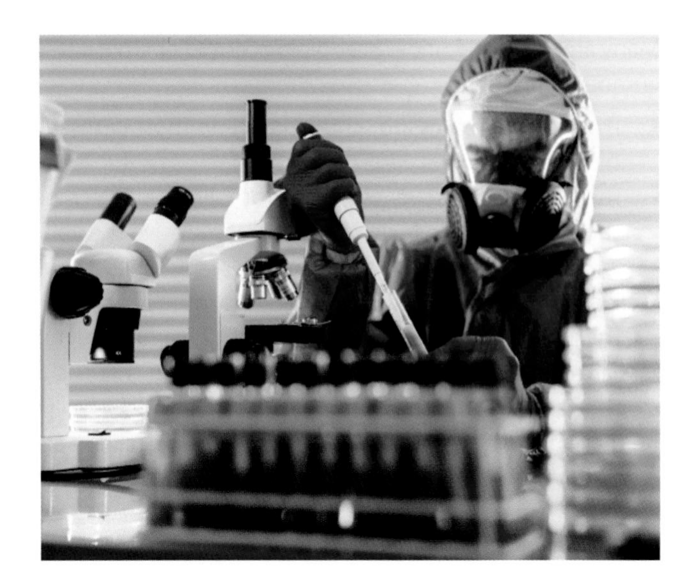

Chemical warfare

There are many chemical substances which can be toxic to humans and/or animals/crops. These come in a range of forms and can have a range of effects. Like biological warfare, they can target living things leaving non-living things intact – useful perhaps if your war is linked to gaining resources. These too might disable rather than kill your enemy – enabling you to win the war in more traditional ways quickly and effectively.

Advantages of chemical warfare

- Similarly there is no need for much by way of military engagement as chemical weapons can be deployed using a range of strategies which do not need to involve humans.
- Also, chemical weapons can attack living things but have no effect on non-living things.
- They can be cheap and very simple to deploy.
- Their all-pervading nature means that they could be used to kill vast numbers of your enemy – often quite horribly – which might act as a deterrent for any of your other enemies.

Disadvantages of chemical warfare

- Again, no direct involvement of humans in deploying these weapons might lead to being able to casually distance yourself from the pain and suffering of your enemy. This could prolong conflict rather than shorten it.
- The creation, storage and deployment of chemical weapons could still have risks for your population.
- Although many chemical weapons can be 'cleaned up', some linger for a very long time and this may result in you not making the gains you want to make from warfare.
- Like biological weapons, chemical weapons might easily find their way into the hands of those you'd rather didn't have access to them. This might lead to them using your weapons against you.

Talk Point

Is chemical/biological warfare morally acceptable?

Many argue that technological, biological and chemical strategies of war are particularly morally unacceptable for a number of reasons:

- They target victims indiscriminately – in most cases when applied you have no control over who is killed or injured.
- They take control over war away from direct involvement by humans. Some might argue that this is a moral benefit, of course, but human involvement may involve the ability to express compassion and mercy – purely technological solutions may not have this capability – and of course, the more control technology has, the greater perhaps the likelihood that one day that could be turned against humans.
- The long-lasting effects of these forms of warfare are morally problematic – nuclear radiation, biological mutation, harmful chemical residues – all of these mean that the war is never truly 'over'.
- They are not proportionate – in a war the aim is usually not to kill the entire population of your enemy, just destroy their military capability. Technological, biological and chemical weapons are therefore more than is needed in most cases. Also, some technological approaches might destroy everything – humans, animals, crops, buildings – is this more than is necessary?
- The threat of these forms of warfare is morally unacceptable in itself – it is never morally permissible to threaten another country or group with utter annihilation or disproportionate action.
- They distance military personnel from the effects of their actions. This might lead to a population which thinks of war as just a game. This could lead to a less caring society and a devaluing of human and other life – which might come back to haunt you if it ends up being turned on your own people by your own people.
- These forms of warfare mean that mistakes made can be on an even bigger scale than in traditional forms of warfare; shooting the wrong person is bad enough, but targeting a few thousand of the wrong people with remote controlled drones is arguably worse.
- Some argue that the nature of the deaths some of these weapons cause is morally unacceptable. Now this one is tricky because it involves deciding if one form of death is worse than another and so whether it is any more morally acceptable to be vaporised in a nuclear detonation or die more slowly as a result of a 'weaponised virus'.

Terrorism

Arguably, terrorism has been around for a very long time, and so it is not particularly a feature of modern warfare. However, 'the war on terrorism' has been used as a justification for military action by some in the recent past, and terrorist actions do seem to have become more commonplace in the last few decades. Perhaps the central moral issue related to terrorism as a strategy of modern warfare is the definition of a terrorist: some might argue that a terrorist is a in fact a 'freedom fighter' and that acts of 'terrorism' are the last resort for those who can find no other way to advance their cause.

Talk Point

Under what circumstances might a terrorist be considered a 'freedom fighter' and does the name applied make any difference?

Terrorism as a strategy for modern warfare is a particularly complex moral issue for a number of reasons:

- With terrorism, it is not always immediately obvious who an attacker is. In traditional warfare, military operatives tend to clearly indicate who they are through uniforms, logos on war machinery and flying flags, for example. Terrorists rarely advertise themselves, making them harder to identify and respond to appropriately.
- This means that responding to terrorism is far more complex than responding to military offensives. In general, terrorist actions only become obvious after they have happened, whereas an army (or a missile) coming towards you is usually very obvious and something you can respond to in advance – even if it is only by taking evasive action if possible.
- In relation to terrorism it can be very difficult to know who to fight back against. Many of the actions of those involved in the 'war on terrorism' have targeted people they claim are terrorists or places where they claim terrorists are to be found – or where they claim terrorism is supported and is considered to originate. However, all of this is very difficult to judge and requires accurate intelligence in order to target 'counter-attacks' appropriately.
- Terrorists often take war to places where wars are not expected. In wars, there are often very clear battle zones drawn up – and it is clear where you shouldn't be if you don't want to be caught up in battle. Terrorist activities can take place anywhere at any time. Of course, terrorists argue that their fight can be taken anywhere since everywhere for them is a battleground.
- Terrorist acts often involve the killing of innocent bystanders and/or those who are generally agreed to be excluded as targets in traditional warfare (e.g. children) – although so too can acts of traditional warfare. Terrorists may disagree with the claim that they kill innocent people because for them, everyone who does not support their cause – or lives in the land of 'their enemy', or shares their enemy's views – can be considered as 'the enemy' and therefore a legitimate target for attack.
- Terrorism as a strategy of modern warfare has complex origins. How someone becomes a terrorist can be a very complicated mixture of circumstances and experiences, beliefs and viewpoints, culture and traditions, historical and political processes and individual and social psychological factors. This can make it very difficult to respond to and address.

Pre-emptive strikes

Again, pre-emptive strikes are not necessarily a feature of modern warfare any more than in any other conflict throughout history. A pre-emptive strike is where a country or group takes the first actively hostile action in response to a real or perceived threat. This can be specifically targeted action against a group or country's military/fighters or it can be a more general attack aimed at 'sending a message' to the potential aggressor (although a pre-emptive strike makes the country/group making it the aggressor). The moral problem here is that the strike is based on the presumption of hostility by another, not any actual hostility (though looking as if you are about to attack might be considered as a hostile act). Morally, it has to be asked whether making such a strike – particularly if it is not directly targeted at an opposing military – is morally acceptable.

However, in defence of a pre-emptive strike a group or country may argue that their action can prevent any further acts of war and so has had a positive outcome which would make it morally justifiable. But this is all very morally problematic since you would have to have clear evidence that your pre-emptive strike was justified and this is often hard to ensure, so it's not always clear if a pre-emptive strike is an aggressive or defensive act. Of course, another issue with pre-emptive strikes is the possibility that they might lead to tensions escalating into a war when otherwise they might not have. This could potentially make a pre-emptive strike even more morally dubious.

Is a pre-emptive strike ever morally acceptable?

Cyber war

One strategy of modern warfare which is very modern is cyber war. This is where a group or country attacks the online infrastructure of another group or country to deliberately cause harm. This might be done in a number of ways – for example, by introducing computer viruses which debilitate a group/country's online infrastructure in some way. It might also be through denying a group or country access to some online facility or process. All of this can have very direct or less direct consequences. You only need to think of how much of our lives now are online: an aggressor in a cyber attack could gather important information, take control of important services, shut down vital services and generally cause all sorts of unpredictable mayhem. This might have direct consequences – for example, it could shut down energy supplies, gather sensitive information, or even turn our weapons against us. In this kind of attack, the aggression could be very obvious, or much more subtle and hidden. It could be pre-emptive or responsive and could be devastating. It could easily escalate, since the attacked group/country might find ways to respond by counter-offensives against the aggressor's cyber structures. This could lead to worldwide chaos and/or an escalation which might eventually lead to a more traditional form of warfare breaking out.

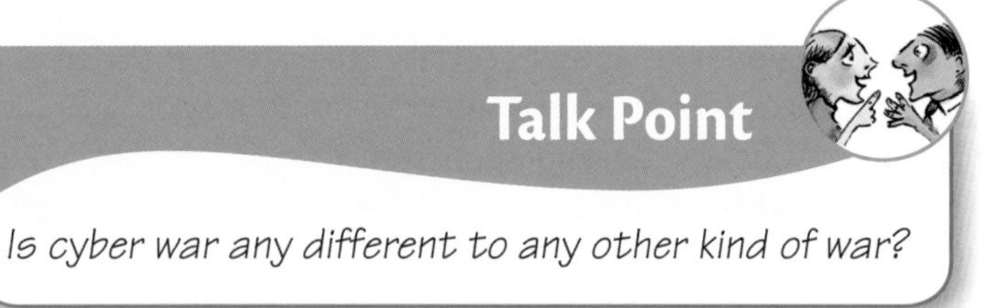

Is cyber war any different to any other kind of war?

There are a number of possible moral issues linked to cyber war:

- If a pre-emptive cyber war is initiated then this would raise the same issues as any pre-emptive strike, even though direct violence is not used – although of course violence (and deaths) could indirectly result, for example you could disable features of air traffic control perhaps and so cause aircraft to crash.
- Whether any cyber attack was pre-emptive or defensive it still raises the moral problem of proportionality – is disabling a country or group's cyber space an action which is focused enough? All sorts of outcomes may follow – over which the attacker may have no control. This might lead to more harm being done than is necessary to achieve the original outcome.
- Perhaps most importantly, cyber attacks may be relatively indiscriminate. In general, the international community tries to agree to ensure wars involve the military and not civilians – and especially not any vulnerable civilians. Cyber attacks could lead to harm for a range of individuals who are not military. For example, if a cyber attack targeted a country's energy supply this could affect everyone, with a wide range of consequences.

Treaties and agreements

To try to address the possibilities made available by increasingly sophisticated technologies as weapons the international community tries to agree certain rules about the use of technology during war. This has resulted in many treaties, agreements and international declarations. The extent to which these are observed during conflict is a matter for discussion. Some of the key treaties and agreements are:

- **The Hague Convention, 1899** This set out basic rules about war, agreements about disarmament and the concept of war crimes.
- **The Geneva Protocol, 1925** This aims to prohibit the use of chemical and biological weapons.
- **Treaty on the Non-Proliferation of Nuclear Weapons, 1968** This aims to prevent the spread of nuclear weapons and work towards their eradication.
- **Convention on Certain Conventional Weapons, 1980** This aims to prohibit or restrict the use of weapons which are indiscriminate or excessively harmful.
- **Ottawa Treaty, 1999** This aims to ban the use of anti-personnel landmines.
- **Convention on Cluster Munitions, 2008** This aims to prohibit the use of cluster bombs during conflict.
- **Arms Trade Treaty, 2014** This aims to regulate international trade in arms.
- **The International Convention against the Taking of Hostages 1979/The International Convention for the Suppression of the Financing of Terrorism 1999** These are examples of specific treaties which relate to specific terrorist activities and support for terrorism.
- While there is no specific treaty on cyber war (although there have been many calls for one), there are conventions on cyber crime, for example **The Convention on Cybercrime 2001**, known as the Budapest Convention, agreed across the Council of Europe.

Whatever the strategies used in any warfare, many of the most important moral questions link to the consequences of war, which we will explore in the next chapter.

Some religious and philosophical perspectives

Christianity

For those Christians who consider that war is sometimes necessary, there would still be views held about what count as morally acceptable strategies in war. In general, it is likely that Christians would want strategies of war to: discriminate between military and civilian personnel; use only as much force as is necessary to achieve the objective; and not be unnecessarily cruel. This would mean that, in practice, Christians would be likely to reject biological and chemical weapons and nuclear weapons. However, they might also argue that any action which is not carefully targeted would also be morally dubious – so even 'traditional' bombing might be included here, as would, potentially, cyber war. Christians could have a variety of views about terrorism as a strategy of war depending upon the definition of 'terrorist action', though terrorism could be included as indiscriminate acts of war and so be rejected completely.

The Church of Scotland

In its Ethics of Defence paper, the Church of Scotland states: *'In the past, the Church of Scotland has persistently viewed nuclear weapons as an evil, and we see no reason to change that perspective'.* It also adds its concerns about the arms trade, suggesting that while the *'UK is one of the largest manufacturers and exporters of military equipment in the world … it surely has a moral responsibility to act in a manner which does not engender unnecessary conflict.'*[107] On nuclear weapons it adds: *'nuclear weapons are so destructive and so harmful to civilians and the natural world that they are inherently evil; to possess, threaten or use such terrible weapons of mass destruction is a dreadful concept which fundamentally threatens the future of humanity as a species.*'[108] The Church strongly denounces nuclear weapons, so it is reasonable to assume that it also rejects the use of chemical and biological weapons and any other strategy of war which is indiscriminate and unnecessarily severe – which could also include cyber war.

The Roman Catholic Church

In 2013 Pope Francis gave an address about the conflict in Syria in which he said: '*With utmost firmness I condemn the use of chemical weapons.*'[109] The Church has a clear position on a wide range of strategies of modern warfare in the Catechism: '*Every act of war directed to the indiscriminate destruction of whole cities or vast areas with inhabitants is a crime against God and man, which merits firm and unequivocal condemnation. A danger of modern warfare is that it provides the opportunity to those who possess modern scientific weapons especially atomic, biological or chemical weapons – to commit such crimes.*' (2314) It also adds: '*Terrorism threatens, wounds and kills indiscriminately: it is gravely against justice and charity.*' (2297) The Church therefore argues that there are definitely strategies of modern warfare which are not legitimate and must consequently be avoided. Therefore the Church would be similarly likely to condemn the indiscriminate and possibly disproportionate nature of cyber war.

Buddhism

Again, there is no one agreed Buddhist position on the use of one strategy of modern warfare as opposed to another. Buddhists would want to ensure that any suffering caused in war was minimised as far as possible, and – probably – excluded those who were not directly involved in the war. Certainly the extent of suffering possible through chemical, biological and nuclear weapons is very significant – and also has the potential to affect non-human life too, which is something which cannot be ignored. The dangers in storing and using some forms of modern warfare are therefore probably too great to justify their existence from a Buddhist perspective. This would also mean that Buddhists would be likely to reject cyber war and terrorist activities. However, again, in Buddhism there is a balance to be struck between compassion, avoiding harm and exercising wisdom. It is therefore not impossible that a Buddhist could potentially support a range of forms of modern warfare and the most skilful ways to bring conflict to an end and so prevent further suffering. For Buddhists, even the threat of using certain strategies in modern warfare could easily be considered as examples of greed, hatred and delusion – three 'poisons' which all Buddhists strive to avoid.

Humanism

Just as have many religious people, Humanists have been very actively involved in antiwar activities for a long time. Additionally, like many religious people, Humanists have taken a strong stand against nuclear, chemical and biological weapons. Humanists argue that: '*Although the distinction between the innocent and less innocent can be a difficult one to make, many people would say that there is something especially wrong with the deliberate targeting of civilians in war. Modern weapons of mass destruction such as nuclear bombs and chemical and biological weapons, whose use would kill thousands, and maybe millions, of ordinary people seem to be impossible to justify.*'[110] So, in common with other perspectives, Humanists think the power and indiscriminate nature of strategies of modern warfare mean they are particularly hard to justify morally. Following this thinking, Humanists would also be likely to reject cyber war since it too could target innocent civilians and also be wide-ranging in its effects. It is likely that Humanists would reject terrorism as a war strategy, since terrorism could be considered by many to be based on ideology and belief. Humanists base their views on reason and evidence and so would be unlikely to support terrorism based on ideology and belief. Of course, terrorists may argue that their 'struggle' is quite reasonable and based on evidence of a need for it – so it's not as clear-cut as it might seem.

Utilitarianism

For a Utilitarian there would be no automatic rejection of any form of warfare. Any strategy and action might be considered morally acceptable if it results in the greatest happiness for the greatest number and/or where the benefits outweigh the costs. Again, the trouble for a Utilitarian would be assessing what the benefits and costs are. Certainly it would be difficult for a Utilitarian to justify indiscriminate killing, killing of civilians and mass destruction – though it would not be impossible. If one strategy of warfare brought a swift end to conflict then perhaps it should be considered

– no matter how awful it is – because it would have beneficial consequences overall. This possible acceptance of any means could include cyber war and terrorism – if they had overall beneficial consequences. However, in practice, many Utilitarians would be likely to reject such unfocused and potentially indiscriminate actions since their indiscriminate nature would make them all the more difficult to measure in terms of their effect on overall happiness.

Personal Reflection

* *Do you think that some strategies of modern warfare are more acceptable than others?*
* *Is going to war part of human nature?*
* *If there was a referendum in Scotland on getting rid of stocks of nuclear, chemical and biological weapons, how would you vote and why?*

Active learning

Check your understanding

1. Describe how war has become more reliant on technology over time.
2. Describe two advantages and two disadvantages of using modern technology in warfare.
3. Describe the possible benefits and drawbacks of chemical and biological weapons.
4. What are the central arguments used by people who oppose having nuclear weapons?
5. What moral issues might be raised by pre-emptive strikes?
6. What is cyber war and what moral issues does it raise?
7. What different viewpoints can there be about the morality of terrorism?
8. How has the international community tried to regulate warfare?
9. What are the key similarities and differences between religions about strategies of modern warfare?
10. How far do religious and non-religious perspectives agree about strategies of modern warfare?

Investigate

1. Different wars throughout history have used different levels of technology. Create an illustrated timeline for display in your class showing how wars have become increasingly technological throughout time.
2. Carry out your own anonymous research into people's views about chemical, biological and nuclear war. Find out how much people know about these, about how they are regulated and their views on whether they are morally acceptable or not.
3. Cyber war is a relatively new threat to peace. Find out more about what a cyber war might involve – how governments and individuals protect themselves against it and the calls for an internationally agreed treaty on cyber war. You should create a presentation about this.
4. The stimulus at the start of this chapter talked about the future. Carry out some research into views about how future wars could potentially be fought. What do people think the future of war will be? What part might technology play? You could create a display of your thoughts, opinions and findings.

Analyse and Evaluate

1 'The issue is going to war in the first place, not how you fight it.' To what extent do you agree?
2 How far is the major moral problem with strategies of modern warfare their potentially indiscriminate nature?
3 'In relation to most strategies of modern warfare there is more agreement between religious and non-religious perspectives than there is disagreement.' To what extent do you agree?

Apply

Choose one of the strategies of modern warfare you have examined in this chapter. Create a FAQs sheet about this strategy.

24 Consequences of war

So, yes, at times it was a pretty tough place to be. But I was a soldier; it was a job; it was what I did; it was what I had chosen to do. You just did what you were trained to do. Yes, there were unpleasant times. And when it was all over, the commanding officers asked us pretty jokingly if we'd 'like any counselling'. We laughed. We were men; we were soldiers; counselling was for movie stars. So I came back home. I left the forces soon after coming back and took a civilian job. I did this job day in, day out for another fifteen years. When I was doing this job, my mind would sometimes wander back to my experiences in battle. I remembered the fierce loyalty and camaraderie of my mates, the laughs and the sometimes very dark humour. I had a family, grandchildren even. Then I took early retirement. That's when it started: just out of nowhere, I'd remember something horrible that happened during the war. Nothing provoked it; I could be standing in a queue for a railway ticket or sitting in a restaurant enjoying a meal. These – flashbacks I know they are now – became more frequent and more horrible – sometimes they were so vivid that I thought they were actually things happening now. I stopped sleeping so well, I lost my appetite – and my interest in a whole load of things I used to really enjoy. My family said I just stopped laughing. I never watched any war movies or anything even close – not even movies with loud bangs.

The memories – I wondered if I was making them up – how could I have seen such things and forgotten them so completely? Did I and my mates do the things I saw myself doing? I went to the doctor – maybe I was losing my mind. Post-traumatic stress disorder is what they call it. It seems that everything I saw, everything I did, I just pushed it away and refused to let myself remember it – or be affected by it. But it refused to stay hidden – it refused to let me forget. Now, yes, I have had counselling. I am coming to terms with what happened to me. Perhaps one day I will be able to cope with the sheer overwhelming scale of what I saw, what I heard … what I did. In many ways when I think about it, it's like a completely different person saw, heard and did all those things. I wish it had been; but no, it was me. And I will have to find a way to live with this.

Talk Point

How might memories of war affect someone throughout their life?

The consequences of war

War has a range of consequences for individuals, families, communities and perhaps society as a whole. These consequences can be very immediate during the time of the conflict and can also be very long-lasting – in fact, lasting many generations. Of course, individual personality styles may influence the extent to which an individual is affected by war – as well as by the exact circumstances of the events – including perhaps how they are recalled by the individual. There is no one way that a person, group, community or society is affected by war, but what is certain is that the consequences of war can be wide-ranging and very serious indeed. It is important to remember that while the consequences of war can be very direct for military personnel, they can be equally direct for civilians caught up in war. They can also be very severe for those who never have any direct experience of the battlefield.

Physical consequences of war

Of course, the most serious physical consequence of war is death. Whether this is one individual or many millions of people, each death is likely to affect someone. The physical pain and suffering of death and of experiences before death can all contribute to what we think of as 'the horrors of war', and the pain of those who lose loved ones during conflict is something which would be hard to understand unless you had experienced it. In wars, there is not much logic about who dies: experienced military personnel can be just as likely to lose their lives as the inexperienced and so too can civilians, including more vulnerable civilians. However, perhaps who dies is less relevant than the fact that *anyone* dies. A person and their loved ones are robbed of their future – a society is robbed of its talent and skills – the human family is robbed of one of its valuable members.

As well as death, the physical consequences of war can be serious and long lasting. Many are injured and disabled by war, and so face the rest of their life carrying the consequences of this injury or disability. Limbs, sight, hearing – so many human physical capacities can be harmed by war, potentially shaping the rest of a person's life, as well as those around them. These physical effects can lead to everyday aspects of life being made much more difficult and plans for the future are forced to change. As well as physical consequences for those who have fought in wars, there can also be similar consequences for those caught up in wars in other ways. Bombing of cities can lead to death and a great deal of physical harm and the effects of certain types of warfare can be even more long lasting. For example, the radiation left behind after the use of nuclear weapons can linger and affect people for generations to come. Chemical and biological warfare can have physical consequences far beyond their immediate effects.

Psychological consequences of war

As well as the physical scars of war the psychological trauma can be equally serious. Post-traumatic stress disorder (PTSD) is one of the more well-known effects – and it is even possible that this psychological trauma links directly to physical difficulties caused by PTSD. War can psychologically affect people in all sorts of ways – which can lead them to become depressed, angry and suicidal, as well as engaging in coping mechanisms which may be harmful to them and/or others.

Talk Point

What do you think a 'coping mechanism' for the psychological effects of war might be?

Not all of the psychological effects of war are, perhaps, recognised psychological conditions, but the long-lasting psychological legacy of the stress of war is very real. It is important to remember that the psychological trauma which results from war can affect those who were involved in a variety of ways. Witnesses to atrocities, as well as those who experience the atrocities, can all suffer psychological effects. Similarly, those who carry out acts of war are also open to the psychological trauma associated with war. Interestingly, in the previous chapter we considered whether being able to inflict damage 'remotely' (for example, by pressing a missile launch button in a control room) was more or less morally problematic than directly killing a person: it was claimed that one of the pilots of the aircraft which dropped an atomic bomb on Hiroshima and Nagasaki in 1945 suffered serious psychological problems later as a result of his feeling the responsibility for so much death and suffering.[111] The psychological trauma of war can therefore be very immediate, but it can also be very long lasting and affect people in many different ways.

One important psychological effect of war can be what psychologists refer to as 'desensitisation': this means that those involved in war become 'immune' to the horrors around them. This is most likely a coping mechanism, but can mean that a person loses their sensitivity to the horrors of war which can, in turn, lead to them committing (further) atrocities themselves or not responding appropriately to atrocities they witness or experience. This can lead to all sorts of further consequences – for example, guilt at their actions (or inaction), anger and a desire for retribution: the last point is an important one. Some have argued that the psychological anger caused by war has great potential to create a mindset which is prepared to continue carrying out atrocities. Some have argued, for example, that the psychological trauma of war is a perfect 'breeding ground' for those who will go on to commit further atrocities – in relation to terrorism and other extreme forms of behaviour, perhaps. One recent area of interest in relation to the psychological effects of war is claims by some descendants of those who suffered in war that they too have suffered trauma. The claim is that although they were not directly involved in the experience, they have been brought up with their grandparents/parents talking about it all through their lives and so they have been traumatised by this experience. It will be interesting in years to come to see if this claim is pursued further and what reactions to it there might be.

Social consequences of war

War and conflict generally involves sides. The side you are on may partly determine your actions during war and your response to it afterwards. Wars have the tendency to polarise groups and to force people to line up with one side or another. Where wars are between countries this is usually based on national identity, but civil wars and conflicts based on ethnic (or perceived ethnic) differences, can lead to conflict between individuals and groups who have grown up alongside each other and lived in peace alongside each other for many years. Some argue that where wars involve these factors, returning to 'how it was before' is very difficult if not impossible. Once groups have been identified and pitted against each other in a society, it is hard to recover from that. This means that wars have important social consequences for how people live and work alongside each other. Suspicion, anger, hatred and retribution can be very difficult to eradicate after any war – and there can often be a feeling of animosity between groups now at peace who were formerly at war. This can lead to ongoing lack of trust between groups and communities which can take a long time to heal.

Refugees as a consequence of war

One of the most recent social consequences of war – although it has been present in many wars throughout history – is the mass migration of refugees away from areas of conflict. This has led to huge numbers of people recently moving from war-torn areas in the Middle East and North Africa to (mainly) Europe hoping to escape conflict and make a better life for themselves somewhere else. This can then lead to any receiving country finding itself in a moral dilemma: on the one hand it may want to respond to such a humanitarian crisis by welcoming and supporting refugees in such circumstances; on the other hand it may want to preserve its own economy and avoid any issues which might arise as a result of a large increase in a refugee population within its own borders. Many have been trying to encourage the international community to take a common stand on this issue, rather than leaving it to be dealt with predominantly by those states which are 'on the front line' for the arrival of refugees. Some argue that as well as a humanitarian concern, the issue of refugee migration could have the effect of destabilising relationships between countries as a result of their differences of opinion about how best to respond to refugees.

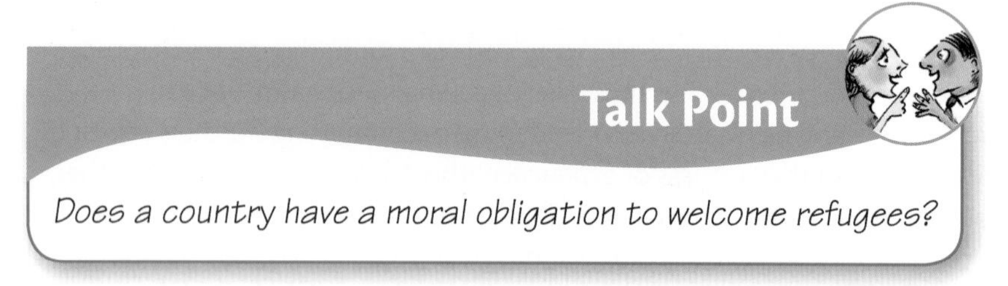

Economic consequences of war

Wars cost money, time, energy, resources and personnel: while the war drains a country or group of these valuable things it means that they are not being used to build and maintain an economy and so provide people with a proper lifestyle. This can have obvious effects on the economy as the country is no longer able to compete in world markets to the same extent: many countries, industries and individuals would be wary of trading with a country or group at war – since this might not be very economically stable from their point of view. In the country or region at war, as everything is directed to 'the war effort' this can mean that it is all directed away from everything else. This can, in turn, have wide-ranging effects on all sorts of other things.

For example, if a country's economy is focused on the war effort then it may be less able to provide adequate levels of health care, welfare, education and so on. All of this can lead to negative consequences for the population generally and, importantly, it can take a very long time to recover from this once the war or conflict has ended. In short, war and conflict can lead to a great deal of economic instability which can have effect far beyond the direct effects of war.

Of course, one of the most serious possible effects is the economic spiral towards poverty which can be the direct or indirect consequence of war. Through death, injury and illness, war can remove huge numbers of people from the workforce who are no longer able to contribute to a country's economy. Add to this the negative effects on a society's infrastructure (roads, transport, etc.), the destruction of natural resources and resources which a country can exploit for its economic gain and you have a very complex picture, the end result of which can be serious poverty. This can then lead to greater economic (and political) instability in a country or region which then acts to keep this vicious cycle going further. Add to this the possibility that poverty itself can be something which stimulates resentment, anger and frustration and this in itself can be a contributory factor in maintaining or initiating war.

Consequences of war on the natural environment

War can also be very destructive to the natural environment. Ecosystems are finely balanced and complex – harm to one element of an ecosystem can have far-reaching and unpredictable consequences for the ecosystem as a whole. This can be harmful to nature itself or to those whose livelihood and survival depend upon the natural environment. Agricultural production can be harmed, as can more wild places and water systems and air quality and the suitability of land for growing crops. This can all have direct effects on human, plant and animal life, as well as on the Earth's wider natural systems. It can also have less direct effects – for example, by affecting a country's economic stability through harm to its ability to make use of the environment. Also, a country's natural resources can be badly affected by war – since they could be used up for the 'war effort', destroyed or taken by enemies, or made unusable through acts of war. Again, such consequences can be far-reaching and unpredictable – for some the loss of some species as a result of war might seem inconsequential given the other things which can be lost in war, but harm to species can lead to changes in natural systems, which themselves can lead to wider and unforeseen changes.

Consequences of war on the built environment

Again, some might argue that harm to buildings is not very important given the terrible human costs of war. However, the identity of individuals, groups and societies can often be intimately linked to the built environment and damage to the built environment can be very harmful for those for whom it matters. Buildings, structures and objects of cultural importance may be lost or harmed during war. This might be intentional – as a way to demoralise the enemy – or a by-product of war which no one really planned. It can lead to life being less easy to live in a war zone – for example, if schools and hospitals are destroyed – but it can also link to a people's sense of themselves if great monuments, works of art and cultural artefacts are destroyed.

Talk Point

Should people be concerned about the destruction of works of art during war?

International agreements relating to the consequences of war

There are a number of international agreements which try to limit the consequences of war as far as possible. These agreements are generally signed up to by members of the international community – though some argue that during war, it is hard to monitor how effectively these agreements are being observed. There are a number of treaties and agreements which aim to limit the negative effects of war. Some are very specific and some quite general:

- **War crimes** One attempt to ensure that the consequences of war do not go beyond the war itself is the existence of agreements that, even during war, there can be actions carried out as 'part of war' which are still treated as crimes. These can then be punished like any other crime. War crimes can include: killing which is not part of a necessary military offensive, torture, unnecessary destruction of property, depriving prisoners of war of a range of rights, attacking civilians or peacekeepers, killing anyone who has surrendered, using civilians as 'human shields', using child soldiers, attacking medical personnel – and there are many others. The aim of war crimes is to ensure that even in war, some rules of humanity are observed, which might also have the beneficial effect of avoiding retribution atrocities for years to come and in addressing some aspects of war trauma. The various versions and protocols of the Geneva Convention from 1864 right through to 2005 cover a range of issues related to war crimes.

- **Protection of cultural artefacts** The Hague Convention in 1954 aimed to prevent the deliberate targeting of cultural artefacts during conflict.
- **Protection of the natural environment** Articles 35 and 55 of Protocol I additional to the Geneva Conventions of 1949, for example, make specific reference to protecting the environment during conflict where it is made clear that the environment should be protected from the possibility of long-term damage and 'acts of reprisal' against the natural environment are prohibited.[112]

Many of the other treaties and agreements signed by members of the international community are designed to ensure that wars are engaged in according to rules. These rules are closely linked to the reasons for going to war as well as the behaviour of nations, groups and individuals during war. Many of the aims of these rules and agreements are to ensure that the consequences of war are limited as far as possible, so that the consequences of war, in the short- and long-term, are minimised.

Some religious and philosophical perspectives

Christianity

Christians would want the effects of any war minimised – whether this was effects on military personnel or civilians, physical or psychological. Christians would also want any consequences of war on the natural environment and also on culture, tradition and heritage to be minimised. Some Christians regard war as a necessary evil in some unavoidable circumstances while others reject all kinds of war in all kinds of circumstances. Regardless of the view taken, Christians would want the effects of war to be as few and as harmless as they could possibly be and to end once the war is over. Even Christians who accept the need for war in some circumstances would agree that war crimes should be punished wherever and whenever they occur.

The Church of Scotland

In response to what was often referred to as the 'migrant crisis', the Moderator of the Church of Scotland said in 2015: *'For too long we have wilfully ignored the cries of those in the world who are at the very bottom ... It is a tragedy that it takes deaths on such a scale to get us to realise what is going on.'*[113] The Moderator therefore stated a common concern among Christians about the effects of war particularly on those most vulnerable and unable to respond to it. Christians do take the view that the consequences of war can often be most serious for the most vulnerable members of society, so we have a moral responsibility to ensure that this is not the case. However, the Church would want all the negative consequences of war to be minimised as far as possible. The Church adds that the costs of war *'to everyone should be considered ... for civilians as well as military; in damage to the environment and human rights; financial costs for war and reconstruction'*[114].

The Roman Catholic Church

The Catechism states: *'The Church and human reason both assert the permanent validity of the moral law during armed conflict. The mere fact that war has regrettably broken out does not mean that everything becomes licit between the warring parties.'* (2312) This is a clear statement that the Church considers that war does not mean that we can simply ignore right and wrong just because 'there is a war on'. In practice, this would mean that every attempt to minimise the harm caused by war should be taken as far as possible and so consequences for anyone and anything caught up in war should be limited as far as they possibly can be – anything else, according to the Church, would not respect the dignity of human beings and God's creation.

Buddhism

In common with Buddhist responses to other aspects of war, Buddhists would want to minimise pain and suffering however they were caused in war. The Buddhist principle of non-violence is obviously applicable to combat during war, but violence can take many forms: the suffering of individuals physically and psychologically could be considered as violence – as could any harmful effects on nature, culture and so on. Buddhists would consider the whole range of possible suffering which can come as a result of war and would want this to be as little as possible. The consequences of war are likely to result in negative kamma and so, again, they should be minimised as far as possible.

Humanism

Humanists argue: *'Humanists would think very carefully before supporting any war, because of the loss of life involved. Wars are hugely destructive, ruining lives, wasting resources and degrading the environment ... All too often wars achieve nothing except terrible suffering, leaving a legacy of bitterness which sows the seeds of future wars'*[115]. So Humanists argue that the consequences of war go beyond death and physical suffering and include effects on humans and non-human life too. Perhaps, for Humanists, the consequences of war take on a special significance because for them, there is no possibility of any afterlife and so the consequences of war are very final for those who lose their lives. Perhaps also because Humanists believe that we only have one life this could have greater significance for a life negatively affected by war.

Utilitarianism

Utilitarians are typically caught up in something of a philosophical difficulty. Since Utilitarians could argue that any action during war was morally justified if it led to the maximisation of happiness, they would also have to accept that any consequence might follow. Perhaps, therefore, in Utilitarian thinking, certain consequences might be both unavoidable and maybe even essential. However, in more practical terms, most Utilitarians would accept that serious and sustained negative consequences of war – no matter what form they took and who they affected – would be hard to say were of benefit to the majority and/or maximised happiness.

Personal Reflection

* *Are some of the consequences of war 'more serious' than others?*
* *Should those who committed war crimes be punished no matter how long ago the war was?*
* *Should certain 'vulnerable groups' be better protected from the consequences of war than others?*

Active learning

Check your understanding

1. What is PTSD and how does it affect someone experiencing it?
2. Describe two physical consequences of war.
3. Describe one psychological consequence of war other than PTSD.
4. What are the possible social consequences of war?
5. What are the possible consequences of war on the economy and the environment?

→

6 Why might someone argue that we should not target cultural artefacts during war?
7 What counts as a war crime?
8 How far are religious people agreed that the consequences of war should be minimised as far as possible?
9 What might a Humanist mean by saying that the legacy of war can sow the seeds for future conflict?
10 Must a Utilitarian accept all potential consequences of war?

Investigate

1 PTSD has been known by a number of names throughout history – from 'nostalgia', to 'shell shock' to 'battle fatigue' and 'Gulf War syndrome'. Choose a conflict from history and explore what views were held about those who returned from war with the psychological scars of war. How were they viewed? How were they treated? How did the treatment provided for such people change over time?
2 Throughout 2015, the movement of refugees from war-torn areas was called by some 'the greatest crisis the world has faced since the world wars'. Carry out your own research into the causes and effects of what became known as the 'migrant crisis'. What were its possible causes and consequences? How did various countries – including Scotland – respond? You could create an exhibition of your research and provide guides to show people around your exhibition. Remember that this may be a sensitive subject for many – you may in fact have pupils who were refugees in your school – so consider this carefully in your work.
3 Throughout history there have been many cases of people being charged with war crimes; some of these, such as Adolf Eichmann, are very high profile. Find out about the case of one war criminal who was found and tried. Tell the story of this process and explain the complexities around finding and prosecuting alleged war criminals.
4 Throughout wars, religious and other belief groups have taken various positions in relation to the war – from objecting completely, to taking part in resistance activities, to supporting countries at war. Choose one religious or belief group and carry out your own research into its activities during war.

Analyse and Evaluate

1 'What is most important is the consequences of war on humans.' To what extent do you agree?
2 Evaluate the view that there is a greater duty to protect civilians from the consequences of war than the military.
3 'International agreements which try to limit the negative consequences of war have failed.' Discuss.

Apply

Carry out some further research into the treatments offered to those suffering from PTSD as a result of war/conflict. Create your own short information leaflet explaining the key approaches and including information about where sufferers of PTSD might obtain help.

25 Responses to conflict and alternatives to war

'Coward', 'traitor', 'sympathiser' ... these were just some of the less harsh words I heard every day; there were many others, which I suppose you can easily imagine. They came from women, men, and even small children far too young to even know what the words meant. I was spat on so many times – sometimes by ladies so posh you would never have imagined them spitting on anything. Little stones often came my way, and a few big ones too – there were plenty of times I went home bloodied and bruised. Sometimes, someone could get quite hysterical with me in the middle of the street – usually this would be someone who had already lost a loved one in the war – and I tried to understand their position, the pain they must have felt and the anger they must have been feeling towards me. 'You should be ashamed of yourself!' 'You should be hanged!' 'How will you ever know the suffering others have gone through so you can hide here at home, while they die for you?'

But ... you see ... the thing was, I did know the suffering they were going through: I had seen it for myself. I had pulled bodies from the mud back to our lines. I had held men as their life slipped away from them – not quietly, but in loud, screaming pain and utter anguish – in their knowing that their life was ebbing away from them. I had talked to them as they cried, sobbed like infants – realising that they would never see their wives, their children, ever again. I had gathered up the body parts of men – men who would never have a burial place since they had been blown out of all human recognition. Men who had not even had those last moments to send their final few words back home: men who had advanced and then fallen as they stood – what they had experienced, no one will ever know. I had saved some too – for this they gave me a medal, the highest military honour they called it – and the injury I received when doing this meant I could not return to battle – though I wanted to as there were many more to save.

I have never fired a gun. I never will. I have never harmed a living thing. I never will. I wore the red cross in battle and went unarmed – that's what some conscientious objectors like me did. I was no more or less afraid than any on the front lines, but I will not take life – only preserve it. The men there understood in a way that those back here at home don't. 'Coward', 'traitor' 'sympathiser', perhaps the gentler words I hear every day ...

Conscientious objection

One response to war is to refuse to fight in it. Throughout history it is likely that there have always been those who have refused to fight because of their beliefs. Sometimes this is based on religious belief and other times on non-religious beliefs and/or political views. Such people refused to fight on 'grounds of conscience' and so became known as 'conscientious objectors'. In some cases, these objectors refused to take part in anything which supported the war effort – for example, they might refuse to work in any industry which was linked to the creation of weapons (they were known as 'absolutists'). Some, however, did work in such industries – their refusal was only to fight or take part in battle. Some did go to war – but acted in support capacities and did not engage in combat (known as 'alternativists').

Conscientious objectors could often be treated very harshly at home by those who saw them as cowards and traitors – 'unwilling to fight for the freedoms they would enjoy as the result of the fighting engaged in by others'. Some were imprisoned for their refusal to take part. In some wars, there was conscription – which meant you were 'called up' to go to war – even though you had never been a soldier. There could be exclusions to being called up – for example, if you were vital to an industry which was needed for the war effort. However, if you refused to be called up on grounds of conscience, you had to go before a 'local tribunal' and explain yourself and they would decide what happened to you. In one instance it was reported that when a conscientious objector told the tribunal that he was 18, the tribunal responded by saying: *'In that case you're not old enough to have a conscience. Case dismissed*[116]*'*. Once your case was dismissed you were now considered to have enlisted in the military and so could be tried by the military for any refusal to follow orders. Of course, some objectors suffered more than others. They could be treated very harshly by the public and often those imprisoned experienced very great difficulties while in prison. It is important to remember that not all conscientious objectors are against self-defence (though some are in all cases) – it is just that fighting 'an enemy' in war means fighting against someone who is not a direct threat to you and your loved ones and can involve acting as an agent of a leader or government which is not morally acceptable in their opinion.

Talk Point

What do you think of the idea of conscientious objection?

There were, of course, and are still perhaps, a great deal of responses to the idea of conscientious objection:

- **It is morally acceptable to be a conscientious objector** Society should protect the rights of those who do not wish to support war on grounds of belief – this is a mark of a fair society.
- **It is not morally acceptable to be a conscientious objector** We each have a responsibility to protect the weak and vulnerable – and sometimes this is what wars are about. No one has the right to refuse to take part in this kind of war.
- **Some versions of conscientious objection are morally acceptable** It is possible to support a war effort in a variety of ways which do not involve fighting – perhaps by working in a war-related industry or in a medical support unit on the battlefield, for example. As this does not involve fighting it enables a conscientious objector to 'support the war effort' while not personally engaging in violence.

Pacifism

Many conscientious objectors would have been considered pacifists, which is another alternative to war. Pacifists can also be 'absolutists' or 'alternativists'. A pacifist who is an absolutist would have nothing to do with any action which might support war, while an alternativist would not engage in any combat, but would otherwise be involved in aspects of war which did not involve fighting. Again, some pacifists would argue that fighting back against an aggressor is acceptable when the threat is directly to you or others, while others would reject this completely. There are further degrees of pacifism, for example, some pacifists object only to certain kinds of war – such as wars using weapons of mass destruction – while others object to war in general but might consider that in some circumstances it is the lesser of a range of evils.

Some argue that pacifism is an ideal situation – and of course would work well – as long as everyone agreed to be a pacifist. However, others claim that the reality of war is that it is sometimes necessary to respond to aggressors through war and conflict. In these instances, a pacifist response would be ineffective – and morally wrong since it would not allow society to protect itself: also, it is possible that a pacifist response could potentially make an aggressor even more likely to act aggressively if a country or its leader considers that the pacifist country they want to attack won't fight back.

Again, pacifism as a position in life might be based on a variety of beliefs. Some pacifists are religious – in Christianity, for example, the principle of 'turn the other cheek' implies that someone should never return violence with violence. Similarly in Buddhism, the kammic consequences of returning violence with more violence would seem to go against the main teachings of this faith and so support a pacifist response to life. Many pacifists have also been non-religious people, basing their views on a range of philosophies – for example, consequentialist ethics, which state that the outcome of war is so great that the most effective response is not to engage in it in the first place.

Is pacifism a meaningful alternative to conflict?

Diplomacy

One possible response to conflict and alternative to war is diplomacy. Winston Churchill famously said: *'Jaw-jaw is always better than war-war'* (or some variation of this statement). By this he meant that talking over issues which could lead to war is always the best option. This is known as diplomacy and is where leaders, governments and so on engage in discussion about issues to try to stop war from breaking out. Of course, almost all wars and conflicts are likely to involve some kind of diplomacy at some point in the conflict – except, perhaps, for those which break out more suddenly and unexpectedly. Most world governments and organisations probably want to avoid war as far as possible and if talking through issues prevents war, then this is the right thing to do. One difficulty with diplomacy is that as well as talking, it may have to involve the offer of certain things in order to avert war. A country or group may be required to give up something which they consider theirs in order to prevent war breaking out. Such negotiations are usually very sensitive and very complex and can lead to a country having to balance up the needs of one group in society with the needs of others in order to avoid war breaking out.

Diplomacy can also sometimes use intermediaries – people who act as 'go-betweens' for the two sides who may end up at war. All of this is very complex and can be very long-drawn-out, but if it succeeds and avoids war, then of course it is a sensible approach. Some do argue that diplomacy is all very well, but it can have unwanted consequences: it might lead to your country making concessions which are harmful for its people; it might make your country look weak in that you do not immediately jump to engaging in warfare; it might also importantly give your enemy more time to prepare for war (while you talk) and so make victory all the more likely for them in the end. So, diplomacy can play a part in preventing and bringing war to an end, but it is a subtle, delicate and complicated process.

Trade and other sanctions

Sanctions are often used against countries or groups taking an aggressive stance which might result in war (or have already engaged in conflict). Sanctions involve the international community agreeing to a set of actions directed at the aggressor in order to persuade them to give up their aggressive plans or actions. Sanctions are designed in some ways to 'cut-off' the offending nation or group from the international community and so make the nation or group think again about their plans or actions. These sanctions are generally agreed by the UN Security Council and therefore across the international community. However, individual nation-states have also imposed sanctions without the agreement of the international community. There are various kinds of sanctions.

Trade/economic sanctions

According to the UK Government, there are various types of trade or economic sanctions:

- Placing restrictions (embargoes) on exporting or supplying arms and associated technical assistance, trading and financing.
- A ban on exporting equipment that might be used for internal repression.
- Financial sanctions on individuals in government, government bodies and associated companies, or terrorist groups and individuals associated with those groups.
- Travel bans on named individuals.
- Bans on imports of raw materials or goods from the sanctions' target[117].

It is important to remember that trade and/or economic sanctions can be applied both to countries importing goods and services as well as those exporting them. In addition to this there can be other economic sanctions such as the removal of aid support for a country, or the 'freezing of international assets' so a country or group cannot use them to support their activities. Supporters of economic sanctions argue that they send a message and weaken the offending country's economy, which could prevent it engaging in any further preparation for or acts of war. Opponents argue that trade and economic sanctions do most harm to ordinary people and believe this is wrong and is more likely to make those ordinary people angry and willing to fight back.

Diplomatic sanctions

This is where diplomatic relations between countries may be suspended temporarily or permanently. This may involve sending diplomatic staff in your country back to their country or recalling your diplomatic staff from another country. It might also mean excluding diplomats from international groups and bodies – effectively not talking to them. Some argue that this sends a clear message that one country is not prepared to accept the behaviour of another and is so serious about this that it no longer discusses anything with the offending country. Also, exclusion from international groups and bodies might lead to the excluded country having less of a say on important international issues – effectively isolating it. Critics of diplomatic sanctions would argue that imposing diplomatic sanctions is exactly the wrong thing to do to avoid conflict. This is because once diplomatic sanctions have been applied it is possible that the lines of communication between countries will have been significantly weakened – and this cannot be helpful in trying to negotiate the avoidance of conflict.

Military sanctions

Military sanctions can involve specific military action short of all-out war. This might be targeted air strikes, limited military activities or other military actions. Supporters argue that this also sends a message to a country about what they can expect if war does break out; it can also reduce a country's ability to fight back by targeting specific aspects of their ability which will reduce their capability to respond if war does break out. Critics argue that military sanctions are effectively 'pre-emptive strikes' and so are acts of war. In addition, they could claim that such strikes do not always target what they should and that civilian casualties are always possible in such situations. Apart from being wrong in itself, this could lead to civilians in the country under attack being more likely to support whatever it is which is potentially leading to war. Also, some would argue that actions like these are more likely to escalate the situation rather than defuse it. Striking a country or group in this way puts them in a position where, perhaps, their pride has been harmed and they may feel the need to escalate the violence even if they don't particularly want to.

Cultural sanctions

In some circumstances, cultural sanctions might be applied to isolate a country within the international community. For example, there may be bans and/or boycotts on a country's athletes taking part in international sporting events and/or athletes from other countries may not compete in the offending country. Supporters of this argue that it sends a powerful message to the country experiencing the ban/boycott about the international community's dislike of its actions. This involves no direct harm to people and certainly no violence. Critics argue that this is not very effective and, besides, targets individuals rather than countries. In addition, perhaps allowing a country to take part in such international events might make it look more carefully at its actions and consider changing them. If it is 'left out' then it is less likely to do so.

Talk Point

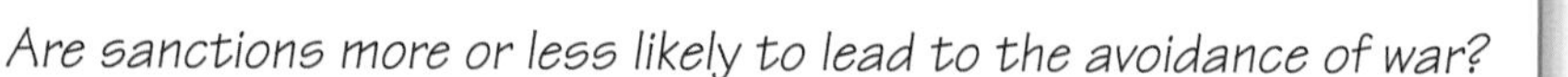

Are sanctions more or less likely to lead to the avoidance of war?

The aim of all sanctions is to have an effect on the targeted group or country, with the ultimate aim of making it change its ways about going to war or engaging in conflict (or other activities undesirable from the point of view of whoever is imposing the sanctions). Supporters argue that sanctions stop short of full-scale war and so might prevent full-scale war breaking out. However, opponents argue that sanctions do not necessarily produce the results they are intended to produce because they may not be 'strong' enough in the first place; they may target the wrong people; and they may have negative effects on a government, group or people which might end up leading to war instead.

Some final alternatives to war ... for the future?

Perhaps there could be ways to engage in war in the future without any violence involving people or other living things, any destruction to natural or built environments – but such solutions would have to be agreed and accepted: perhaps humans could settle their differences through technology. Perhaps we could turn war into something which happens between robots or maybe even have our wars fought by technology outside Earth's orbit and we just have to accept whichever group's/country's technology wins. Of course, this could lead to technology becoming something which works against us rather than for us. Perhaps we might get to a point where anger and aggression are things of the past and we settle our differences through competition: we could maybe compete, not in violence, fighting or warfare, but through producing the most beautiful art, the most harmonious music, the greatest sporting achievements. Perhaps we could settle our differences through creating the most inspiring literature, creating the most incredible buildings, or racing to solve the most pressing problems of life on our planet. Perhaps countries could compete with each other to see which can provide the best education, the best health care, the best care. Perhaps we could compete with each other as groups and countries to see who can be first to eradicate poverty, to end disease and to make everyone feel that they matter. Perhaps we could simply recognise our common humanity and see no one as an enemy, but all as fellow travellers on this home we call Earth. Let's hope so.

Some religious and philosophical perspectives

Christianity

Christians would actively support any alternatives to war where these were likely to avoid war, or reduce its negative impact. Within Christianity, however, there are differences of opinion about pacifism and conscientious objection in all their forms. Some Christians would support both a pacifist approach and the principle of conscientious objection – while some would not. Although Christians generally support the principle of 'turn the other cheek', they may also think that people have a responsibility to respond appropriately to evil, violence and aggression and to defend themselves and others when needed. Christians could therefore reach a range of conclusions on the issues you have explored in this chapter.

The Church of Scotland

In 2015, a campaign calling on Edinburgh City Council to create a memorial in Edinburgh to conscientious objectors was backed by the Church and Society Council of the Church of Scotland. On 10 June 2015, the Council agreed to this. The Church of Scotland therefore clearly supports the right of individuals to take a stance based on conscientious objection. In common with other Christian groups, the Church would be supportive of measures which aimed to avoid war; however, it would also want to ensure that any such measures had the effect they were intended to have and did not affect the weak and vulnerable instead – which can, for example, happen in certain types of sanctions. The Church supports avoiding military action where possible. In a letter to the UK Defence Secretary in 2012 about the escalating situation in Syria, the Convenor of the Church and Society Council stated: '*I urge you to do all that is within your power to prevent the further militarisation of this conflict. Peace comes through mutual trust, reconciliation and acceptance, and not by continuing to promote ways for human beings to kill other human beings.*[118]'

The Roman Catholic Church

The Church recognises the right of individuals to be conscientious objectors and to take a pacifist stance if they choose to. The Catechism states: '*Public authorities should make equitable provision for those who for reasons of conscience refuse to bear arms; these are nonetheless obliged to serve the community in some other way.*' (2311) In relation to alternatives to war the Catechism is equally clear in that it does support the option of military activity, but states: '*All other means of putting an end to [war] must have been shown to be impractical or ineffective.*' (2309) So clearly the Church would support any alternative to war to the point where it no longer seemed to work. However, the Church also stresses throughout its teaching the dignity of human beings and the special need to protect those who are most vulnerable. This would mean that any sanctions imposed on a country or group would need to take into account the potential effects of these sanctions on the people of the country so that they do not have serious effects on their wellbeing.

Buddhism

The Dhammapada states: '*All tremble at violence; all fear death. Putting oneself in the place of another, one should not kill nor cause another to kill.*' Arguably, Buddhism could perhaps represent the belief group most likely to take a pacifist stance since one of the key Buddhist principles is the avoidance of harm to any living thing. In practice, many Buddhists are absolute pacifists for this reason – and prepared to accept their own deaths peacefully to safeguard this central belief. However, again, Buddhists can exercise 'skilful means' in relation to taking part in war if they believe that this might reduce suffering in the long term and, in practice, many Buddhists argue that fighting for a just cause is an acceptable Buddhist standpoint. However, Buddhists would argue that every possible alternative to war should have been absolutely exhausted before any military action is undertaken – and many would argue that even after every alternative had been tried, war is wrong and a pacifist stance is the only authentic Buddhist response.

Humanism

The British Humanist Association states: '*If all wars involve killing the innocent, aren't we back with the impossibility of justifying war at all? Shouldn't we all be pacifists? It is difficult for Humanists to lay down an absolute principle on this ... Humanists have to accept that however terrible war may be, it's at least possible that sometimes a refusal to go to war may be even worse*[119].' In saying this, the British Humanist Association identifies the problem which many belief groups have in relation to war: on one hand war should be avoided where possible; on the other perhaps there are times when it is not possible to avoid war. In relation to individual choices, Humanists take the view that each person makes their own decision on this based on reason and evidence. In practice, many Humanists are pacifists of one variety or another and during wars many conscientious objectors based their stance on Humanist principles. Like many religious groups, Humanists would be prepared to support sanctions to try to avoid war – however, they too would want to ensure that such sanctions did not cause unnecessary harm.

Utilitarianism

J. S. Mill stated: '*War is an ugly thing, but not the ugliest of things: the decayed and degraded state of moral and patriotic feeling which thinks that nothing is worth a war is much worse ... A man who has nothing which he is willing to fight for, nothing which he cares more about than he does about his personal safety, is a miserable creature who has no chance of being free, unless made and kept so by better men than himself ... human beings must be willing, when need is, to do battle for the one against the other.*[120]' Mill clearly seems to have little time for the idea of conscientious objection. In addition, Mill's predecessor, Utilitarian Jeremy Bentham, considered that: '*All war is in essence ruinous, mischief upon the largest scale*' and he proposed a whole range of alternatives to each possible cause of war[121]. This basically explored a whole range of possible causes of war, for each one of which Bentham suggested an alternative approach. For all of the alternatives to war and responses to conflict in this chapter Utilitarians could support or reject these: the judgement each Utilitarian must reach would be decided by how far each alternative or response to war was likely to lead to the maximisation of positive consequences and the happiness of the majority.

Personal Reflection

* *If your country went to war, would you fight?*
* *What do you think is the most effective way to avoid war?*
* *Will humans ever find an alternative to war which is acceptable to all?*

Active learning

Check your understanding

1. Describe some of the ways in which conscientious objectors have been treated in the past.
2. Why might someone choose to be a conscientious objector and what might they do as an alternative to fighting in conflict?
3. What different forms of pacifism are there?
4. How might diplomacy be used to avoid war?
5. Describe what is meant by trade/economic sanctions and explain how effective you think they are.
6. What other sanctions might the international community (and individual countries) use? Which of these do you think are likely to be effective/not effective?
7. What other possible ways might humans settle their differences in the future and what issues might these raise?
8. How far are religious and non-religious perspectives agreed about pacifism and conscientious objection?
9. How do religions respond to the use of sanctions as a way to avoid war?
10. Would a Utilitarian be prepared to accept any response/alternative to war?

Investigate

1. The Imperial War Museums have a range of accounts of the experiences of conscientious objectors at www.iwm.org.uk Listen to some of these and read the transcripts. Now create a display of these accounts in your class.
2. A range of sanctions is used by the international community. Find out how these sanctions are chosen and applied. Consider how far these sanctions have achieved their outcome or not. You can prepare a presentation on your findings.
3. Sanctions on sporting activities have been common throughout history as a way for the international community to express its views. Choose one example of this and find out more about what happened and why. You could look, for example, at boycotts of South African sport during the apartheid era, or boycotts of various Olympic Games in relation to various world situations. You should prepare an illustrated report of your findings.
4. Religious and non-religious people have supported pacifism – and continue to do so. Carry out your own research and explain in more detail the similarities and differences between religious and non-religious 'forms of pacifism'.

Analyse and Evaluate

1 'Pacifism is a weak response to aggression and does not work.' To what extent do you agree?
2 Discuss the view that alternatives to war have only limited success.
3 Compare religious and non-religious perspectives on the morality of being a pacifist in the face of war.

Apply

The world has decided that it has had enough of war, but it is not sure what to replace it with. Prepare a speech for the United Nations in which you explain your alternative to war.

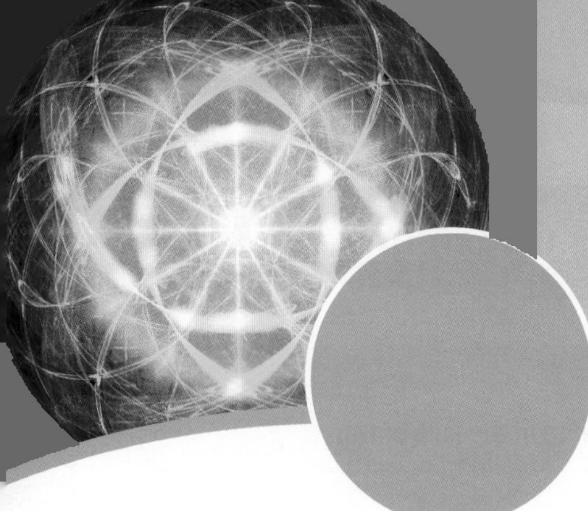

Revision guidance and exam-type questions

Some SQA and other guidance

According to the SQA, this unit of work is all about '*... evaluating and presenting clear arguments about moral issues: Learners will be required to understand and communicate the relationship between religious beliefs and moral viewpoints as well as the similarities and differences between religious and non-religious moral thinking.*'[122] The SQA also points out correctly that within a religion there is not always agreement about moral issues – this is true of non-religious perspectives too. It is hoped that you will build up a balanced and well-understood picture of moral issues and how religious and non-religious groups respond to these. This will also – and very importantly – help you to further develop your own beliefs and values which Curriculum for Excellence Religious and Moral Education has been helping you to do since you were in Early Years. Now that you are in your senior phase of education, you should be building on the prior learning you have been engaged in since you were very young. This doesn't stop at the end of your Higher RMPS, of course (or Advanced Higher if you go on to give that a go), it is a lifelong process. It is hoped that studying this course will develop very important skills for learning, life and work and support you throughout your life.

How to revise?

There is not just one way to revise – everyone learns in different ways, and different ways of revising work for different people. You have to find the method(s) which work best for you. Whatever its form, revision means *processing* the information, facts and figures, viewpoints, opinions and so on in this course. Processing means engaging you in a range of skills which will help you to understand the materials you have covered in this course: processing is a circular and so never-ending process and is sometimes reduced to the term 'Plan, Do, Review'. In practice, one way of thinking about processing is this:

- **Gather your information** Use this book and as many other resources as you have time to make use of. Pull together the information and make careful notes about where it comes from.
- **Organise your information** Put the information together under the following headings: facts, figures, opinions, beliefs, arguments, counter-arguments; then sort it into categories of 'for' and 'against', 'religious', 'non-religious' and whatever other categories make sense to you.
- **Review your information** What is everything you have gathered telling you? How do you know if what you have gathered is true, authentic, valid, reliable and representative? How up to date is your information – where did it come from? Who said it? What might that person (or group) have to gain by saying this?
- **Assess your information** How does what you have gathered increase your understanding? What questions remain and how will you answer these?
- **Redraft your information** Processing of information is often helped by redrafting the information you have gathered. This forms new neural connections in your brain and so helps you to understand the material better (and probably remember it better too). So, can you turn your information into a picture, a diagram, a song, a speech, a doodle, a wordle, a 'thing', a painting, a sculpture, a dance ...? The more you can do with your information, the more neural connections you're making and so the more effectively you will learn it.

- **Use your information** Devise a range of questions about your issue/topic and use your information to answer these. Think creatively – you could come up with some very serious questions (Why does X agree with euthanasia?) or some less serious ones (Would a joiner be more likely to cause global warming than a teacher?) to help you get a different perspective on an issue.

It's worth pointing out that a lot of thinking at the moment says that we are far more likely to learn effectively when we do it in collaboration with others. This might not be true for everyone, of course, but learning with others can be helpful and enjoyable – so working together can help you to develop your understanding even further as you debate, argue, discuss and support each other in your learning.

You can buy lots of books on revision skills and techniques and there are many websites which help with revision skills. You can also get hold of past papers in RMPS from the SQA website as well as a range of other guidance about RMPS. As for past exam papers, the 'New' Higher RMPS is still relatively 'new' – as the years go on, more papers will become available for you to learn from for assessment purposes.

Exam-type questions

At the time of the writing of this book, the first 'new' Higher RMPS exam had just been sat by the first candidates (2015) and so the only guidance on the exam came from that paper and what are called the 'Specimen Paper' and 'Exemplar Paper', which gave some guidance about what exam questions and answers would look like. You can find this paper and the marking instructions on the SQA website and subsequent papers and marking instructions will be there too.

All questions in the Morality and Belief section will be worth 10 marks only. The skills assessed here will be Knowledge and Understanding; Analysis or Knowledge; and Understanding and Evaluation. There are no 20-mark questions in the Morality and Belief section.

In the exam paper the SQA is assessing the following skills:

Critical analysis

The SQA states: *'This means identifying parts, the relationship between them, and their relationship with the whole. It can also involve drawing out and relating implications.'*

In practice this means:

- *Making links between different components*
- *Making links between components and the whole*
- *Making links between components and related concepts*
- *Similarities and contradictions*
- *Consistency and inconsistency*
- *Different views/interpretations*
- *Possible causes/implications*
- *The relative importance of components*
- *Understanding the underlying order or structure*

This means using what the SQA calls 'question stems' which are: *In what ways …?; Analyse; Compare.*

It is important to remember that all the question stems which follow are for example only, and so you should keep up to date with the kinds of question stems which are used in future RMPS exams.

Also, the SQA can only ask questions in the examination which link to the mandatory content of the course as set out in the Course Assessment Specification. Therefore, some of the questions below are just for you to use to help your learning rather than as possible exam questions. **Make sure you check with your teacher as to which questions could appear in an exam and which questions could not.**

So here are some examples:

NB: You should assume that the exam-type questions in this section are each worth 10 marks. Don't forget – there are no 20-mark questions in the Morality and Belief section!

- In what ways might religious people respond to attempts to bring back capital punishment to the UK?
- In what ways might religious and non-religious people differ in their views about assisted suicide?
- In what ways might religious people respond differently to environmental crises?
- In what ways might there be differences in opinion between religious and non-religious people about same-sex marriage?
- 'The responsibility of caring for the poor belongs to us all.' In what ways might religious perspectives respond to this statement?
- In what ways are the views of non-religious people likely to be the same on the issue of the 'right to die'?
- Compare religious and non-religious perspectives on the effectiveness of sentencing in the UK.
- Compare different religious views about the causes of crime.
- 'Men and women are equal but different.' Compare different religious responses to this statement.
- 'Euthanasia is always morally acceptable.' Compare the views of non-religious perspectives on this statement.
- 'Fair trade is better than free trade.' Analyse this statement.
- 'End of life decisions are about quality of life'. Analyse this statement in relation to religious and non-religious viewpoints.
- Analyse the view that offenders need support not punishment.

Evaluation

The SQA states that this involves: *'making a judgement based on criteria and making reasoned evaluative comments relating to, for example:*

- *The relevance/importance/usefulness, e.g. of a viewpoint or source*
- *Positive and negative aspects*
- *Strengths and weaknesses*
- *Any other evaluative comment.'*

The 'question stems' here are: *Evaluate; How valid ...?*

So here are some examples:

- How valid is the view that all life is sacred?
- How valid are religious perspectives on capital punishment?
- 'Capital punishment is morally unacceptable.' How valid is this view?
- 'Religious people should reject same-sex marriage.' How valid is this view?
- How valid is the view that punishments should 'make an example' of offenders?
- How valid is the view that our life is ours to end as we choose?
- 'Non-religious perspectives would always support organ donation.' How valid is this statement?
- 'Life is sacred so should be preserved in all circumstances. Embryos are living beings.' How valid is this statement in relation to religious views on the status and treatment of embryos?
- Evaluate the claim that religious perspectives are confused about their views on passive euthanasia.
- 'Only human action can solve environmental crises.' Evaluate this claim.
- 'War can never be justified.' Evaluate this claim including religious and non-religious perspectives in your answer.

Constructing your exam answer

The SQA provides clear marking instructions for those who will mark your exam. The marking instructions are in two groups, General Marking Instructions and Specific Marking Instructions.

General marking instructions

These give very broad principles which markers will apply when assessing your answer. The ten marks are available for analysis and there are six marks available for Knowledge and Understanding *which is relevant to the question and to the answer.*

So for a 10 mark question ...

8–10 marks

- **A 'sophisticated answer'** This means that the ideas and argument in the answer flow and work together well. They link knowledge and understanding (KU) to analysis in a clear and meaningful way.
- **A 'full answer'** This means that the answer covers all that the question asks in good detail.
- **KU is accurate and relevant** The KU in the answer about the question asked is accurate and relevant to the question.
- **The analytical points are 'well-considered'** This means that careful thought has gone into the analytical points and they make sense in relation to the overall answer.
- **The analytical points may be 'insightful'** This means that the answer is so good that it might even come up with some new ideas, points about, or responses to the issue under consideration. The marker might read it and think 'I've never really thought about it like that!'

6–7 marks

- **A 'good answer'** This means that the answer has good points but is not as sophisticated and full as it could be.
- **The answer has 'some analysis'** This means that analysis is present, but is not as in-depth or wide-ranging enough to gain higher marks.
- **KU is mainly relevant and accurate** This means that some slight inaccuracies have crept in to the answer and on occasion it might stray off the point a bit.
- **'Analytical points are appropriate but may be incomplete at times'** This means that the basic analysis is there, but it hasn't gone as far as it could and so left the reader high and dry.

4–5 marks

- **'A borderline answer'** This means, when thinking about all of the above, it's not clear if the answer has done enough in each category to answer the question and so it is on the fence between being an effective answer and not.
- **Includes some basic analysis** This means that analysis is there, but it just doesn't go far enough to do the job of analysing the issue in the question.
- **It has weaknesses in KU** This could mean that some of the KU is just wrong or not accurate enough or just not at all relevant to the question – or it may be very generalised and not specific enough to the question.
- **It has weaknesses in the analysis** This means the analysis is not developed fully enough, although it is probably appropriate.

0–3 marks

- **A 'weak or poor answer'** This means that the answer doesn't tackle the question or does so pretty badly.
- **Answer is descriptive with little or no analysis** This means that the answer (although it might be long) is just a list of facts, figures, viewpoints and so on which all might be not really related to the question. It might 'tell a story' but not analyse any aspects of that 'story'.
- **The focus of the answer is not consistently on the question** This means that the answer is probably rambling and tends towards the 'writing all you know about' whether it is relevant to the question or not.
- **The answer is 'vague'** This usually means that the person writing the answer doesn't really know what they are writing about and so skirts around the edges making weak stabs at something which might link to the answer. Generally this indicates that the candidate doesn't understand the question or does, but hasn't a clue about how to answer it. It may also show that the person answering the question knows nothing much about the issue at all.

Specific marking instructions

These guide markers towards knowing what should be present in an answer and therefore what an excellent/good/awful answer looks like.

To help you with this, we'll use a typical exam-type question.

- **Question** 'It should be compulsory for everyone to carry an organ donor card'. To what extent do you agree?
- **Purpose** The purpose of the question is to give candidates (you) the opportunity to explore the moral debates surrounding the issue of organ donation, which could include the background to organ donation and a range of moral responses to it.

Specific instructions

Knowledge and Understanding may include:

- Causes of the debate surrounding organ donation.
- Types of organs which can be donated and their uses.
- The debate around shortages of organs.

Evaluative Information may include:

- The extent to which organ donation should be compulsory/opt-in/opt-out.
- The morality of different types of organ donation.
- Religious and non-religious perspectives on organ donation.
- Consistency and inconsistency in viewpoints around organ donation.

Other assessments in RMPS

Assessments in RMPS are now far more likely to be *'holistic'* and *'naturally occurring'*. In simple terms, *'holistic'* means that assessments are likely to cover a range of outcomes all at once, rather than picking each outcome apart and tackling it in isolation.

'Naturally occurring' means that assessments will take place as you work through the Unit – they will not always take place at a fixed point (in the past this was often at the end of the Unit). Also, assessments should be linked to what you are doing naturally – so, for example, many of the 'Active learning' activities in this book could build towards use in assessing your progress and achievement. Whatever happens, assessment is partly *formative* – which means it is there to help 'diagnose' where you have strengths and where you have things which still need a little attention – and then help you to do what you need to do next to improve and achieve success.

A final word

Hopefully this course will mean more to you than an 'A' pass – though that would be nice too. Hopefully it will help you to understand yourself and others better and so get more out of life and give more in life. The whole point of learning is to make the world a better place. I hope you do.

References

Chapter 1

1 – 'A Humanist discussion of … war' (2015) British Humanist Association [online] **www.humanismforschools.org.uk**

Chapter 2

2 – 'A Humanist Discussion of Crime and Punishment' (2015) [online] **www.humanismforschools.org.uk**

3 – 'The Amsterdam Declaration' (2002) as cited in *About Humanism* (2015) [online] **www.humanism-scotland.org.uk**

Chapter 3

4 – **www.ccpas.co.uk**

5 – 'Grangemouth Minister forgives his mother's killers' The Church of Scotland (2013) [online] **www.churchofscotland.org.uk**

6 – 'What's the alternative?' The Church of Scotland Church and society Council (2007) [online] **www.churchofscotland.org.uk**

7 – 'Our Vision: Imagining Scotland's Future' Church of Scotland Church and Society Council (2014) [online] **www.churchofscotland.org.uk**

8 – 'Pope Francis: God always forgives everything' Vatican Radio (2015) [online] **en.radiovaticana.va**

9 – 'Francis: We must love and forgive our enemies as the Gospel tells us to' Vatican Insider (2013) [online] **www.lastampa.it/vaticaninsider/eng**

10 – HH The Dalai Lama (2001) *An Open Heart* London, Hodder & Stoughton, p111;

11 – 'A Humanist discussion of evil and suffering' (2015) British Humanist Association [online] **www.humanismforschools.org.uk**

12 – 'A Humanist discussion of crime and punishment' (2015) British Humanist Association [Online] **www.humanismforschools.org.uk**

Chapter 4

13 – 'The Death Penalty' (2008): Church of Scotland Church and Society Council [Online] **www.churchofscotland.org.uk**

14 – 'Pope Francis: No matter what the crime, 'the death penalty is inadmissible" The Catholic News Agency (2015) [online] **www.catholicnewsagency.com**

Chapter 5

15 – 'What's the alternative?' (2007) The Church of Scotland Church and Society Council [Online] **www.churchofscotland.org.uk**

16 – 'Responsibility and rehabilitation: A catholic perspective on Crime and Criminal Justice' (2000) United States Conference of Catholic Bishops [Online] **www.usccb.org**

Chapter 6

17 – **www.amnestyusa.org**

18 – **www.gov.scot**

19 – 'Evaluating the effectiveness of home detention curfew and open prison in Scotland' (2011) Crime and Justice: Social Research No 32 [Online] **www.gov.scot**

Chapter 7

20 – National Records of Scotland at **www.nrscotland.gov.uk**

21 – Family Matters: Living together in Scotland **www.gov.scot**

22 – Marriage and Civil Partnership (Scotland) Act 2014: Advice from the Principal Clerk **www.churchofscotland.org.uk**

23 – Catechism of the Catholic Church: 1637

24 – **http://www.humanismforschools.org.uk/pdfs/Family%20Matters.pdf**

Chapter 8

25 – **www.bbc.co.uk**

26 – **http://www.vatican.va/archive/ccc_css/archive/catechism/p3s2c2a6.htm**

27 – **http://www.churchofscotland.org.uk/__data/assets/pdf_file/0014/13811/20_THEOLOGICAL_2013.pdf**

28 – **http://www.humanism-scotland.org.uk/content/policy_same_sex_marriage/**

29 – **http://www.utilitarian.net/singer/by/200610--.htm**

30 – **http://www.humanism-scotland.org.uk/content/about_society/**

Chapter 9

31 – Sternberg, R. (1986) 'A triangular theory of love', Psychological Review, 93,119–35

32 – Byrne, D. (1971) *The Attraction Paradigm*. New York: Academic Press

33 – Wiseman, R. (2012) *Rip it Up* London: PanMacmillan

34 – Cochran, J. K., and Beeghley, L. (1991). 'The influence of religion on attitudes towards non-martial sexuality: a preliminary assessment of reference group theory'. Journal for the Scientific Study of Religion, 30, 45–62

35 – 'Enhancing Sexual Wellbeing in Scotland: A sexual Health relationship Strategy' (2001): Scottish Executive [Online] **www.gov.scot**

36 – **www.americanhumanist.org**

37 – Humanist Manifesto II at **www.americanhumanist.org**

Chapter 10

38 – LoBlue,V. and DeLoache, J. (2011) 'Pretty in Pink: The development of gender-stereotyped colour preferences'. British Journal of Developmental Psychology, 29 (3), 656–667

39 – **www.gov.scot**

40 – **www.un.org**

41 – 'Moderator says Church will strive for gender Justice' [online] **www.churchofscotland.org.uk** 10 December 2014

42 – **www.vatican.va**

43 – 'A Humanist discussion of … Family Matters' British Humanist Association [online] **www.humanismforschools.org.uk**

Chapter 11

44 – **www.ukfeminista.org.uk (2015)**

45 – Action of Churches Together in Scotland: Anti-Human Trafficking Ecumenical Group: Church of Scotland 2011 [online] **www.churchofscotland.org.uk**

46 – In peace message, Pope takes aim at modern-day slavery (2015) Catholic news agency, [online] **www.catholicnewsagency.com**

47 – 'Position Statement on Vulnerability and Inequality' CAFOD, 2015 [online] **www.cafod.org.uk**

48 – **www.humanism.org.uk**

Chapter 12

49 – 'Responding to Climate Change Project' (2009) The Church of Scotland [online] **www.churchofscotland.org.uk**

50 – 'Theology and the Environment' Scotland (2015) Eco-congregation [online] **www.ecocongregationscotland.org**

51 – Encyclical letter Laudato Si' of the Holy Father Francis On our care for our common home (2015) The Holy See [online] **www.vatican.va**

52 – Excerpt from 'My Tibet' (1990) in *Universal Responsibility and the Environment* (2015) [online] **www.dalailama.com**

53 – 'A Humanist discussion of' ... environmental issues' (2015) British Humanist Association [online] **www.humanismforschools.org.uk**

Chapter 13

54 – 'Church of Scotland welcomes Pope Francis' statements on climate change' (2015) [online] **www.churchofscotland.org.uk**

55 – 'God's own Country: Rural Theologies' (2015) The Church of Scotland [online] **www.churchofscotland.org.uk**

56 – Encyclical letter Laudato Si' of the Holy Father Francis On our care for our common home (2015) The Holy See [online] **www.vatican.va**

57 – Brown, P. (2015) 'Buddhism and the Ecocrisis' [Online] **www.buddhanet.net**

58 – Mason, M. 'Why humanists should act together on climate change- and why we need another humanist interest group' (2015) [online] **www.humanism.org.uk**

59 – Sagan, S. (1991) in 'Humanists on the environment' (2015) [online] **www.humanism.org.uk**

60 – Singer, S. (1998) *Practical Ethics* Cambridge University Press, p286

61 – *ibid* p288

Chapter 14

62 – 'A Right Relationship with Money' Church of Scotland special commission on the purposes of economic activity (2012) [Online] **www.churchofscotland.org.uk**

63 – Norman, R (2015) 'The need for Humanist action on global poverty and injustice' [online] **www.humanism.org.uk**

64 – 'A Humanist discussion of Human Rights' (2015) British Humanist Association [online] **www.humanismforschools.org.uk**

Chapter 15

65 – 'Fast Facts: The Faces of Poverty' (2015): The UN development Group [online] **www.unmillenniumproject.org**

66 – 'Poverty in the UK' (2015) Oxfam [online] **policy-practice.oxfam.org.uk**

67 – 'Church called to challenge poverty' (2015) The Church of Scotland [online] **www.churchofscotland.org.uk**

68 – 'A right relationship with money' (2012) The Church of Scotland special commission on the purposes of economic activity p15 [online] **www.churchofscotland.org.uk**

69 – Human Rights, Democracy and Freedom; The Dalai Lama (2015) [online] **www.dalailama.com**

70 – 'A Humanist Discussion of ... World Poverty' (2015) The British Humanist Association [online] **www.humanismforschools.org.uk**

71 – Singer, P. *op cit*, p222

Chapter 16

72 – Maimonides eight levels of charity [online] **http://www.chabad.org/library/article_cdo/aid/45907/jewish/Eight-Levels-of-Charity**

73 – 'Structural Readjustment Programmes', (2015) World Health Organization [online] **www.who.int**

74 – 'Our Mission: (2015) Buddhist Global relief' [online] **https://buddhistglobalrelief.org/active/ourHistory**

75 – 'Good causes and Charities: Humanist Charities?' (2015) The British Humanist Association [online] **https://humanism.org.uk/humanism/humanism-today/humanists-doing/good-causes-and-charities/**

Chapter 17

76 – 'End of life issues: A Christian perspective'. (2015) The Church of Scotland [Online] **www.churchofscotland.org.uk**

77 – Supplementary report of the Church and Society Council: End of Life Assistance (Scotland) Bill May 2010: proposed deliverance. The Church of Scotland (2010) [online] **www.churchofscotland.org.uk**

78 – Keown, D. 'Buddhism and Suicide: The Case of Channa' Journal of Buddhist Ethics, Vol 3 1996 [online] **www.urbandharma.org**

79 – 'My life, my death, my choice: Why we want change' (2010) The British Humanist Association [online] **www.lifedeathchoice.org.uk**

80 – Singer, S. (1994) *Rethinking Life and Death* Oxford University press p4

Chapter 18

81 – 'Euthanasia: A Christian Perspective' (1995) The Church of Scotland, Board of Social Responsibility [online] **www.churchofscotland.org.uk**

82 – 'End of Life Issues' (2009) Church of Scotland Church and Society Council [Online] **www.churchofscotland.org.uk**

83 – (and previous quote) 'A Humanist Discussion of Euthanasia' (2015) British Humanist Association [Online] **www.humanismforschoools.org.uk**

Chapter 19

84 – 'Content of the information brochure of DIGNITAS' DIGNITAS (2015) [online] **www.dignitas.ch**

85 – Assisted Suicide (Scotland) Bill [As Introduced] (2015) [online] **www.scottish.parliament.uk**

86 – 'Church reaffirms opposition to assisted suicide bill following health committee report' (2015) The Church of Scotland [online] **www.churchofscotland.org.uk**

87 – Assisted Suicide (Scotland) Bill 2013: Response of the Catholic Bishop's Conference of Scotland to the Health and Sports Committee for Evidence: [online] **www.dioceseofaberdeen.org**

88 – 'Assisted dying policy and campaigns' (2015) The Humanist Society of Scotland [online] **www.humanism.scot**

Chapter 20

89 – 'Organ Donation – How it works' (2015) NHS Choices [Online] **http://www.nhs.uk/Conditions/Organ-donation/Pages/Donationprocess.aspx**

90 – 'Response to Transplantation Scotland Bill' (2015) Church and Society Council of the Church of Scotland [online] **www.scottish.parliament.uk**

91 – 'Organ Donation and Religious Beliefs: a Guide to Organ Donation and Buddhist beliefs'–Mention N. Ireland? (2015) Public Health Agency/NHS [online] **www.organdonationni.info**

92 – 'Organ Donation' (2015) BHA [online] **www.humanism.org.uk**

93 – 'British Humanist Association response to the House of Lord select committee on the European Union's call for evidence': (2008) BHA [online] **www.humanism.org.uk**

Chapter 21

94 – HFEA (2015) [Online] **www.hfea.gov.uk**

95 – Chinese Scientists genetically modify human embryos: Cyranoski, D. & Reardon, S. (2015) in Nature [online] **www.nature.com/news/chinese-scientists-genetically-modify-human-embryos-1.17378**

96 – 'Scientists seek permission to genetically modify embryos' (2015) BBC News [online] **www.bbc.co.uk**

97 – 'Embryonic and Adult Stem Celles: Ethical Dilemmas' (2015) The Church of Scotland [online] **www.churchofscotland.org.uk**

98 – 'Embryo research, Human Stem Cells and Cloned Embryos: Summary report from the Church and Society Council to the 2006 Church of Scotland General Assembly' (2006) [online] **www.srtp.org.uk**

99 – Embryo Research, Human Stem Cells and Cloned Embryos Report May 2006 Society, Religion and Technology Project (2015) [online] **www.srtp.org.uk**

100 – (and immediately previous quote) Instruction on respect for human life in its origin and on the dignity of procreation relies to certain questions of the day Congregation for the Doctrine of the Faith (1987) [online] **www.vatican.va**

101 – Sivaraman, M. A. F. and Noor, S. N. M. (2014) *'Ethics of embryonic stem cell research according to Buddhist, Hindu, Catholic and Islamic religions: perspectives from Malaysia'* in Asian Biomedicine Vol8, no 1 43–52 [online] **www.e-journals.org**

102 – (and previous Humanist quotes in this section) 'A Humanist Discussion on Embryo Research' (2015) British Humanist Association [online] **www.humanism.org.uk**

103 – Analysis: Why it's irrational to risk women's lives for the sake of the unborn Singer, P. (2012) [online] **www.scotsman.com**

Chapter 22

104 – 'Ethics of Defence' (2009) Church of Scotland Church and Society Council [online] **www.churchofscotland.org.uk**

105 – 'Just war Criteria and the War in Afghanistan' ACTS Church and Society Network (2011) [online] **www.churchofscotland.org.uk**

106 – 'A Humanist Discussion of … War' (2015) British Humanist Association [online] **www.humanismforschools.org.uk**

Chapter 23

107 – 'Ethics of Defence' (2009) Church of Scotland Church and Society Council [online] **www.churchofscotland.org.uk**

108 – 'Nuclear Weapons' (2015) Church and Society Council, The Church of Scotland [online] **www.churchofscotland.org.uk**

109 – 'Francis calls for prayer and fasting for peace in Syria' (2013) National Catholic Reporter [online] **www.ncronline.org**

110 – 'A Humanist Discussion of … War' (2015) British Humanist Association [online] **www.humanismforschools.org.uk**

Chapter 24

111 – Hirsch, S. *et al.* (Eds) (1974) *Madness: Network News reader*. San Francisco: Glide Publications

112 – 'Protection of the natural environment in time of armed conflict' Bouvier, A., (1991) International Review of the Red Cross, No 285 [online] **www.icrc.org**

113 – 'Moderator calls for humanitarian action to solve migrant crisis' (2015) [online] **www.churchofscotland.org.uk**

114 – 'Ethics of Defence' (2009) Church of Scotland Church and Society Council [online] **www.churchofscotland.org.uk**

115 – 'A Humanist Discussion of … War' (2015) British Humanist Association [online] **www.humanismforschools.org.uk**

Chapter 25

116 – Brooks, M. (2015) *Conscientious Objectors in their own words* Imperial War Museums [online] **www.iwm.org.uk**

117 – 'Sanctions, embargoes and restrictions – Business and enterprise guidance' (2015) The UK Government [online] **www.gov.uk**

118 – Letter to William Hague; Foster-Fulton, S., (2012) The Church of Scotland [online] **www.churchofscotland.org.uk**

119 – 'A Humanist Discussions of … War' (2015) British Humanist Association [online] **www.humanismforschools.org.uk**

120 – Mill, J. S. (1848) *Principles of Political Economy*, London, John W. Parker

121 – Bentham, J. 'Of War, Considered in Respect of its Causes and Consequences' in *The Principles of International Law, Essay 3* [online] **www.laits.utexas.edu**

Revision Guidance & Exam-type Questions

122 – Unit Support Notes – Morality and Belief (Higher) p55 The Scottish Qualifications Authority (2015 [online] **www.sqa.org.uk**

Index

F

G

H

I